THE WORKS
AND CORRESPONDENCE OF
DAVID RICARDO

VOLUME XI

PLAN OF THE EDITION

VOLUME

   I.   Principles of Political Economy and Taxation;
       pp. lxiii, 447

   II.   Notes on Malthus; pp. xxi, 463

   III.   Pamphlets and Papers, 1809–1811; pp. viii, 437

   IV.   Pamphlets and Papers, 1815–1823; pp. vii, 422

   V.   Speeches and Evidence; pp. xxiv, 534

   VI.   Letters, 1810–1815; pp. xliii, 353

   VII.   Letters, 1816–1818; pp. xi, 387

   VIII.   Letters, 1819–June 1821; pp. xi, 403

   IX.   Letters, July 1821–1823; pp. xi, 401

   X.   Biographical Miscellany; pp. x, 424

   XI.   General Index; pp. xxxii, 114

THE WORKS
AND CORRESPONDENCE OF
DAVID RICARDO

EDITED BY
PIERO SRAFFA
WITH THE COLLABORATION OF
M. H. DOBB

VOLUME XI
GENERAL INDEX

CAMBRIDGE
AT THE UNIVERSITY PRESS
FOR THE ROYAL ECONOMIC SOCIETY
1973

PUBLISHED BY THE SYNDICS OF THE CAMBRIDGE
UNIVERSITY PRESS
Bentley House, 200 Euston Road, London NW1 2DB
American Branch: 32 East 57th Street, New York, N.Y.10022

© Cambridge University Press 1973

Library of Congress Catalogue Card Number: 51–12245

ISBN: 0 521 20039 3

Printed in Great Britain at the University Printing House, Cambridge
(Brooke Crutchley, University Printer)

CONTENTS OF VOLUME XI

ADDITIONAL LETTERS

3 a	Ricardo to S. Beckett	21 June 1810	*page* ix
137a	Ricardo to Joseph Hume	8 Nov. 1815	ix
197a	Malthus to Ricardo	11 January 1817	x
259a	Ricardo to Torrens	15 June 1818	xi
418a	Ricardo to Miss Bayley	30 January 1821	xii
492a	Ricardo to Thomas Booth	28 March 1822	xiii
516a	Ricardo to Wilmot Horton	19 January 1823	xv
517a	Mallet to Ricardo	24 February 1823	xvii
517b	Ricardo to Mallet	25 February 1823	xxi
531a	Townsend to Ricardo	20 July 1823	xxii
531b	Ricardo to Townsend	25 July 1823	xxiv
	Ricardo to Wright	22 August 1823	xxv
	Tooke to John Murray	8 January 1824	xxvi

ADDITIONAL NOTES

David Hume's supposed notes on the Wealth of Nations	xxvii
Changes in location of Manuscripts	xxvii
First publication of J. S. Mill's letter on his studies	xxvii
Identification of 'Piercy Ravenstone'	xxviii
Authorship of 'Life of Huskisson'	xxix
Marriage of Ricardo's grandfather	xxix
Pirated edition of 'Plan for a National Bank'	xxix
Build-up of mistakes in French editions of 'Principles'	xxix
A second freak copy of 'Principles'	xxx
Swift's Church of England Man	xxx
Authorship of 'Reply to Mr. Say'	xxx

CORRECTIONS TO VOLUMES I–X

(additional to the list in Volume X, p. 411) xxxi

INDEX

PREFATORY NOTE

THIS much delayed Index completes the edition of Ricardo's *Works*. Of the previous attempts at making an index, only one, sketched out with the help of Professor A. Heertje, proved useful for the final version. For the rest I am indebted to Mrs Barbara Lowe, who returned to Cambridge to help to complete the work begun many years ago.

P. S.

ADDITIONAL LETTERS

3a. RICARDO TO HIS SUPERIOR OFFICER, S. BECKETT[1]

New Grove Mile end
21ˢᵗ June 1810

Sir

I received your letter dated the 18ᵗʰ inst, directed to the Commander of the Sᵗ Leonard Volunteers, with instructions concerning assembling the Corps this day at 4 oClock.— I think it necessary again to acquaint you, that the Bromley Sᵗ Leonard Volunteer Corps, which I had the honour to command, has been disbanded nearly six months

I am Sir
Your obedᵗ humble Servᵗ
DAVID RICARDO

S. Beckett Esqʳ

137a. RICARDO TO JOSEPH HUME[2]

Gatcomb Park
8ᵗʰ Novʳ 1815

My Dear Sir

It is with the greatest concern that I inform you I am obliged to go to London on Sunday next[3] by the Gloucester

---

[1] MS in Public Record Office, "H.O.42–107". I am indebted to Sir Leon Radzinowicz for calling my attention to it.

Ricardo joined the Bromley and St. Leonards Volunteers in 1803, and was commissioned as Captain in the same year. See above, X, 47 & n.

[2] Addressed: "Joseph Hume Esqʳ / Cheltenham".—MS, International Autographs, New York, Cat. 15, 1964, item 292.

Joseph Hume (1777–1855), from 1818 M.P. for Aberdeen. At the time of this letter he had, at Mill's suggestion, planned to bring his newly wedded wife to Gatcomb. On a previous occasion he had arrived there only to find the family away. (See above, VI, 158, 310, 313, 325.) He became later one of Ricardo's chief allies in parliament.

[3] 12 November.

Mail, and that on Saturday I am going to Gloucester to pass that day with a friend of mine to whom I had written to secure me a place in the Mail. I very much regret that I am again disappointed in not having the pleasure of seeing you here, particularly as Mrs. Ricardo and I would have been happy in the opportunity which your visit would have afforded us of becoming acquainted with Mrs. Hume. There appears to be a fatality attending our meeting in this part of the world,—I hope we shall become better acquainted in London. I am writing immediately after the receipt of your letter, but have some doubts whether I shall be in time for the Post

I am My dear Sir
Yours very truly
DAVID RICARDO

197a. MALTHUS TO RICARDO[1]
[Reply to Letter 197.—Answered by 199]

[11 Jan. 1817]

[. . .] I am sorry to find from what you say that you do not feel yourself able to approach nearer to those opinions, which I still continue after repeated consideration to think correct.

Everything that has occurred lately appears to favour my idea of the all powerful efficacy of demand, and to shew that is very far indeed from depending merely on supply. I quite

[1] Addressed: "D. Ricardo Esqr. / Upper Brook Street / Grosvenor Square". Incomplete, dated from postmark.

MS in the Rothschild Library, n. 1388 of the Catalogue.

Ricardo had asked Malthus for his opinion on the plan lately adopted for the relief of the poor by employing them on public works. He himself did not think it a very efficacious mode of relief, as it diverted funds from other employments. (Above, VII, 116.)

agree with you in thinking that the funds raised for the support of the poor (though perhaps necessary at the moment) essentially interfere with other employments. But this opinion appears to me to accord with my view of the subject, more than with yours. According to you and Say, if people were willing to subscribe and convert their *revenue* into *capital*, there ought to be no difficulty, if the sole want is the want of supply; but in my view of the subject there ought to be a difficulty, from the want of a proportionate demand.

I shall be most happy to visit you in Brook street the very first time I am in Town; but I have now been a truant for some time and must stay at home a little.

Mrs M joins me in kind regards to Mrs Ricardo

Ever truly Yours

T. R. MALTHUS

259a.   RICARDO TO TORRENS[1]

London, Upper Brook St.,
15 June, 1818, 5 o'Clock

My Dear Sir,

I have this moment returned home, and find your letter[2] dated from the King's Head Inn, Rochester (13th June) on my table.

Mr. Philips[3] is in Sussex, attending his own election, and therefore he cannot be applied to attest that you are a fit and proper person to serve in Parliament,[4] in time to be of any

[1] This letter was quoted by Torrens in an election speech in 1832, and printed in full in the *Bolton Chronicle* of 17 November 1832. It was discovered by Mr B. A. Corry and published by him in *Economica*, 1957, pp. 71-2.

[2] Torrens' letter is not extant.

[3] Probably G. R. Phillips (as spelt three lines below), M.P. for Horsham.

[4] Torrens was contesting Rochester in the general election of 1818.

use to you,—but from my knowledge of Mr. Phillips opinion of you, I can attest that those are his sentiments, and if he were in town I am sure he would say that and much more in your favour. My own acquaintance with you entitles me to give it as my opinion that you would render great service to your country in the House of Commons. From your knowledge of Political Economy, your advice would be of essential use in all financial questions, and at present there appears to be a great dearth of that sort of talent amongst our legislators. It will give me great pleasure to hear of your success.

As High Sheriff for the County of Gloucester, I shall be obliged to leave town the latter end of the week, to preside at the election of members for that county.

I am sorry that I did not see your friend.

I am, most truly yours,

DAVID RICARDO

418a. RICARDO TO MISS BAYLEY[1]

London 30 Jan.ʸ 1821

My Dear Miss Bayley

I shall be happy to forward your letters whenever you will favor me with them;—that which you enclosed to me this morning was immediately after I received it despatched by the 3ᵈ post to its address.—I promise to do this, or any other kindness in my power for you, although I should not be flattered by the account of such favorable opinions as Mr. Corrie expressed of my arguments in favor of my own

[1] MS in the Houghton Library, here printed by permission of the Harvard College Library. I am indebted to Professor Frank W. Fetter for calling my attention to it. Ricardo had met the Bayley sisters, Sarah, Elizabeth and Ann, at Easton Grey, the home of Thomas Smith. See above, X, 350 & n.

doctrines on the disputed points in Political Economy. In truth however I am pleased that they had some effect on him.

You will like to know what Mr. McCulloch said of my notes. He thinks that I should not publish them in their present form—they are in his opinion too controversial, and although he considers them as establishing the doctrine of the effects of accumulation on the ground on which I had previously placed it, before Mr. Malthus wrote his work, he thinks I should lower my reputation if I became a commentator of every erroneous opinion which I might think I discovered in the writings of another political economist.[1]

I shall therefore I think proceed no further with the notes. They are now in the possession of Mr. Malthus and if they have any influence with him in inducing him to make corrections in his next edition they will not have been written in vain.

Pray give our united regards to Mrs. and Mr. Smith and Miss Mary Ann Bayley,[2] and accept them yourself from our family circle. I hope you will hear good accounts of your sister Anne.

Y^{rs} with great esteem

DAVID RICARDO

492a. RICARDO TO THOMAS BOOTH[3]

London 28 March 1822

Sir

I am very much obliged to you for the frank communication of your sentiments respecting the probability of

---

[1] See McCulloch's letter of 22 Jan., above, VIII, 338–40.
[2] Probably to be identified with the "Miss Mary Ann" of Ricardo's letter of 20 April 1822, above, X, 164–6.

[3] Addressed: 'Thomas Booth Esqre / Foxteth Lodge / near / Liverpool'. MS in Sotheby's sale, 28 July 1964, lot 534.

success, if I were disposed to listen to Mr. Hodgson's suggestion of becoming a candidate to represent in Parliament the town of Liverpool.[1] With your means of information I cannot have the least doubt that the opinion you have formed is a correct one. If I were well disposed to enter into so fearful a contest, your letter would make me pause and hesitate, as on the whole it does not hold out much promise of success; but since I had the pleasure of seeing Mr. Hodgson I have given the subject the most serious consideration, the result of which is that I must give up all thoughts of commencing a contest for which I am so unfit. I should be sacrificing my peace of mind for a considerable time for an object which I should not probably after all attain. I should be exchanging a seat of comparatively little trouble for one which would require constant attention, if I were to succeed. It is true that I should have the honour, which I know how to value, of representing a very important place, but I doubt whether I could be altogether as useful in my humble line, fettered as I should be by the particular views and opinions of my constituents, as I am now.

The reflection that Mr. Hodgson and a few of his friends thought so favourably of me as to be willing to give me their aid in elevating me to the rank of a representative of Liverpool will always be a source of satisfaction to me.

I remain

Sir

Your obed[t] and humble Serv[t]

DAVID RICARDO

[1] See Ricardo's letter to David Hodgson, declining the invitation to stand for Liverpool, above, IX, 182.

516a. RICARDO TO WILMOT HORTON[1]

Widcomb House, Bath
19 Jan.ʸ 1823

My dear Sir

My servant at Gatcomb Park having neglected to send my letters after me, I did not receive your note, with the pamphlets accompanying it, till this morning.

You know I am frequently reproached with being a theorist, and if those who so reproach me, mean that I am not conversant with the practical details of the subjects which have engaged my attention, they are right. The subject of the Poor-laws for instance is one intimately connected with the science of Political Economy, but nobody is so little acquainted with them, as forming a part of parish economy, as I am.

The question you refer to me relates wholly to Parish economy, and therefore I am not qualified to give a good opinion on it.

I can have very little doubt but that the plan[2] would be favorable to parishes. With the waste and extravagance of our system of poor laws an able bodied pauper must cost the parishes more than £35.[3] It is said in the "Outline"[4] that each able bodied pauper costs the parish £10 p.ʳ Ann.ᵐ, but

---

[1] MS in Central Library, Derby: it was located by Mr R. N. Ghosh (*Economica*, 1963, p. 47n.).

The letter was first printed in Wilmot Horton's pamphlet, *Causes and Remedies of Pauperism, Part I* (London, Murray, 1829), but was overlooked until Lord Robbins found it and reprinted it in *Economica*, 1956, pp. 172–3.

Robert John Wilmot Horton (1784–1841), M.P., was at the

time Under-Secretary for War and the Colonies.

[2] The plan was to mortgage the poor rates in order to finance the emigration of paupers to Upper Canada.

[3] The sum calculated as necessary to get a man to Canada and keep him until he was self-supporting.

[4] *Outline of a Plan of Emigration to Upper Canada* (*printed, but not published, Jan. 1823*).

against this must be set the value of the work which such pauper may be made to do for the parish, and also the general saving in the wages of labour which accompany the present system. If the farmer who pays £10, saves £5 in the wages of the rest of his workmen, his real contribution is only £5, and the real saving to the parish will be only a like sum.

With every emigrant we are to divest ourselves of £35 capital. If employed at home, with that portion of capital, he could replace it with a profit, England would be a loser by the proposed plan. The enemies of the plan will say that he could do so, and if they could make that appear I would rather adopt their plan, than the one recommended.

At the present moment however we are to compare the emigration plan to the system actually existing, and I can have no doubt that it would be attended with great advantages over it. The plan would be economical; it would enable us to get rid of the most objectionable part of the poor laws, the relieving able bodied men; and what is to me by far the most important consideration, it could not fail to make the wages of labour more adequate to the support of the labourer and his family, besides giving him that as wages which is now given to him as charity.

I told you how incompetent I was to say any thing worthy of your attention on this subject and I have now convinced you of it.

Believe me
Very truly yours
DAVID RICARDO

If you wish to have the pamphlets returned I will give them to you when we meet in London.

517a. MALLET TO RICARDO[1]
[Answered by 517b]

Upper Gower Street
24 Feb.ʸ 1823.

My dear Sir,

Mr Hume has given notice of a motion relative to Savings Banks, which has excited the attention of some of the principal Managers of these Institutions in London, and given them some anxiety. In the first place, we think that a habit of minute regulation, and of frequent Legislative interference is unfavorable to the experiment we are trying.

So far as could be collected from Newspaper Reports, Mr Hume's observations related to the rate of interest granted by Government to Depositors in Savings Banks, which he seemed to think unreasonable and wasteful. But I did not understand whether the observations were intended to apply to the rate of interest originally granted, or whether Mr Hume thought that the circumstances of the Country, or the state of the Banks, called for a reduction of the rate of interest.

On the first supposition, I should beg him to observe, that altho' the rate of interest originally granted and now enjoyed by the Banks £4.12 per cent was beneficial as compared with the rate of interest on other Public Securities, it was not materially so; the 5 per cents being then (June 1817) at 104¾ or 105 the 3 per cent consol. 74. Then there are comparatively speaking, a few cases only in which the

---

[1] MS in R.P.—This letter was published in Ricardo's *Minor Papers*, ed. by J. H. Hollander, 1932, pp. 210–13, but was not included in the present edition. Ricardo's reply having since come to light, the two letters are now published together.

John Lewis Mallet, son of Mallet du Pan; his diaries have been frequently quoted in these volumes. On Mallet's and Ricardo's common interest in Savings Banks, see above, VII, 50 n.

Depositors receive the whole amount of the interest granted by Government; the expenses of management of the Banks being generally defrayed out of the allowance of interest. The Depositors in two of the largest Banks in London, receive a rate of interest, not exceeding £3.17 per annum, which is in fact less than the interest they would have received had they invested their money in 3 per cent consol. If it be asked why so large a deduction is made, and why Government should bear this expence, the answer is that it is incidental to the proper management and security of such Establishments in large towns; and particularly in London. It is of the greatest importance that the Persons who conduct these Institutions should be men of the greatest respectability and at the same time, men of business. I speak from long experience when I say that it is extremely difficult to find Persons of this description who can give up any part of their time and that those with whom I am acquainted, and who attend to the Saving Banks in the City and in Southampton Row, are considerable Merchants, or men engaged in active professional pursuits. Now, when it is considered, that from the year 1817 to the year 1822, 6472 accounts were opened at the Bank in Southampton Row; which accounts must be kept with the greatest regularity, checked with the Depositors Book, the interest computed, the repayments entered; when it is further considered that notices of every repayment are to be given at least a week previously to the receipt of the Money; that these notices are all entered, and contain the particulars of the name and situation of the Depositor, his place of residence, the amount of his deposit; and that they are to be compared with the original entries of the Depositor, the signature of the depositor, and the Ledgers: it may easily be conceived, that independently of the labour of the Cash transactions of the Bank, which

partly occupy 2 or 3 Managers and four Clerks, twice in the week, the business of such an Establishment cannot be conducted without efficient and regular assistance; other than can be expected from the Managers themselves. But this is not all. The actuary and Clerks are necessarily entrusted to a considerable extent with the custody of Money; and we therefore require securities: their salaries are therefore necessarily higher. Again, convenient and large premises are required; both with reference to the great number of Persons who attend the Bank, and the number of Ledgers and Desks in constant use, and the propriety of decent accommodation for the Managers. Under all these circumstances, a large deduction from the rate of interest granted by Government seems unavoidable.

On the second supposition: namely that the circumstances of the country or of the Banks, or both, are so far altered, as to require a reconsideration of the rates of interest, I should say that the present state of Public Securities, affords no grounds for any change in this respect. The price of 3 per cents is the same as it was when the 57 Geo. 3ᵈ. Ch. 130 was passed: and in proof of the greater advantage derived from investments in Stock, I would mention that a great number of the larger Depositors in Savings Banks in London, have lately withdrawn their deposits, to place them in the funds. Our repayments for several weeks have exceeded by several hundred Pounds every week the amount of our receipts. With regard to the large accumulation of deposits in Savings Banks, amounting to several Millions; and the idea generally entertained that a portion of these deposits are received from an improper description of Persons, I beg leave to observe with reference to my former remarks, that Depositors do not at present derive, and are not likely to derive any advantage from

depositing their Money in Savings Banks instead of purchasing stock; and that this is not therefore a proper time for proposing any alteration in the rate of interest granted by Government. The sacrifice made by Government has been inconsiderable; particularly with reference to the great importance of the experiment now going on, and to the excellent effects which have already resulted from the Establishment of these Institutions. I think I may safely refer to the enclosed Report in support of this opinion.

Upon the whole I cannot but conceive that the agitation of the question as to Government keeping the terms upon which the Banks have been established, cannot but be productive of harm; and that any alteration in those terms would greatly check the progress of these useful Institutions, shake confidence and embarass and discourage to a very great degree, the Persons who have devoted to them so much of their time and attention.

Convinced as I am that Mr Hume has no other object than the Public good in view, I trust that if you will have the goodness to communicate these observations to him, he will not be unmindful of the circumstances to which I have taken the liberty of requesting your attention.

Believe me my dear sir

Your's very faithfully

J. L. MALLET

517b. RICARDO TO MALLET[1]
[*Reply to* 517a]

Upper Brook Street
25 Feb.ʸ 1823

My Dear Sir

Your very judicious remarks upon Savings Banks shall be communicated to Mr. Hume, and I have no doubt he will think with you that it will not be expedient to agitate the question of interest at the present moment. I heard the observations he made in the House—his objection was against the rate of interest allowed by Government, he said that a considerable loss was sustained by the public between the rate allowed, and that obtained by the Commissioners by investing the money in Stock. For the reasons you give I think the present not a favourable time to make any alteration in the rate of interest. Mr. Woodrow, the author of an annuity plan,[2] is very desirous of giving the working classes the opportunity of purchasing annuities on the lives of their children to commence after the children arrive at a certain age: I once mentioned the plan in the House. If any alteration were made in the Savings Bank Act I think I should again suggest this annuity plan.

Ever My Dear Sir
Yours very faithfully
DAVID RICARDO

J. L. Mallet Esqʳ

[1] MS in Sotheby's sale of 19 Feb. 1963, part of lot 456.

[2] On Woodrow's annuity plan, see above, V, 121, 128–9.

531a. TOWNSEND TO RICARDO[1]
[Answered by 531b]

Figgs Marsh, Mitcham
July 20th 1823

Sir

Altho' I have not the honour of knowing you, permit me to offer you my best thanks for the manner in which you have advocated the cause of religious freedom, and the important point of free discussion, and the liberty of the Press, whenever those topics have come under the consideration of the House of Commons during the present Session: and however much I might regret that your efforts, combined with those of Mr. Hume, and Sir Francis Burdett, proved of no avail in the House, I rejoice in the assurance that they were duly appreciated by the enlightened part of the Community out of it. Your Arguments, together with those Gentlemen who delivered their Sentiments on the same side, against the folly, as well as the injustice, of punishing Men for their Opinions, were, as the Examiner justly observed, admirable, clear, powerful conclusive-convincing, and the effect arising from the impression which they must have made upon the minds of those who perused them I have no doubt will ere long be fully evinced.

To Yourself Sir, as also to the above named Gentlemen,

---

[1] Addressed: 'David Ricardo Esq[r] M.P. / Upper Brook St.' Both Townsend's and Ricardo's letters were published in Richard Carlile's paper, *The Republican*, 26 Sept. 1823, Vol. 8, pp. 369–70.

Townsend's letter is here printed from the MS in *R.P.* It differs from the published version in being dated from Figgs Marsh, Mitcham (instead of from London), and containing the postscript.

Carlile came again to the defence of Ricardo in *The Republican*, 16 Jan. 1824, pp. 65–9, in a review of a pamphlet by the Rev. William Baily Whitehead, *Prosecution of Infidel Blasphemers, briefly vindicated in a letter to David Ricardo, Esq., M.P.*

all those Individuals who know how to estimate the importance of Political and Religious liberty, cannot but feel
greatly indebted, for the open and candid manner which you
have shown yourselves the enemies to every species of
persecution; and when I see Gentlemen of talents, fortune,
and integrity, standing up and holding such just and liberal
Sentiments, undismayed by the taunts of the bigot, and the
frowns of the interested; I say, when I behold Gentlemen
sitting in Parliament manfully contending for the rights of
the people, and that too, in a strain of reasoning that cannot
be refuted, I am (notwithstanding the gloom which at present
obscures the political horizon) led to cherish the hope that
by such exertions, I shall yet see the day when there will be
a less expensive and more happy form of Government
established in this Country than at present; and that in
fact, when Tyranny and Superstition shall be banished from
our Thresholds, and never more venture to violate our
Sanctuaries.

To conclude, as one of a numerous body of Men who
profess Republican principles, I cannot withhold my ad-
miration of your conduct with respect to that much injured,
and much calumniated, and misrepresented Individual,
Mr Carlile; and whose Sister's Petition you so ably supported. It is in pursuing such a course as this Sir, that you
secure the affections of all honest and well-meaning Men;
and as you appear to be actuated by a sense of the manifest
wrong, in imposing penalties for opinions expressed, either
with regard to Theology, or Politics, I cannot suppose for
a moment that you will relax in your endeavours to effect
free toleration, or that you will permit yourself to be deterred
therefrom, by any insults which the fanatic, and the place-
man, may think proper to offer you; but that you will prove
the Patriot, to stand by and advocate the great cause of free

discussion as alone calculated to elicit truth, and that you will not fail to denounce the iniquitous and cruel proceedings which continue to be exercised towards those, who seek for the Reformation of the Government.—I am Sir

With the highest respect

Your mo. Obed.^t Serv.

J<small>N</small> P. T<small>OWNSEND</small>

David Ricardo Esqr M.P.

P.S. My situation in life precludes me from openly declaring my Opinions, and therefore I write this in perfect confidence; but there are several Letters of mine in the "Republican", with no other Address than that of "London", I will, if you see no objection thereto, procure this to be inserted likewise, but certainly not without your permission.

531b. RICARDO TO TOWNSEND[1]

[Reply to 531a]

Gatcomb Park, Minchinhampton
July 25, 1823.

Sir,

I am happy that the sentiments which I expressed, on the occasion of the late discussion in the House of Commons on religious freedom[2] are approved by you: I trust I shall ever be found advocating the same cause, whenever it shall be submitted to the consideration of the House.

With respect to the publication of the letter, which you have done me the honour to address to me, in the Republican, you will be so good as to decide on the expediency yourself: being a friend to free discussion I leave every one

[1] The MS of Ricardo's letter is not extant. It is here reprinted from *The Republican*. See above, p. xxi n.

[2] See above, V, 324–31, and cp. 277–80.

to praise or censure my public conduct as he may think fit.

I remain, Sir, your obedient and humble Servant,

DAVID RICARDO

To Mr. John Townsend, London.

RICARDO TO WRIGHT[1]

Gatcomb Park
Minchinhampton
22 Aug. 1823

Sir

The speech on Mr. Western's motion[2] of which you wish to have a correct copy for the *Parliamentary Debates* contained a great many remarks on Mr. Western's pamphlet,[3] which besides being in my opinion very attackable on its own merits, was at variance with the frequently declared opinions of that gentleman. As I have not that pamphlet here I cannot refer to it, nor is it perhaps desirable that all those remarks should be published. I will look over the newspaper reports, and will, within the time you mention, send them back either with the printed report corrected, or with the speech written out as far as I can recollect it.

I am Sir

Your obed[t] servant

DAVID RICARDO

[1] Addressed: 'J. Wright Esq[r] / 112 Regent Street / London.— MS in Sotheby's sale of books 4 Nov. 1969, part of lot 274.

This letter is in reply to one (printed above, V, xxx) from John Wright, editor of *Hansard's Parliamentary Debates*, who had asked for a transcript of Ricardo's speech on Western's motion of 10 July 1823.

[2] Above, V, 309–21.

[3] *Second Address to the Landowners...*, by C. C. Western, 1822. See above, V, 317 & n. and cp. 522–8.

THOMAS TOOKE TO JOHN MURRAY[1]

Russell Square
Jan. 8, 1824

My dear Sir

Some manuscript papers of the late Mr Ricardo have by his executors been placed in the hands of my friend Mr. Mill with a view to his determining whether they are deserving of publication and if so in what form they should appear. One of these papers entitled "a plan for the establishment of a national bank"[2] is in a perfectly finished state:— It is very short but very clear and every way worthy of the Author's reputation.

Mr Mill is desirous, as you published for our late friend when living, that you should undertake this his posthumous work. I propose that he (Mr. Mill) and myself should meet if agreeable to you in Albemarle Street for the purpose of arranging the materials and the form of publication. I have accordingly to beg you that you will let me know whether it will suit you to receive Mr. Mill and me on Monday morning at a little before 10 and to devote half an hour to the object in question—With my best regards to Mrs. Murray believe me to be

Dr Sir

Most truly yrs
THO^s TOOKE

---

[1] MS in the possession of John Murray, the publishers. I am indebted to Professor F.W. Fetter for drawing my attention to it. A postscript dealing with a second edition of a work by Tooke himself is here omitted; Murray was at this time his publisher.

[2] Above, IV, 271–300.

ADDITIONAL NOTES

VOLUME I

[p. vii] DAVID HUME'S SUPPOSED NOTES on the 'WEALTH OF NATIONS'. An allusion by Professor Foxwell to the destruction of Hume's notes on the *Wealth of Nations* was quoted in the General Preface (I, vii). It should be made clear that the lost notes which Foxwell assumed to be by David Hume, the philosopher, were in fact by his nephew and namesake, a Scottish judge. See *Letters of Eminent Persons addressed to David Hume*, ed. by Hill Burton, 1849, pp. 315–17.

VOLUME VI

MARIA EDGEWORTH'S PAPERS (above, VI, xxxii–xxxiii, X, 387–8 & n.). At Mrs Harriet J. Butler's death, these papers passed to her son, the late Professor Harold Edgeworth Butler. In his will he expressed the hope that the MSS would be given to the British Museum, without, however, making it binding on his executors.

FRANCIS HORNER'S PAPERS (above, VI, xxxv). The bulk of these papers, lately in the possession of Lady Langman, have been deposited in the Library of the London School of Economics. Others, including the letters of Ricardo used for this edition, were retained by the family.

RICHARD SHARP'S PAPERS (above, VI, xxxvii). At the death of the Hon. Mrs Eustace Hills (Nina Kay-Shuttleworth), the MS of her biography of Richard Sharp was deposited in the Bodleian Library, Oxford. The papers of Sharp were dispersed, some being bought by Miss Myers, autograph dealer, of Dover Street, London.

VOLUME VIII

[p. 198 n.] J. S. MILL'S LETTER ON HIS STUDIES, FIRST PUBLICATION. J. S. Mill's boyhood letter to Sir Samuel Bentham was said (above, VIII, 198 n.) to have been published 'apparently for the first time' in A. Bain's biography of J. S. Mill, 1882. It has

now been found that the letter was first printed in *The Sheffield Telegraph* of 13 Feb. 1877, and reprinted in *The Times* two days later.

VOLUME IX

[p. 45] IDENTIFICATION OF 'PIERCY RAVENSTONE, M.A.' Ricardo refers several times with interest to the book, *A few Doubts as to the Correctness of some Opinions generally entertained on the subjects of Population and Political Economy*, 'by Piercy Ravenstone, M.A.'[1] It has been generally accepted that 'Piercy Ravenstone' is a pseudonym,[2] and it is now possible to give the author's real name.

A copy of *A few Doubts* has come to light, on the title-page of which 'Piercy Ravenstone, M.A.' has been crossed out, and 'Richard Puller' written in; 'Puller on Political Economy' is lettered on the spine of the binding, which is contemporary; this may well have been the author's own copy. Another copy, which is in the Feltrinelli Library in Milan, is inscribed on the fly-leaf: 'The real author of this book was Richard Puller, brother of Sir Christopher Puller, Chief-Justice of Bengal, and uncle of Christopher Puller, member for Hertfordshire about 1858. The present head of the family is Charles Puller, of Youngsbury, Herts.'[3]

Of Richard Puller little else is known. He is mentioned in the will (dated 2 October 1789) of his grandfather, Christopher Puller (1707–89), a director of the Bank of England; on 7 February 1827 he was given the administration of the estate of his father, Richard Puller (1746–1826), of Painswick Court, Glos., a director of the South Sea Company. His signature and his address, Park Street, Grosvenor Square, appear on an affidavit, dated 10 October 1831, in

---

[1] London, J. Andrews, 1821. See above, IX, 45, 59–60, 62–3, 64.
[2] See Max Beer, *History of British Socialism*, Vol. 1, p. 251, and Kenneth Smith, *The Malthusian Controversy*, p. 142. Professor J. Dorfman, in his Introduction to the reprint of *A few Doubts* (A. M. Kelley, New York, 1966), has suggested that Ravenstone was the Anglican minister, Edward Edwards, but there appears to be no evidence to support this conjecture.
[3] Charles Puller inherited Youngsbury in 1885 and died in 1892— which fixes the time limits for this inscription.

connection with the will of his sister, Charlotte Louisa Puller, of Painswick Court.

[p. 270n.] AUTHORSHIP OF THE LIFE OF HUSKISSON. The author of the biography of William Huskisson prefixed to his *Speeches* is E. Leeves, and not, as stated above, IX, 270 n., John Wright, who only edited these speeches. See British Museum Catalogue of Add. MSS 1911–15, p. 230.

VOLUME X

[p. 19] MARRIAGE OF RICARDO'S GRANDFATHER. Joseph Israel Ricardo was not married twice, as said above, X, 19, but only once, to Hannah Abaz. There were, however, two marriage ceremonies, the civil, in which his wife's name is recorded as Hannah Abaz, and the Synagogue, in which it appears as Hannah Israel. (Information from the Amsterdam records supplied by Professor A. Heertje.)

[p. 367] PIRATED EDITION OF 'PLAN FOR A NATIONAL BANK', 1824. An unrecorded printing, no doubt pirated, of this pamphlet has turned up. The pagination is [i]–iv, [5]–31 with a blank page at the end; as opposed to that of the original, which is [i]–vi, [1]–32 with two unnumbered pages of advertisements at the end. The only 'signatures' shown in the pirated edition are '2' on p. 9 and '3' on p. 17, whereas the original has the regular signatures, 'A' on p. [v], 'A2' on p. [1], 'B' on p. 15, 'B2' on p. 17, and 'C' on p. 31. Although the lay-out of the title-page is the same in both editions, the depth of the type area is $6\frac{3}{8}''$ in the 'pirate', as against $5\frac{3}{8}''$ in the original. The copy in question was supplied by Mr Ambaras, antiquarian bookseller of New York, and it seems likely that this pirated edition is American.

[p. 376] FRENCH TRANSLATION OF THE 'PRINCIPLES'. A build-up of mistakes in successive French editions of Ricardo's *Principles* resulted in a total travesty of his original statement on the effects of machinery. He had written: 'the opinion entertained by the labouring class, that the employment of machinery is frequently detrimental to their interests, is not founded on prejudice and error, but is conformable to the correct principles of political economy.' (I, 392.)

The chapter on Machinery (which was added in ed. 3 of the *Principles*, 1821) was first translated into French in the Paris edition of 1847, and the above passage read as follows: 'l'opinion des classes ouvrières sur les machines qu'ils croient fatales à leurs intérêts, ne repose pas *seulement* sur l'erreur et les préjugés, mais sur les principes les plus fermes, les plus nets de l'Économie politique.'[1] (Editor's italics.)

The intrusion of the word 'seulement' made nonsense of the whole statement. The editor of the next French edition (1882) tried to put it right without referring to the original English; and taking it for granted that Ricardo must have held the orthodox view, amended the passage to read: 'l'opinion des classes ouvrières sur les machines qu'ils croient fatales à leurs intérêts, ne repose pas *seulement* sur l'erreur et les préjugés, mais sur *l'ignorance* des principes les plus fermes, les plus nets, de l'Économie politique.'[2] (Editor's italics.) Thus the revised version represented Ricardo as saying precisely the opposite of what he had actually said.

This travesty held the field for half a century. The correct version was first given in C. Debyser's translation of the *Principles*, Paris, Costes, 1933–4, p. 217.

[p. 394, line 21] The 'work in English' referred to is Swift's *Sentiments of a Church of England Man*.

[p. 403] A second freak copy of Ricardo's *Principles*, 1817, containing pp. 219–22 in both the original state and the 'cancel' state (as described above, X, 403 ff.), has been found by Professor Heertje of Amsterdam, and is now in his possession.

[p. 405] The author of the anonymous pamphlet, *A Reply to Mr. Say's Letters to Mr. Malthus* (annotated by Ricardo) is John Cazenove, who has been mentioned as the author of another anonymous pamphlet above, III, 428 n. 1. See Halkett and Laing's *Dictionary of Anonyms*.

---

[1] *Œuvres complètes de David Ricardo* (in *Collection des principaux économistes*), Paris, 1847, p. 367.

[2] *Œuvres complètes de David Ricardo* (in *Collection des principaux économistes*), Paris, 1882, p. 329.

CORRECTIONS TO THE
FIRST PRINTING OF VOLUMES I–X
(*Additional to the list in Vol. X, p. 411*)

VOLUME I

p. xxxviii, note 3, *for* n. 2 *read* n. 3
p. 99, n. 2, line 4, *for* 1815 *read* 1816
p. 248, n. 3, last line, *for* 40, n. 2, *read* 41, n. 1
p. 421, n. 2, col. 2, end of last line, *for* rent. *read* rent,

VOLUME II

p. 336, line 7 from bottom, *for* cause *read* causes
p. 455, col. 1, under Distribution, lines 2–3, *for* introduction *read* production

VOLUME III

p. 165, line 8, *for* 'disadvantages' [misquoted by Ricardo] *read* 'advantages'
p. 179, n. 3, line 2, *for* An II *read* An XI
p. 345, line 2 and line 6, *for* October *read* September
p. 345, n. 2, lines 1–4, *for* 'Advertisement in *Monthly Literary Advertiser*, 10 Oct. 1810: a new edition was advertised on 10 Jan. 1811' *read* 'Advt. in *The Times*, 23 Sept. 1810; and a new ed., *ib.* 13 Dec. 1810 [nos. 2 and 4 in F. W. Fetter's 'Editions of the Bullion Report', *Economica*, 1955, pp. 153–4]'

VOLUME IV

p. 45, line 20, *for* their *read* its
p. 100, n. 2, last line, *for* 1926 *read* 1826
p. 125, line 3, *for* 1814 *read* 1804
p. 126, note †, *for* p. [120] *read* p. [122]
p. 157, line 14, *for* fifty- *read* sixty- (error in *Enc. Brit.*)
p. 162, line 26, *for* 793, 343 *read* 793, 348 (misprint in *Enc. Brit.*)
p. 274, line 11, *for* 14 pages *read* 14 leaves
p. 420, in heading, *for* Editions 1–2 *read* Edition 2

VOLUME V

p. xx, n. 4, *for* 197–8 *read* 246
p. xxix, n. 2, for *Cobbett's Parliamentary Debates* read *Cobbett's Parliamentary Register*
p. 369, n. 1, for *Abbott* read *Abbot*
p. 432, no. 54, *for* as *read* has
no. 5 read5, *for* found sound

p. 461, lines 4 and 12, *for* Catley *read* Cattley
p. 522, n. 3, *for* vol. X *read* X, 349
p. 530, col. 1, 3 lines from bottom, *for* Catley, Mr *read* Cattley, Stephen
    col. 2, line 21, *for* 491 n. *read* 492 n.
    col. 2, line 29, *for* 364, *read* 365
p. 532, col. 2, under Marcet, *for* 353–4 *read* 352–3
p. 534, col. 1, line 7, *for* Sidney *read* Sydney

VOLUME VI

p. viii, letter 103, *for* 1915 *read* 1815
p. xvi, n. 1, *for* VIII *read* VII
p. 337, 14 lines from bottom, at end of line, comma instead of full stop

VOLUME VII

p. 120, n. 3, line 2, *for* 10 *read* 410
p. 121, n. 1, *add* [But see XI, x–xi]
p. 197, n., col. 2, last line, *for* 1779 *read* 1781
p. 244, line 6, *for* difficult *read* different

VOLUME VIII

p. 116, n. 1, line 4, *for* 116 *read* 261
p. 207, n. 1, *for* I *read* II
p. 208, n. 3, *for* 22–4 *read* 122–4

VOLUME X

p. 359, entry [1 *h*], line 2, *for* [12] *read* [13]. (The same correction to be made on p. 360, entry [2 *c*], line 2; p. 361, entry [3 *d*], line 3; and p. 366, entry [6 *f*], line 2.)
p. 363, entry [5 *a*], the paragraph headed *Variant* should not be under the First Edition of *Principles* but under the Third Edition on p. 364, entry [5 *c*]
p. 397, line 11 from bottom, *for* 179 *read* 197
p. 400, line 11, *for* Supplement, 1811 *read* Supplement, 1810

INDEX

Abaz, Hannah (Ricardo's grand-mother), X, 19, XI, xxix

Abbot, Charles, Lord Colchester, *Diary and Correspondence*, V, 369 n.

Abe, Hiroshi, X, 384

Abercomby, James, M.P. for Calne, VII, 264 & n., see also V, 351, 352, 354

Aberdeen magistracy, VII, 303 & n.

Abrahams, Dudley, on 'Jew Brokers of the City of London', X, 22 n., 57 n.

Absentees in foreign parts, petition for tax on, V, 186–8

Absolute price, I, 63; absolute revenue, III, 281–2; absolute value of money, V, 209

Absolute value and exchangeable value, papers on, IV, 357–412. See also Value, absolute

Abstract currency:
abstract pound sterling, VIII, 32
ledger pound, VII, 44
imaginary currency (Blake), IX, 286
currency without a standard (Sir James Steuart), IV, 59–62

Abundance: effect of, on price of corn, IV, 219–22, see also V, 318–20, 523, IX, 378; different effects of, on money and on commodities, V, 169–71; see also Agricultural distress

Accarias de Serionne, Jacques, *La Richesse de la Hollande*, 1778, IX, 135 n.

Accounts, public: methods of keeping V, 67–8, 100, 115–16, 139; committee on, V, xxv–xxvi; balance-sheet form adopted at Ricardo's suggestion, V, 145

Accumulated and immediate labour, I, 34, 410, IV, 379, 386, VII, 316 n., IX, 307, 338–9, 343, 365

Accumulation: a misleading word, II, 320 n.; of capital and of produce distinguished, VI, 155, 164. See Capital

Acland, Sir Thomas Dyke, M.P. for Devonshire, V, 278

Acres, W. M., *The Bank of England from Within*, IV, 97 n.

Addington, Henry, later Lord Sidmouth, IV, 153–4, 165, VI, 261

Addison, Joseph, VI, 279

Address to the Nation...on the Doctrines lately advanced by Mr Malthus, 1815, VI, 269–70 n.

'Adjustment of property', V, 266, and cp. 21, 34–5, 126, VIII, 147 & n. See National debt, Ricardo's plan

Adler, secretary to Prince of Denmark, IX, 195

Administration of the Affairs of Great Britain, 1823 (attributed to J. S. Copley), V, 250 n., IX, 269 & n.

Agents of production (McCulloch on), IX, 342–3, 356–7, 359, 367–8

Agio: on British money, III, 288, on Napoleons, IX, 224

Agiotage, VII, 352

Agricultural Committee, 1820, V, 48, 56 & n., see also xxiv

Agricultural Committee, 1821, IV, 203–4, V, xxiv–xxv
speech on motion for, V, 81–91, VIII, 352–60
Ricardo a member of, V, 86–7
evidence, IV, 210–11, 221, 228 & n., 231, 241 & n., 259–60, 265, V, 214, 258, VIII, 366–7, 369–74, IX, 1, 66–7, 86–7, 106
Report, IV, 210 n., 244–5, 249, 251–3, V, 114, 151–2, 157, IX, 1, 28
drafted by Huskisson, V, 151 n., VIII, 390
reviewed by McCulloch, IX, 7 & n., by Senior, IX, 109 & n., 122

Agricultural Committee, 1822, IV,
203–4, V, xxv
speech on motion for, V, 129–38,
IX, 163–4, 166, 175
Ricardo a member of, V, 138, 157 n.,
182, 322, IX, 164, 176–7
evidence, V, 173–4, 181–3, 228
Report, IV, 245 & n., 246–50, 253,
V, 148, 155, 162–4, 172, 224–5,
228–9, 235, IX, 180
speeches on, V, 151–3, 155–7, 164–
86, IX, 187–8
Ricardo refuses to concur, V, 182–3;
his Propositions, V, 158–9, 172–
6, 180–1, 184–6, IX, 194 & n.,
197
Report reviewed by McCulloch, IX,
186 & n., 188
see also Corn Laws
Agricultural distress:
speeches on, V, 47–56, 141–2, 148–
54, see also 124–5
due to abundance, IV, 241–2, 258–
61, 263, V, 108, 125, VIII, 371,
IX, 157–8; and to corn-laws, V,
73–4, 79, 151, 170, VIII, 345,
357
not due to currency, IV, 230–1, V,
149–50, 233–4, 241–2, 315, IX,
167; nor to taxation, IV, 255–9,
V, 84, 89, 124, IX, 152, 165–6,
199–200
proposed loans to parishes for, V,
129, 133, 136, see also IV, 235 n.
see also IV, 234 n., IX, 267 n., and
under Labouring classes
Agricultural horses tax, V, 101, see
also IV, 255
Agriculture:
no claim to pre-eminence over manufactures, I, 75, VIII, 102–3; Adam
Smith controverted, I, 76–7 n.,
429, and Malthus, II, 18–22, IV,
37–8; see also VI, 229–30, VII,
270–1, 279
profits of, regulate all profits, VI,
104; dispute with Malthus, VI,
117–18, 133, 139–40, 144–5, 152–
5, 162–3, 167, 170, 182–3, 194

Agriculture (cont.)
withdrawal of capital from the land,
I, 80–2, 267–71, II, 135–6, IV,
28, 248–9
see also Corn, Diminishing returns,
Improvements in agriculture, Land
Aillaud, J.-P., publisher, VIII, 225 & n.
Albury, Malthus family home, his
MSS at, VI, xix–xx, X, 386
Alembert, d', his correspondence with
Voltaire, IX, 335, 374
Alessandria, X, 335, 337
Alexander I of Russia, X, 208
Algiers, V, 495
Ali Bey el Abbassi [pseud.], *Travels in
Morocco*, 1816, VII, 189 & n.
Alien bill, V, xxii
Allardyce, Alexander, IV, 112–13;
*Address to the Proprietors of the
Bank of England*, 1798, IV, 106 n.,
110 n., 415, VI, 242, 260, 265;
Second Address, 1801, IV, 103 n.,
112 & n., VI, 288 n.
Allen, Elizabeth, X, 45 n.
Allen, Jessie, Sismondi's wife, VIII,
25 n.
Allen, John, V, 471 n.
Allen, Mr, X, 285
Alpnach, X, 250
Althorp, Viscount, M.P. for North-
amptonshire, his amendment to
Ricardo's resolutions on the corn
duties, V, 176–8, 184–5, IX, 197;
see also V, 86
America:
Birkbeck's settlement, VII, 257,
259–60
cheap food and population, I, 409
emigration to, IX, 61
English currency in, III, 182–3 & n.
no-rent land in, I, 328, VII, 289, 297
prices of wheat and labour, VI, 232,
234, 236, 241, see also I, 15–16,
395, II, 138, 194–5, 213
relative prices of domestic and
foreign commodities, II, 145–7,
156, 383, IX, 78, 83–4, 91–3, 97–
100
rate of profits, VI, 129, 210, VII, 52, 57

America (*cont.*)
War of Independence, III, 251, 417, 419, V, 24, 215
see also III, 89, X, 271–2, and under Exchange
America, Spanish:
fertility of, II, 28–9, 87, 216, 341–3
day's labour in, II, 272
indolence of labourers, II, 337, 339–40, VII, 184, VIII, 216
gold and silver mines, I, 86, 195–9, III, 111, 127, 171, 362, 375, 391, V, 93 n., 391 n.
see also V, 205, 477
'Amicable arrangement' for national debt, V, 251–4. See Fundholders, gains and losses of
Amsterdam:
Ricardo's ancestors in, X, 18–19, 21
at school in, X, 3, 30–2
visit to, X, 205–12
Bank of, III, 126, 288
Exchange with, III, 73–4, VI, 97–9, 298–9
Anabaptists, Bayle's article on, X, 394
Andréadès, A., *History of the Bank of England*, X, 367–8
Angerstein, John Julius, X, 82
Anholt Mail, VI, 79 n., 80
Annales de législation et d'économie politique, 1822, IX, 245 & n.
Annales de législation et de jurisprudence, 1820, VIII, 376 n.
Annals of Philosophy, 1815, VI, 244 n.
Annual Biography, Memoir of Ricardo, I, xix n., III, 3 n., 4 n., 6 n., 9 n., IV, 273 n., X, 3 n., 14 & n.
Annual parliaments, VIII, 99, 107
Annual Register, for 1819, VIII, 111 n.; for 1822, IX, 195 n.
Annuities:
circulating, VIII, 293–5
life, V, 121, 129, XI, xxi
pensions plan and, V, 160, 191–5, 281
terminable, V, 270–1, IX, 175
see also I, 55–9, 174, III, 93–4, 341, IV, 64, 277
Antwerp, visit in 1817, VII, 160–2; in 1822, X, 191–3

Arbuthnot, Charles, Patronage Secretary, V, xvi, VII, 347
Arcot, Nabob of, VII, 243
Ardoin & Co., Ricardo's bankers in Paris, X, 99–101, 390
Arena for the employment of capital (Malthus), VI, 103 & n., 104, see also II, 140, 293
Aristocracy, political power of, V, 284–6, 496, VII, 323, IX, 86, 217
Aristocratical Conspiracy, Mill on, VIII, 106, 291, 295, 328, IX, 42
Arkwright's cotton-machine, IV, 33
Armstrong, F. E., *The Book of the Stock Exchange*, X, 129 n.
Arth, X, 245
Artificial checks to population, VII, 63, VIII, 71 & n., 80–1, IX, 62 & n.
Ashurst, William Henry, M.P. for Oxfordshire, V, 351, 366
Asiatic Journal, 1822, V, 475 n., 478 n.
Aslett, Robert, embezzler, IV, 97 n.
Aspland, Robert, Unitarian minister:
petition for free discussion of religious opinions, V, 324 n.
Ricardo attends his chapel, X, 40–1
Memoir of, by R. B. Aspland, V, 324 n., X, 40 n.
Assize of bread, V, 109
Astley, Francis Dukinfield, X, 99
Atheists, no justification for silencing, IX, 278, see also V, 277–80, 324–31
Atkinson, Jasper, *Letter to a Member of Parliament*, 1810, X, 401
Attwood, Mathias, M.P. for Callington:
on rise in prices since 1819, V, 105, 108
speech on agricultural distress, V, 162–9
attacks Peel, V, 186
on machinery and unemployment, V, 302
'no cause for triumph' over Ricardo, IX, 265–6
Letter to Lord Archibald Hamilton, V, 321 & n.

Attwood, Thomas, evidence before Agricultural committee, 1821, VIII, 370 & n.; Tooke on its absurdity, VIII, 371; see also V, xxiv, IX, 156

Prosperity Restored, 1817, VII, 151 n.; *The Remedy*, 1817, VII, 151 n.

Auckland, Lord, letter quoted, III, 413 n.

Austin, Anthony (D.R.'s son-in-law), X, 62; on Ricardo's last illness, IX, 388–9; see also VII, 13 n., 54, 325 n., 375, X, 161–3, 261, 348, 350, 352

Austin, Edward, sen., on Fanny Ricardo's marriage, X, 161–4

Austin, Edward (D.R.'s son-in-law), X, 62, see also VII, 325, 335, 350, 375, VIII, 183, X, 161–3, 348

Austin, Fanny, see Ricardo, Fanny

Austin, Humphrey, VIII, 226

Austin, John, introduced to McCulloch, IX, 124–5, 138, 142, 148–9, 187; see also X, 162

Austin, Priscilla, see Ricardo, Priscilla

Austin, William (D.R.'s grandson), X, 54

Austria, V, 77, VIII, 363 n.

Authentic Narrative of the Westminster Election, 1819 (by J. C. Hobhouse and F. Place), VIII, 125 & n.

Automaton Chess Player, V, 368, X, 402

Autun, X, 344–5

Avallon, Ricardo sleeps in the bed of Napoleon, X, 345–6

Axon, E., *The Family of Bayley*, X, 350 n.

Babington, Thomas, M.P. for Leicester, VII, 356

Bacon, Lord, 'Of Ambition', VI, 327; see also VII, 211

Baden, X, 230–1; Grand Duke's palace, VII, 165

Bagshot, Military College, J. S. Mill attends lectures, VII, 313–14, 326

Bagshot heath, VI, 124, VII, 300, 302

Bagster, bookseller, VI, 260

Bailey, Samuel, *Critical Dissertation on Value*, 1825, I, xxi–xxii, IX, 27 n.

Baillie, Joanna, IX, 143 n.

Baillie, Mathew, M.D., VII, 90

Baillie, Mrs, VII, 265, IX, 143

Baily, Francis, VI, 270, VII, 14

Bain, Alexander, *James Mill*, I, xxi n., III, 9 n., VII, 8 n., VIII, 60 n., 84 n., 243 n., 251 n., IX, 6 n., 150 n., 159 n., 280 n., 390 n., 391 n., X, 47 n., 118 n.

J. S. Mill, VII, 313 n., VIII, 198 n., XI, xxvii

Balance of powers in government, VII, 367–9, 374, VIII, 13–14

Balance of trade, III, 54

and balance of payments distinguished, III, 101 n.

unfavourable, always due to redundant currency, III, 59–61, 64 notes, 116, 360–2, V, 394–5, VI, 25–6

see also III, 205–13

Baldwin, C., publisher, VII, 207, 210, IX, 116

Bâle, X, 233

Ballot at Bank Court, VII, 19

Ballot, plan of voting by, V, 504–12, see also V, 112, 285–6, 474, 485, VII, 261, 272–3, 299, VIII, 99, IX, 60, 119

Bangor, VI, 107, 109, 113

Bank Advances bill, V, 23

Bank notes:

circulation of, in 1805–8 and 1812–15, VI, 266 & n.; in 1799–1815, VI, 286; in 1814–15, VI, 260 & n.

country, in relation to Bank of England, notes, III, 26–7, 86–8 & n., 227–35, V, 202, 375, VI, 11–13

deposited in Exchequer, IV, 79 & n., see also 91–2 n.

depreciation of, see Depreciation

economy in use of, III, 378, IV, 109

effects of resumption of cash payments on, VIII, 35 & n., 135 n., IX, 201–2

forgery of, see Forgery

Bank notes (*cont.*)

large and small, different effects of, III, 114–15, 371–2, 395

made legal tender in 1811, V, 316, VI, 45, 68

of insolvent banks, VI, 53, and cp. III, 202 n.

quantity of, relation to price of gold, III, 123–4, V, 423, see also VI, 281 n.; to bullion price of commodities, III, 64; no relation to public deposits, IV, 78–9

Bank of Amsterdam, III, 126, 288

Bank of England:

accounts, publication advocated, IV, 110–14, V, 36, 463–4, 466, VI, 268, 335; tables of, IV, 115–35, VII, 39

an unnecessary establishment, VI, 268, IX, 325–6

balances of cash, 1799–1800, IV, 91 n., 92 n., VI, 257

bargain with Perceval in 1808, IV, 53–4, 81–3, 89–90, VI, 261, 333, 337, 347

Charter, terms of renewal in 1800, IV, 53, 87–8, 91–4, 140–1, VI, 268

proposed extension, 1822, IV, 272, 278, V, 156 & n., 193, 247

report on, 1832, IV, 100 n.

see also IV, 106 n., V, 282, 336, VIII, 35

Court of proprietors, Ricardo's speeches at, V, 461–7, VI, 335–6, 343, VII, 11, 19 & n., 21

see also III, 9, 145, IV, 90, 106, 110, 231–2 & n., VI, 242, 276–8

Directors, their ignorance of the principles of currency, I, 353–4, III, 131–3, 147, 221, 377, IV, 112, 334, V, 14, 18, 201, 207, VIII, 21; their incompetence, V, 12, 76, 134–5, 143–4, 518–19, IX, 15, 176

fearful for the safety of their establishment, III, 62, 75–6; cajoled by ministers, IV, 282, V, 15

their integrity allowed, III, 152, IV, 110, V, 134, 143, VI, 336

Remonstrance on resumption of

Bank of England (*cont.*)

cash payments, IV, 267–70, V, 9 & n., 14 n., VIII, 32 & n.

Resolution on resumption, V, 9 & n., VIII, 21 & n.

discounts, scale of, III, 358 & n., IV, 99, 279, 415–18, V, 12 & n.

dividend, in 1816, VII, 26

Lord King's idea to stop, while gold above mint price, VII, 262–3

reduced in 1822, VIII, 35 & n.

see also III, 95, IV, 103–6, VI, 277–8

gold, Ricardo's advice to sell, and reduce issues gradually (1819) V, 12–13, 105–6, 133; advice ignored, 207; unnecessary purchases, 76, 143–4, 199–200, IX, 140–1; issues too much restricted, IV, 231–2, V, 201, 312, see also V, 61–2

Governor of (1810), III, 193 n., 227–8; see also Dorrien, Harman, Mellish, Pearse, Samuel Thornton, John Whitmore

Grenfell's Resolutions on, 1815, IV, 76–7, 86, 136–7, VI, 242 & n., 276 & n.; his motion, 1816, IV, 51 n., VII, 22, 25–6 & n.

loans to government, V, 35–6, 60, 63, 129, 133, 143–4, VII, 252 & n., VIII, 27, 134–5 & n., see also V, 23

Mellish's Resolutions on, IV, 86–8 & n., 138–41, V, 465 n., VI, 305

moral argument against, IV, 93, VII, 5

number of clerks employed, IV, 83–4, 97, 290, VI, 276 & n., 282–3

Parliamentary papers on: 1808, IV, 54, 81, 89, 90; 1811, V, 462–3 n., VI, 281; 1815, IV, 77, 90, 91–2, VI, 257, 259–60, 266; see also Bank Restriction Act

power of forcing a circulation, III, 214–21, 336, 364, see also VI, 67

profits: calculation of, IV, 96–105, 119–35, V, 433, VI, 282–3, 285, VIII, 34–5; less than expected (1819), V, 14 & n., 62–3, VIII, 27; obligation to distribute, IV, 105–10, V, 463–4, VI, 268, 303, 313; see also V, 193

Bank of England (*cont.*)
proprietors, their timidity, VII, 15–16; kept in ignorance, IV, 113
services overpaid, IV, 76–95, V, 100, 247, VI, 313, 338
stock of, whether to invest in, VIII, 33–5, see also III, 95
Volunteer Corps, IV, 97 n.
Bank of France, IV, 234
Bank of Hamburg, III, 126, 175–6 n., 288, V, 358
Bank of Ireland, III, 370, 398, V, 70, 98–100, 143, VIII, 24
Bank of Scotland, III, 228
Bank Post Bills, III, 117, 123, VI, 259 & n., 260–1, 266 & n., 286
Bank rate, and market rate, V, 97 & n.; lowered to 4% (1822), V, 222–3
Bank reserves, not a fixed proportion of circulation, III, 312–13, 322, VI, 17
Bank Restriction Act, 1797:
report from Commons' Committee, IV, 100 n., V, 175, VI, 8 n.; from Lords' Committee, III, 33, 78 n., 163, 188–90, 238, 364 n., IV, 80 n., 119 n., 283 n., 415, V, 461–2
and depreciation of currency, III, 132, 416–18, V, 143, 217, 236–7
checks to over-issue removed by, III, 17, 78, V, 92
see also I, 368, III, 255, 367, V, 253, 313
Bank Restriction Continuance bill, 1816, IV, 51 n., V, 465, VII, 28, 30 & n.; see also III, 400; in 1818, VII, 262
Lauderdale's Protest against, I, 371 n., VII, 265, 267, VIII, 3
The Bank – The Stock Exchange… An Exposé, 1821 (by J. Lancaster), X, 93–5 & notes, 123–4 & n.
Banks:
adventurers in, III, 335
compared with highways, III, 55
failures in Ireland, V, 70, 99
of credit and banks of deposit, III, 288, V, 437

Banks (*cont.*)
of issue, substitute for a gold mine, III, 54–5, 92, 215–17, 219, 376–7, provide a cheap currency, III, 55, 92 n., IV, 233–4, 276, 298, VII, 42
Scotch, III, 228, **235**, 399, see also VI, xxxvii
see also Country banks
Bankes, Henry, M.P. for Corfe Castle:
on restrictions on the importation of corn, V, 176–80
on religion, V, 329 & n.
see also V, 351, IX, 176, 279
Bannister, John, X, 111
Barclay & Co., bankers, III, 373
Barclay the brewer, VII, 109
Barham, Joseph Foster, M.P., V, 189
Baring, Alexander, M.P. for Taunton:
advocates double standard, V, 45–6, 71, 74–8, 92–6, 106, VIII, 346–7, 349–50
presents merchants' petition, V, 42, VIII, 164, 183 n.; lukewarm friend of free trade, VIII, 197
criticises Ricardo on sinking fund, V, 102, and on capital tax, 265–7
moves for committee on cash payments, V, 105–8; his evidence, 93 n., 352 & n., 356, 358–9, 360–1, VIII, 18 n.; his loans to France and resumption, V, 352 n., VII, 292 n.
moves for reduction of sinking fund, V, 272–3
on law of principal and factor, V, 292
on increased output of silver, V, 391 n.
prefers no gold in circulation, V, 403 n.
see also V, xxv, 48–9, 56 n., 59, 86, 102–3, 247, 335, VI, 244, VIII, 74 n., 361, 378 n.
Baring, Sir Francis, evidence to bullion committee, III, 132, 147, 370–2, 428, X, 93
Baring, Henry, M.P., V, xxiii n.
Baring Brothers & Co., V, 352 n., 355, X, 80, 82, 93, 125

Barnard, Viscount, M.P. for Tregony, V, 185

Barnes, Anne, wife of Benjamin Ricardo, X, 59

Barnes, John, Ricardo's partner as loan-contractor, X, 79–81, 82 n., 125 n.

Barnett, L. D., *Bevis Marks Records*, X, 18 n., 26 n.

Barre, de la, affair, IX, 374

Barrett family, of Hope End, X, 267 n.; big loss in Jamaica, X, 350 & n.

Barrett, Samuel Moulton, M.P., X, 267 & n.

Barrow, John, VIII, 58

Barter, all trade finally a trade of, I, 228, II, 146, 154, VI, 109; see also I, 137, 142, IV, 214, and under Foreign Trade

Barton, C. E., *John Barton, a Memoir*, VII, 155 n.

Barton, John, letter to, VII, 155–9
   view that demand for labour depends only on circulating capital, VII, 157–9; later accepted by Ricardo, I, 395–6 n.
   see also I, lviii–lix, II, 234, 245 n.
   Observations on the Condition of the Labouring Classes, 1817, VII, 155 n., VIII, 171 n.

Basevi, George (or Joshua), sen., VII, 10 & n.
   Ricardo's oldest friend, VII, 336; early studies, X, 34–5
   his visits to Gatcomb, VI, 312, 325, VII, 306, 308, 317, 324
   projected visit to Paris with, in 1803, X, 117
   bequest to, X, 105
   see also VI, 112 n., 190, 245 n., VII, 14, X, 14–15, 50

Basevi, George, jun., architect, VI, 250 & n., IX, 104–5 & n., X, 15 n.

Basevi, Naphtali, visits Say in Paris, VI, 245 & n., 246, 250, 264, 270; see also VII, 336, 351

Bassett, Joseph Davie, VIII, 337–8 n.
   Elementary Thoughts on the Bullion Question, 1820, VIII, 337 n., IX,

Bassett (*cont.*)
   135, 138–9, 156–7, 162, 164, 185, X, 400–1 n.
   Elementary Thoughts on the Principles of Currency and Wealth, 1830, VIII, 337 n.

Bath, visits to, VI, 161, VII, 15, 47, 71, 144, 307, VIII, 55, 329, IX, 101, 104, X, 7, 35–6; Malthus at, VI, 135, 139, 231, 234, 244, VII, 311, IX, 13; see also VI, 137, 157, VII, 55, 222

Bath Institution, VII, 23, 153

Bathurst, Earl, Secretary for War, V, 351, 354, 365

Battye, loan contractor, X, 82, 85

Baumstark, E., X, 377

Bautte, Jean-François, watchmaker, X, 270

Baveno, X, 291

Bayle, Pierre, *Dictionnaire historique et critique*, VII, 190, 196–7 & n., 206; extracts from, X, 393–4
   Pensées diverses, VIII, 49, X, 394

Bayley, Mary Ann, XI, xiii & n.

Bayley, Sarah, Elizabeth and Ann, VIII, 282, X, 350 & n.; letter to Miss Bayley, XI, xii

Bayley, Thomas, X, 350 n.

Beacon, newspaper, IX, 136 & n., 142, 187, 204, 207

Beattie, Dr James, VII, 277

Beaufort, Duke of: family influence in Gloucestershire, VIII, 62, 156, 162–3; hostility to Ricardo, VIII, 157 n.; see also VII, 187 n., 381–2

Beaufort, Francis, X, 167, 172, 174

Beaumont, Thomas Wentworth, M.P. for Northumberland, V, 185

Beauregard, Paul, X, 376

Bebb, Mr, V, 480

Becher, William Wrixton, M.P., V, 185

Beck and Allen, nurserymen, VII, 232

Beckett, S., letter to, XI, ix

Beer, VIII, 275, X, 198; duties on, V, 294–5, 301–2, 322, see also I, 252–4

Beer, Max, *History of British Socialism*, XI, xxviii n.

Beetroot, sugar from, IV, 248, V, 51, 91

Beggars: in Bologna, IX, 223, X, 312; in Flanders, VII, 164, much reduced in 1822, X, 184; in Ireland, VII, 175; in Leghorn, X, 321

Bellot, Pierre-François, X, 281 & n., see also IX, 220

Belsham, Thomas, Unitarian minister, VII, 171 & n.; Ricardo attends his chapel, X, 39–40; see also VII, 187, VIII, 56, 75 & n., 84

Belzoni, Giovanni, IX, 107 & n.

Benefit societies, VII, 12

Benett, John, M.P. for Wiltshire:
  presents agricultural petition, V, 148
  on import duties on corn, V, 173, 175, 181, 196 n.
  taxes on land, V, 131–2, 138, 257–8
  see also, V, 129

Bennet, Henry Grey, M.P. for Shrewsbury:
  on timber imports, V, 103
  taxes and agricultural distress, V, 154
  depreciation of currency, V, 215, 216–17
  national debt reduction, V, 272–3
  wages and machinery, V, 302
  see also V, xxii, 277, IX, 165 n., 194, X, 351

Bentham, Jeremy, VI, xxviii–xxxi
  and Burdett's resolutions, V, 493
  Chrestomathic school, VI, 112, VIII, 191 n., 197–9 & notes, 212
  circulating annuities, VIII, 293–5
  on corruption, V, 507
  Ford Abbey, VI, 124–7; Ricardo's visit to, VI, 156 n., 157 & n., 161 & n.
  Benjamin Franklin's bust, IX, 228 & n.
  list of letters, IX, 393; other letters quoted, VI, 161 n., VII, 273 n.
  marginal contents, VI, 329 n.
  his political economy, III, 261 n.
  MS on profits, X, 388 n.
  Ricardo as disciple, V, xix, VI, xxviii, IX, 52, 239, 259, X, 35
  walks in Green Park, VIII, 191, in Hyde Park, VI, xxviii n., VII, 277
  see also VI, xv–xvi, xxxiii, xxxv, 48, 52, 60, 105–6, 136, 251, 264, 317,

Bentham (cont.)
  VII, 4, 14, 61, 75, 170, 182 n., 183, 192, 285, 355–6, VIII, 17 n., 57, 150, 186 n., 242, IX, 201 n., 219, 248 n., 253, 274
  Chrestomathia, 1816, VI, 112 n.
  Plan of Parliamentary Reform, 1817, VII, 261 & n., 263 & n., 270; 'Bentham made easy', 1818, VIII, 116 & n., and cp. 47
  Table of the Springs of Action, 1815, VI, 314 & n.
  Tactique des assemblées législatives, X, 399
  Théorie des peines et des récompenses, X, 399
  Traité des preuves judiciaires, 1823, X, 277 n.
  Traités de législation, X, 399
  The True Alarm (Sur les prix), 1810, III, 261–6, VI, 13–20; Ricardo's Notes on, III, 259–341
  Works, ed. J. Bowring, III, 262 n., 263 n., V, 493 n., VI, xxviii n., 106, 112 n., 161, VII, 74 n., 167 n., 273 n., VIII, 115 n., 116 n., 293–4 notes

Bentham-and-Mill school, IX, 52, 253, 259

Bentham, Sir Samuel, J. S. Mill's letter to, quoted, VII, 313 n., VIII, 198 & n., XI, xxvii; see also VI, 127

Bentinck, Lord William Henry Cavendish, M.P., motion on Sicilian affairs, V, xxii

Beranger, and Stock Exchange fraud, VI, 106

Berar and Scindia, Rajah of, VII, 243

Bergami, Bartolomeo, VIII, 304, X, 292–3 & n.

Berkeley, Colonel, VII, 221, 223–4, 335

Berkeley, George, his theory of ideas, VII, 229, 235 & n., see also 277
  The Querist, VIII, 353 & n., IX, 231

Berkhamstead, VI, 92

Berlin Decrees, III, 430 & n.

Bernal, Ralph, M.P. for Rochester, VIII, 157 n.

Berne, X, 261–3

Berrow, Ricardo's estate, X, 98, see also VII, 232 & n., 299 n., IX, 108, X, 105

Besterman, T., *The Publishing Firm of Cadell and Davies*, VI, 160 n.

Bex, X, 283

Biaujeaud, H., *Essai sur la théorie ricardienne de la valeur*, I, xxxviii n.

Bills of exchange:
  transfer, never pay, a debt, III, 206, 246, IV, 332, VI, 80, see also III, 54
  effect on prices, III, 323
  and rate of exchange, I, 138–40, 146–9, VIII, 87–9
  marketing of, in London, VIII, 37, 39
  see also X, 29 n.
  for other Bills see under Bank Post, Exchequer, Navy, Ordnance

Bimetallism, see Double standard

Binda, Giuseppe: pearls at an auction, VII, 54 n.; visits Gatcomb, VII, 56; sails to the Brazils, VII, 171–2, 276; see also VII, 114, 139, 144 n.

Bing, A., *Frankfurter Stadttheater*, X, 224 n.

Bingham Richards & Co., X, 318 n.

Binning, Lord, M.P. for Rochester, V, xxvi

Binns, Samuel Thomas, III, 345, 350

Birch, Joseph, M.P. for Nottingham, V, 185

Birkbeck, Morris: *Notes on a Journey in America*, 1818, VII, 257 & n., 259–60; *Letters from Illinois*, 1818, VII, 259 n.; see also VIII, 16 n.

Birmingham merchants' petition, V, 71

Birth control, see Artificial checks, Population, checks to, Prudential habits

Black Dwarf, VIII, 329 n.

Black, John, editor of the *Morning Chronicle*, IX, 201 & n.

Blackwood's Magazine:
  on Ricardo's *Principles*, VII, 316 & n., 326, 332, 362

Blackwood's (cont.)
  on McCulloch and the Scottish Whigs, VIII, 25 & n., 205 n., IX, 205–6 n.

Blair, Hugh, *Lectures on Rhetoric*, 1783, VI, 326 & n.

Blake, William, F.R.S., VI, 206 & n.
  Observations on . . . the Course of Exchange, 1810, III, 173 n., 209–10, IX, 284 & n.
  Observations on the Effects Produced by the Expenditure of Government, 1823, IV, 325; Ricardo's Notes on, with Blake's replies, IV, 323–52; Ricardo's unpublished review of, IV, 353–6; discussion of, IX, 271–2, 275–7, 284–7, 289, 293, see also 301 n., 312, 345, 362
  letter to McCulloch, IX, 302
  see also III, 11, IV, 396 n., V, 352, VII, 28–9, X, 49–50, 271, 392 n., 400 n.

Bland, Maria Teresa, X, 111

Blanqui, Jérôme Adolphe, X, 375–6, 380

Blasphemous Libels Act, V, xxii, VIII, 148 n.

Bleasdale, Lowless & Crosse, Ricardo's solicitors, V, xvii n., xviii n., VII, 306, 327, 382, X, 42, 98–9, 390

Block, Maurice, X, 376

Bloom, H. I., *Economic Activities of the Jews of Amsterdam*, X, 19 n.

Boats, at Gatcomb, VII, 51, 55–6, 68, 71, 76; Malthus's four-oar, VIII, 64

Boddington, Miss, V, 352

Boddington, Samuel, VII, 291 & n., see also V, 352, VI, xxxvi, VIII, 152 n.

Bognor, VII, 171

Bologna, X, 311–13; beggars, IX, 223, sausages, X, 303

Bolton Chronicle, XI, xi

Bonaparte, Louis, King of Holland, IX, 210

Bonaparte, Napoleon:
  prevents export of corn from Russia, IV, 28; permits it from France to England, IV, 29

Bonaparte, Napoleon (*cont.*)
scheme for producing sugar from
beet, V, 51, 90–1, VIII, 356
return from Elba, VI, 194 & n., 199,
229, X, 345–7, see also VI, 188,
344
Waterloo, VI, 231–2 & n., 235, 238,
280–1, X, 333
death, IX, 6, 12
anecdotes, X, 211
marks of his genius everywhere, X,
289, 299, see also IX, 221–2, 234
and *High Price of Bullion*, X, 374
see also VI, 255, VII, 267, IX, 247 n.,
X, 324, 335
Bonar, James, on the ingot plan, V,
369; see also II, xiv n., III, 406,
IV, 415, VI, xx–xxi, 159 n., VIII,
35 n., IX, 174 n., X, 370, 371, 399
Bonazza ('Banasso'), X, 307
Bonelli, Vincenzo, his bust of Ricardo,
V, 1, X, 53 & n., 318 & n.
Bonn, X, 217
Book society, VIII, 134
Bookers of Edmonton, coachmakers,
VI, 131
Booth, Thomas, letter to, XI, xiii
Borghetto, X, 327, 345
Bornsteinowa, M., X, 379
Borough system, V, 509
Mallett on, VII, 254 n.
vested rights in, V, 285
boroughmongers, VIII, 74 n.
Scots burgh system, VIII, 326
Whig boroughs, VIII, 336
Borromeo, Count, X, 291
Bosanquet, Charles, *Practical Obser-
vations on the Report of the Bullion
Committee*, 1810, III, 10–11, 159 &
n., X, 400, ed. 2, with Supplement,
III, 204 n., 247 & n.; Ricardo's
Reply to, III, 155–256
Bosanquet, Jacob, East India Direc-
tor, VII, 135–6, 139
Bossi, Giuseppe, X, 301 & n.
Bounties, I, 301–26
Adam Smith on, I, 304–10, see also
VII, 100, 107–8
divert capital, I, 314, 339

Bounties (*cont.*)
drawbacks and, distinguished, IV,
243–4
on export of corn, I, 301–4, when
justified, VIII, 359; on export of
manufactures, I, 312–14, of Irish
linen, V, 57–8 & notes
on production of corn, I, 321–5, of
other commodities, 325–6
see also I, 142, 179
Bourbons, VI, 235
Bourne, William Sturges, M.P. for
Christchurch:
his committee on the poor laws, VII,
209 n.
poor rates misapplication bill, V, 1,
6–7, VIII, 25, 74 n.
settlement of the poor bill, VIII, 30,
32
see also V, xxiv, 86
Bouverie and Antrobus, bankers, VI,
277 n.
Bouverie, Philip Pleydell, VI, 277 & n.
sides with Ricardo at Bank Court, IV,
106, V, 463, 466–7, VI, 335 n., 336
see also VII, 11, 15–16, 19 n.
Bow, VI, 84, VII, 80, X, 24–5, 36
Bowles, John, *Provident Institutions*,
1817, VII, 130
Bowood, VII, 191, 198 & n., 284, 311,
X, 37 n.
Bowring, John, X, 58
Autobiographical Recollections, VI,
xxviii, IX, 228 n., X, 73–4
see also Bentham, J., *Works*
Boyd, Benfield & Co., loan contrac-
tors, X, 75 n.
Boyd, Walter, banker, III, 364 n., VI,
9 & n.; *Letter to W. Pitt*, 1801,
III, 4, 261–2 & n.
Bradford, Wilts, VI, 100 & n.
Brady, A., *William Huskisson*, III,
427 n.
Brand, T., M.P., IV, 5 n.
Brandon, Raphael, X, 25 n.
Brassage, V, 431
Bray, Miss, VII, 253
Bray, Mrs (Malthus's sister), VI, xx n.,
322, VII, 265

Bray, R., VI, 322
Bray, R. A., II, xiii n., VI, xx n.
Brazils, V, 477, VII, 171–2, 276
Bread:
early view that tax on, raises price of every commodity, III, 270; later view, I, 302; see also under Price
demand for, not affected by price, I, 385, nor by tax, I, 237 n.
as measure of value, X, 185
price regulated by loaf that pays no rent, II, 42–4, IX, 171–2
Breakfast parties at Ricardo's: Maria Edgeworth, IX, 230 & n., X, 172–3; Grote, VI, xxxiv; Malthus, VI, xix, 28–9, 31, 77, VII, 35; Mill, VI, xxxiv, VII, 188; Mushet, VI, 88; Sharp, VI, xix, 28–9, 31, 77; Trower, VIII, 19, 345
Breda, gentlemanly bookseller at, X, 193–4
Brescia, X, 300–2
Brieg, X, 285, 288
Brientz, Lake of, X, 255
Bright, Henry, M.P. for Bristol, V, 306–7
Brighton, Ricardo family at, in 1795, X, 109–12; in 1810, X, 118; in 1820, VIII, 206, 213; in 1823, IX, 279–80
see also VIII, 318, X, 336
Brinsop Court and Manor of Brinsop, Ricardo's property, VII, 217, X, 98, 105
British Press, newspaper, V, 31 n., 81 n., 93 n., 97 n., VIII, 357
British Review:
review of Ricardo's Principles and Say's Traité, I, li, 60–1 n., VII, 219, 222, 229, 231, 235, 256, 259, 289 n.
on Poor Law report, 1817, VII, 219, 248–9
Broad Street Buildings, family home at the time of Ricardo's birth, X, 29 & n.
Broadley, John, letters, VII, 39–44
his Ledger pound, VII, 44
Pandora's Box, 1801, VII, 39 n.

Brodie, John, agriculturist, IV, 260
Broglie, Duc de, IX, 242 n.
supports Ricardo against Sismondi, IX, 218, 235, 242–3, 248, X, 277–8, 281–2, and against Bentham, III, 261 n.
Souvenirs 1785–1870, IX, 242 n.
see also VIII, 224, IX, 219–20, 230, 236, X, 178, 269, 351
Broglie, Duchesse de, IX, 218, 235, 243, 248, X, 277–9
Bromesberrow, Manor of, Ricardo's property, VII, 232 n., X, 97, 98, 104 & n.
Bromesberrow Place, X, 97, Osman Ricardo's residence, VIII, 48–9
Mill prefers it to Gatcomb, VIII, 51, 231
Ricardo papers at, I, viii, II, xv
see also VI, xxxii, IX, 27, 37, 41, 90, 101, 104, 115 n., 263, X, 64, 386
Bromley and St Leonard Volunteers, Ricardo captain in, X, 47, XI, ix
Brook Street, see Upper Brook Street
Brooksbank, Thomas, VI, 43 n.
Brooks's club, VIII, 28 & n., 163, X, 50; Memorials of Brooks's, VIII, 28 n., X, 50 n.
Brougham, Henry, M.P. for Winchelsea, later Lord Brougham:
sketch of Ricardo, V, xxxii; calls him 'an oracle', V, 40, 'dropped from the clouds', V, 56, 85
negotiations for Ricardo's seat, V, xvi–xvii, VII, 293, 300, 304, 306–7, 355, 358–9, 362–3, 371, 373, VIII, 326–7
on Owen's plan, V, 30, 32
opposes Ricardo's plan for capital tax, V, 40, 268, VIII, 239
advocates reduction of taxation, V, 124–7 & n., 132–3, 137
on usury laws, V, 335
on effect of agricultural taxes, IV, 239–40 & n., V, 131
on Ricardo's resolutions on agriculture, V, 176, 177–8, 182
Report on education of the poor, VII, 150 n., 303–4 & n., 306, X, 262 n.

Brougham, Henry (*cont.*)
model infant school, VII, 356–7 & n.,
  359–60, 363, 371
travels in Italy, VII, 61, 74
scandal about him, VII, 84, 86
vacillations on reform, VII, 266–7,
  274, 303
his bad political economy, IX, 164,
  167, 207
see also I, 269 n., V, xxiii, 86, 185,
  302 n., VI, 127, 180, 280, VII, 89,
  179 n., 285, 305, 382, VIII, 59,
  63–4, 148, 196, 204, 289, 328, IX,
  197, 265, X, 41 n., 50
Historical Sketches of Statesmen, V,
  xxxii–xxxiv, X, 53
Broughton, Lord, *Recollections of a
  Long Life*, X, 36 n., 228 n., 273 n.
  See Hobhouse, John Cam
Brown, James, letters, VIII, 94–104,
  see also X, 391 n.
Brown, Thomas, VI, 113 n.
Browne, Denis, M.P. for Kilkenny, V,
  87
Brunnen, X, 245–8
Brussels, X, 187–90
Bruttini, Dr (?Butini), IX, 218, X, 271
Buchanan, David: his edition of
  Wealth of Nations, with Notes and
  an additional volume, 1814, VI,
  159 & n.; Ricardo re-reads, VII,
  101, 115, VIII, 4; Mill on, VII, 108;
  McCulloch on, VII, 353, IX, 206
bounties, I, 314–15
debased currency, I, 355–6, 370
rent, I, 77 n., 398–9, 400, II, 119,
  VII, 120
taxes on raw produce, I, 251–4, on
  wages, 218–20
wages and price of provisions, I,
  216–18, 315, 382
see also I, 106 n., 334, II, 105, VII,
  279, 316 n., X, 399
Buchanan's articles on Ricardo in
  Caledonian Mercury, IX, 206 & n.
Buckingham, Duke of, *Memoirs of
  George IV*, V, xxiii n.
Buckland, C. S. B., *Metternich and the
  British Government*, III, 432–4 notes

Budget, speeches on, (1819) V, 20;
  (1820) 63; (1821) 115; (1822) 220;
  (1823) 248
Bulky commodities and foreign trade,
  I, 144, II, 86, VI, 22, 27, IX, 81,
  98, 285
Bullion:
its value regulated like any other
  commodity, VI, 24–5
effects of peace and war on price of,
  VI, 344
Bullion Controversy, III, 3–12, see
  also VII, 246
Price of Gold, Ricardo's letters on,
  III, 13–46
High Price of Bullion, III, 47–99
Horner's motion for committee, VI,
  xxxiv–xxxv, IX, 123 n., X, 8,
  14–15, 92; letter to Horner, VI,
  1–7
Bullion Report, 1810, III, 8, IV,
  416–18; recommends reducing
  circulating medium, III, 142–3
Malthus's review, III, 10–12, 99–
  114, 120–3, VI, 50 & n., takes
  middle course, II, 150–1
Ricardo's *Three Letters* on, III,
  129–53; his Notes on, III, 345–78
Reply to Bosanquet, III, 155–256
Mill's paper on, VI, 49–50, 60;
  Malthus on Mill's paper, VI, 61–2
see also III, 116, 118, 123–4, 295,
  380, 385–6, 392–3, 397–401, 427–
  34, IV, 99, V, 461–2, VI, 43,
  VIII, 89 & n., 140, IX, 289, X, 399,
  401
Horner's Resolutions, III, 413 & n.,
  414
Vansittart's Counter-resolutions, III,
  413–14 & n., Ricardo's Observa-
  tions on, III, 415–23
'Bullion Committee' of 1819, V, xxxii,
  VIII, 152 n.; see Resumption of
  Cash Payments
Bullion merchants, III, 71, 73, 140,
  165, VI, 90
Bullion plan, Ricardo's, IV, 65–73;
  see Ingot plan
Bullionists, II, 150–1, VI, 328, 343–4

Buonaparte, Napoleon, IV, 28–9, V, 51, VI, 229, 235. See Bonaparte
Burdett, Sir Francis, M.P. for Westminster, VI, 181 & n.
resolutions for reform in 1818, V, 493 n., VII, 266 & n., see also VIII, 47 n.
election, 1818, VII, 269–70 & n.
see also V, xxii, 169, 170, 474, 484, VII, 273 n., 274, 307 n., VIII, 6, 59, IX, 268, X, 397, XI, xxii
Burgess, H., project for an extra post, V, 148
Burke, Edmund, VIII, 385
Thoughts on the Cause of the Present Discontents, 1770, VII, 261
Works, X, 397
Burning of corn in the country, VII, 45, 49
Burton, J. Hill, *Letters of Eminent Persons to David Hume*, XI, xxvii
Bury Court, Manor of, Ricardo's property, X, 97, 104
Bury street, St Mary Axe, Ricardo's childhood home, X, 30, 36
Bushe, Charles Kendal, IX, 274
Butcher's meat, I, 424, VIII, 99, 103, see also 371–2
Butini, Dr Pierre, X, 271 n., and cp. IX, 218
Butler, Harold Edgeworth, I, xi, VI, xxxiii, VIII, 56 n., X, x, 33 n., 167, XI, xxvii
Butler, Mrs Harriet J., VI, xxxiii, IX, 203, XI, xxvii
Butterworth, Joseph, M.P. for Dover, V, 330 n.
Buxton, Thomas Fowell, M.P. for Weymouth and Melcombe Regis, defends Spitalfields Acts, V, 295, 296, 306, 307
Memoirs, 1848, X, 90 n.
Byron, Lord, his house in Venice, X, 309; see also VII, 131 n., IX, 199 n.

Cadenabbia, IX, 221, X, 292
Caff, Mr, IX, 116 & n.
Cairnes, John Elliott, I, ix, VI, xvii–xviii & n., X, 391

Calais, VII, 160, X, 182–4
Calas affair, IX, 374
Calcraft, John, M.P. for Rochester, later for Wareham, V, 84, 89, 109, VII, 252
Caledonian Mercury, IX, 206 n.
Calvert, Nicolson, M.P. for Hertford, V, 183
Cambridge: visit to Osman Ricardo at, X, 136–40; David jun. at, VIII, 284, 293, 297; see also VI, 31 & n., IX, 280 n.
Cambridge University Library, Ricardo MSS at, X, 386
Camden, Lord, X, 169
Campbell, Lord, *Life*, V, xxviii n.
Campbell, Miss, X, 272 n.
Campbell, Thomas, VIII, 152 n.
Campolongo, A., X, 355
Canada: distress in, V, 144–5; emigration to, XI, xv n.; timber trade, V, 104, 306; see also X, 395
Canals, I, 133, 152, 251, II, 368, V, 32, VIII, 155; in Venice, IX, 222, X, 309
Canard, N. F., *Principes d'économie politique*, X, 399
Cancels in first edition of *Principles*, I, xxviii–xxx, X, 403–4, XI, xxx
Candide, VII, 102
Candles, duties on, IV, 257, V, 146–7; as necessaries of labourers, I, 20, 104, 224, 234, 275, 306
Cannan, Edwin:
A Review of Economic Theory, I, xxv, xxxvi, xxxviii, xl, 20 n.
History of the Theories of Production and Distribution, VII, 3 n.
The Paper Pound of 1797–1821, III, 427
'Ricardo in Parliament', V, xxii–xxiii, 490
review of *Notes on Malthus*, II, xvi
Canning, George, M.P., President of the India Board till Jan. 1821, Foreign Secretary from Sept. 1822:
on corn bill, V, 195
reform of Parliament, V, 285–8

Canning, George (*cont.*)
in committee on resumption of cash
payments, V, 350, 354, 365
his eloquence in debate, VIII, 148
resigns from Government on Queen's
trial, VIII, 326 & n.
the King bars him from Cabinet, IX,
115, 120, 124
and Governorship of India, IX, 116–
17 & n., 146–7, 182 n., 215
see also III, 413 n., 432, V, xix n.,
197, 250 n., VII, 51 & n., 305,
VIII, 20, 68 & n., IX, 270 n., X,
305
Capadose, Dr Abraham, X, 210–11
& n., *Conversion de M. Capadose*,
1837, X, 207 n.
Capadose, Dr Immanuel, X, 32, 210–
11
Capital:
defined, I, 95
accumulation of, I, 131, II, 391, 417,
V, 438, VIII, 102–3, see also II,
315, VI, 16–17, 164
due to productive consumption,
not to non-consumption, I, 150–1
& n., II, 326–7
profit as motive for, I, 122, 290,
334, 411, II, 310–11, 331, IV,
16 n., 35, VI, 121; foreign trade as
incentive to, I, 133
effects on profits, I, 126, 289–96,
II, 221–2, V, 137, VI, 95, 103–5,
146–9, 162, VIII, 208–9; curious
effect on rent and profits, IV, 16
limited by diminishing returns from
land, I, 98, II, 302, 321, IV, 179
impeded by taxation, I, 152 & n.,
160, 166, VIII, 168–70
not affected by depreciation of
money, III, 273
never injurious to a country, II,
329, 365, 438, V, 118, VIII, 217;
still advantageous in England, III,
274; increased in spite of war, I,
151, V, 95, VI, 94–5
and power to employ labour, I, 79,
95, 104, II, 352–3, V, 501, VI,
148, VIII, 258, 270

Capital (*cont.*)
Malthus's most objectionable chapter, VIII, 181, 185, 212, 378
agricultural capital, I, 117, 269, VI,
226; security and respectability of,
IV, 38
and free import of corn, I, 269 n.,
IV, 32–3, 242, 248–9, V, 83–6,
88–90, 256, VIII, 108, 130
and manufacturing capital, I, 76 n.
in revulsions of trade, I, 266–71
apportionment of capital between
trades, I, 88–91
arena for the employment of, II, 140,
293, VI, 103 & n., 104
circulating and fixed: distinguished,
I, 31, 52 & n., 150, 207, 266; proportions of, I, 396 n.
circulating: demand for labour depends on, II, 234, see also I, 95;
wages as, I, 32, 52
fixed capital: curious effect of wage-
rise on products of, VII, 82–3, 98
and cp. I, 35, 43
does not reduce employment (early
view), VII, 157–9; Barton's contrary view accepted, I, 395–6 n.
motives for substitution of fixed for
circulating capital, VIII, 389
effect of substitution of labour for,
II, 237–9
definition of fixed capital extended,
IV, 312, see also 306
constant and variable, IV, 306
demand for, unlimited, VI, 301, 318,
see also I, 293–4
diminution, effects of, I, 78, 165,
VI, 110–11, 113–14, 116–17, 119–
21, 123, 142
distribution of a country's, I, 154,
267, IV, 32, 35, V, 501, VI, 345, of
world capital, I, 172
emigration of, I, 136–7, 247–8, III, 274
encouraged by high price of corn,
IV, 16 n., 237, V, 33, 38, 50, by
low rate of interest, VII, 171, by
taxation, II, 452
in 1820–1, VIII, 152–3 n., 353,
357–8, 364–5

Capital (*cont.*)

floating capital, I, 89

whether a capital employs as much labour in foreign as in home trade, I, 350–1

labour and capital cannot both be redundant, II, 241, 339, 426–7, VIII, 181, 185, 278

Malthus's view that the proportion of capital to labour determines profits, VII, 52, 69, 77, 80, 215; opposed by Ricardo, VII, 57, 72, 78–9, 81–2

measure of capital, VI, 249, 272, 274

equal capitals and equal value of products, I, 42, 62 n., 207, IV, 307, 309–15, VII, 315 n.

difficulty of defining equal capitals, IV, 393–5, IX, 357, 359–60 & n.

mobility of, I, 134, 136–7, 191–2, 268–9 & nn., II, 87, 351, IV, 25, 28

capital not increased by increase of money, I, 143, III, 390

capital and money, proportion between, III, 54, 92–3

that pays no rent, I, 72, 74, 110, 328–9, 412–13 n., II, 73, 166–7, 172, IV, 38, 240, VI, 177, 198, VII, 372, VIII, 4, 149

proportion of, to population, V, 32; see also under Wages

of the stockholder not productive, I, 249 n.

Capital punishment, V, xxi

Capitalist, I, 90–1, 136, 424–6, II, 62, III, 165, IV, 230–1, V, 32, IX, 13, of the mine, I, 197–8

capitalists and cheap corn, IV, 35; and monopolies, II, 409

Capper, Henry, X, 55

Card, Mrs, milliner in Pall Mall, X, 145, 148, 151–3, 157–8

Carli, Tommaso, banker in Milan, IX, 224

Carlile, Mary Ann, speech for her release, V, 277–80, see also 325 n., XI, xxiii

Carlile, Richard, prosecution of, V, 325

Carlile, R. (*cont.*)

publishes Ricardo's letter in *The Republican*, XI, xxii n.

see also V, 277, 330 n.

Carlsruhe, VII, 163–5, X, 229

Caroline, Queen (till 1820 Princess of Wales):

notices Ricardo's child, X, 112

her residence on Lake Como, IX, 221, X, 292–5

her trial, V, 69, VIII, 199–200, 206, 220–1, 223, 226, 230, 237, 250, 259, 276, 284, 287–91, 314, 335, 347

barred from Coronation, IX, 30 & n.

a 'persecuted woman', VIII, 299, 303–4

popular support for, V, 469, VIII, 241–4, 295–6; higher and middle classes further separated, VIII, 308

her death and funeral, IX, 38–9, 41, 69 n., 88 & n.

see also V, 64 n., VII, 208 n., VIII, 324, 326 n., IX, 6, 12, 115

Carriages:

Malthus's low gig, VI, 130, 131, 133

low phaeton, VIII, 231–2, X, 240

carriage for the Continent, X, 177, 188–9, 197

barouche, X, 231–2

covered carriage, X, 261

charabanc, X, 250, 273

duc de Broglie's equipage, X, 281

see also I, 242, V, 148, VII, 82, 254, IX, 377, X, 208, 306, 319, 347

Carrington, Lord and Lady, X, 169–70, see also VII, 356

Carruthers, Mr, V, 477

Carrying trade, I, 293–4, 349, V, 102, 305, VI, 93

Carter, John, M.P., V, 185

Cash accounts in Scotland, I, 365–6

Cash payments bill, see Resumption of cash payments

Cassel, VII, 160, X, 183

Castlereagh, Viscount, Foreign Secretary:

in committee on resumption, V, 350, 354, 365

Castlereagh (*cont.*)
and Catholic question, VIII, 362
see also V, 17, 28, 86, 124, VIII, 374
from 1821, see Londonderry, Marquis of
Catholic emancipation, see Roman Catholics
Cato Street plot, VIII, 163 & n.
Cattle: that pay no rent, II, 70, 73; fall in value of (1822), V, 164, IX, 166; see also VIII, 371–2
Cattley, Stephen, V, 461
Cavendish, Lord George, M.P. for Derbyshire, X, 302, 305, 327
Cavendish-Bentinck, see Bentinck
Cazenove, John: *Reply to Mr Say's Letters to Mr Malthus*, 1820 (anon.), annotated by Ricardo, X, 405–10; see also X, 401 n., XI, xxx
The Evidence that WOULD *have been given by Mr* ——, 1832 (anon.), III, 428 n.
Chambers, William Cecil, evidence before bullion committee, III, 362–4, 429 n.
Chambéry, X, 340
Chamonix (Chamouny), X, 273–5
Champion, The, Torrens's newspaper, IX, 113–14 & n., 120, 122
Chancellor of the Exchequer (N. Vansittart till Jan. 1823, thereafter F. J. Robinson):
on public deposits and Bank profits, IV, 83, 87 n., 90, VI, 334
defends sinking fund, V, 5
on resumption of cash payments, V, 8, 91
denies leakage, V, 18–19
announces new loan, V, 20–2
on reduction in currency, V, 23
moves for new taxes, V, 23
on Owen's plan, V, 30
lowering of import duties, V, 57
criticised by Ricardo over Budget and sinking fund, V, 63–5, 67–8, 115–19, 138–9, 220–2, 259–65
on integrity of sinking fund, V, 79, 194

Chancellor (*cont.*)
commutation of Navy five per cents, V, 140–1
financial situation of the country, V, 248, 250 n.
new sinking fund, V, 266, 271
on condition of the people, V, 492 n.
negotiations for loans, X, 75–6, 78, 81–3, 85–90
see also II, 433, IV, 227, V, 35, 58, 61, 70, 96, 105, 108, 129, 145, 148, 156, 247, 301, 335, VI, 261, VII, 116 n., 252 n., 292 n., VIII, 29–30, 134 n., 332, IX, 291 n.
Chandler, Elizabeth, see Smith, Mrs Thomas
Chandler, Mrs, VIII, 63 n., 75
Channel of circulation, III, 148–50
Channel of currency, III, 219
Charities, I, 73 & n., VII, 248, see also VIII, 171, XI, xvi
Charlotte, Princess, VII, 207–8, 218
Charlotte, Queen, VII, 222 n., 372
Charterhouse, Osman at, X, 61; David jun. at, VI, 128 n., 239, X, 62
Chatham, Lord, VIII, 74 n.
Chaumette, L. A. de la, VI, 112 n.
Cheap currency, IV, 234, VI, 36, 41–2, VII, 42; see also Redundancy of currency
Checks, banker's, III, 237, IV, 58, whether included in money, III, 298; checks issued upon the government, V, 39
Cheltenham, visits to, VI, 135, 161, VII, 70, 358, 361; see also VIII, 243–4
Chepstow, VIII, 231, IX, 27
Chernishev, D. R., X, 382
Chesterfield, Lord, IX, 105
Chetwynd, George, M.P., IX, 181
Cheyt Sing, VII, 237
Children employed in the Manufactories, report on, 1816, VII, 146, 150
Chillon, IX, 220
Chinard, G., *Jefferson et les Idéologues*, X, 372
Chlenov, S. B., X, 383

Chrestomathic School:
  Bentham's plan for, VI, xxviii–xxxi,
    112 n.
  subscriptions to, VI, 112–13 n.
  buying ground for, VII, 184, 190,
    198 & n., VIII, 191 n.
  plan abandoned, VIII, 197–9 & notes
  see also VI, xxxvi & n., 127, VII,
    182 n., VIII, 212, IX, 58 n.
Christian VIII, IX, 195 n.; see Den-
  mark, Crown Prince of
Christians' petition for free discussion,
  V, 324, XI, xxiv
Chuan Shih Li, X, 385
Church and State breed, VII, 211, see
  also VIII, 284
Circulating annuities, VIII, 293–5
Circulating medium, III, 74
  real amount of, III, 143, IV, 58
  distribution of, III, 120–2
  checks and bonds not included, III,
    298
  see also Money
Clarendon, Lord, *History of the
  Rebellion*, IX, 45
Clarens, IX, 220
Clark, J. M., article on Distribution,
  IV, 6 n.
Classes:
  higher, influence of, at elections, V,
    485
  rich class, existence of, ensured by
    rent, IX, 126
  middle classes: not created by national
    debt, II, 444–5; their exertions
    justly praised, IX, 55; see also
    VIII, 308, 314
  inferior class of tradesmen, their
    votes influenced by threats, V, 285
  working classes: combination laws
    unjust to, VIII, 316; often calum-
    niated, IX, 54–5 & n.; see also IV,
    347, V, 303, 308, XI, xxi, and
    Labouring classes
  struggle between rich and poor, IX,
    42, 45
Clerk, George Russell, student of
  Malthus, VI, 240 & n., 291, 295,
  VII, 114

Clerk, Mr, VI, 240
Cleves, X, 213
Clive, E. B., V, 471
Clubs of London, The, 1828, VI, 87 n.
Clubs, Ricardo's, X, 49–51
Clutterbuck, Account of the Family of,
  by M. Witchell and C. Huddleston,
  X, 62 n.
Clutterbuck, Daniel, X, 62, 96 n.,
  162
Clutterbuck, Edmund, VIII, 243
Clutterbuck, Henrietta, see Ricardo,
  Henrietta
Clutterbuck, James, VIII, 243–4
Clutterbuck, Thomas (D.R.'s son-in-
  law), X, 62; buys Hardenhuish
  Park, X, 315–16; see also VI, 100,
  219, 312, 323–5, VII, 48, 84, 110,
  262, 269, 304, VIII, 56, 183, 329,
  IX, 44–5, 103, X, 12, 162, 261,
  319, 348, 352
Coaches:
  Bath and Exeter, VI, 127, 157, 320
  Brighton Slap-bang, X, 110
  Salisbury mail, VII, 148
  Gloucester mail, XI, ix–x
  London to Gatcomb, VII, 277, 331,
    VIII, 310
  see also VI, 186, 242, 281, 285, 299,
    302, VIII, 211
Coal duties, V, 275
Coal mines, I, 68, 330–2, V, 218, see
  also II, 22, X, 99; coal hewers,
  VIII, 99
Cobbett, William:
  first clash with Ricardo, III, 26 & n.;
    dubs him the 'Oracle', V, 40–1 n.;
    continues attacks, VIII, 74 & n.,
    IX, 140–1 & n., 228, 250, 266–7
    & n.
  dispute with Burdett, VIII, 6 & n.
  on Tooke, IX, 106 & n.
  defends use of machinery, V, 302–3
    & n.
  on gold as standard, IX, 123 & n.
  the all-devouring monster (the fund-
    holder), IV, 229 & n.
  advises hoarding sovereigns, IX,
    166–7 & n., 176 & n.

Cobbett, William (*cont.*)
see also II, 360 n., V, xxv, 166 n.,
VII, 75, VIII, 314, 317, IX, 120,
153, 265 & n., X, 185, 333 n.
Cobbett's Parliamentary Register,
1820, V, xxix n., 43 n., 48 n., 64 n.
Cobbett's Weekly Political Register,
III, 26 n., IV, 229 n., V, xxvii,
41 n., 302 n., VIII, 74 n., 144 n.,
IX, 106 n., 123 n., 141 n., 166 n.,
167 n., 176 n., 250 n.
Coblentz, VII, 165, IX, 211–12, X,
218–21
Coburg, Prince of, VIII, 347
Cochrane, Lord, and hoax on the
Stock Exchange, VI, 106–7, VII,
62–3 & notes, IX, 111 & n., see
also X, 41 n., 69, 124
The Trial of Lord Cochrane, 1814, X,
399
see Dundonald, Earl of
Cockburn, H., *Memorials of his Time*,
VIII, 167 n., IX, 136 n., 187 n.
Cockerell, Samuel Pepys, architect
employed by Ricardo, VII, 17–18
& n., X, 48
Codrington, Sir Edward, V, 352, X,
189–90
Coin:
law against exporting or melting
gold coin, III, 18, 24, 25 n., 56, 60,
63, 125–6, 187–9, 415–16, V, 381,
430–1, 511–12, VI, 2; repealed in
1819, V, 490
silver coins legal tender till 1816, I,
368–9 & n., 371 n., V, 16–17 & n.,
VIII, 3
resumption of cash payments and
gold coinage, V, 97, 206, 255,
VIII, 21, 39, IX, 202
recoinage: of 1695, failure of, III,
202, see also III, 31, 69, 141, 177,
V, 215, VIII, 24; of 1774, III, 32,
40, 70 n.; of 1816, V, 386–7, X,
201
see also III, 36–7, 68–9, IX, 201–2
Coke, Thomas William, M.P. for
Norfolk, his Sheep Shearing, IX,
46; see also IX, 265

Cologne, VII, 160, X, 215; pont
volant at, X, 216; see also IX, 209,
211
Colonial trade, I, 338–46
cannot affect rate of profits, I, 344–5,
VII, 202
restrictions on, V, 144–5, 188–90,
298, IX, 130–1
see also Canada, Sugar
Colquhoun, Patrick, *Treatise on the
Wealth of the British Empire*, 1814,
VIII, 94
Colthurst, Sir Nicholas Conway,
M.P. for Cork, V, 218
Combermere, Lord, X, 185
Combination of workmen, effect on
wages, VII, 203 & n.
Combination laws, opposed by Ricardo, V, xx, 332, VIII, 313, 316,
338, IX, 55 & n., 61; see also V,
296
Commerce:
adds to utility, not to value, I,
264 n., II, 389–95, see also I,
271
profits of, regulated by profits of
agriculture, IV, 23–4, VI, 167,
170
more liable to stagnation than
agriculture, IV, 254–5
see also Foreign trade, Trade
Commerce, treaties of, I, 340–2
Commercial distress, 1819, speech on,
V, 37–41; see also Distress
Committees, parliamentary:
on which Ricardo served, V, xxiii–
xxv. See Accounts, public; Agricultural, 1821; Agricultural, 1822;
Ireland, labouring poor in; Law
Merchant; Poor law; Sewers;
Stationery
to which he gave evidence, see Resumption of cash payments; Usury
laws
other parliamentary committees, see
Agricultural, 1820; Bullion; Corn
laws; Corn trade; Finance; Foreign trade; Poor laws; Wine
trade

Commodities:

are purchased with commodities, II, 395, see also 308 n., 393, IV, 214

whose only merit is their high cost in labour, II, 357–8

commodities generally (in general), I, 228 n., IV, 61, V, 374, IX, 79; see also Mass of commodities

Community of goods (Owen), IV, 222, V, 31, VIII, 46

Como, and Lake of, X, 292–7, see also IX, 224

Comparative costs and foreign trade, I, 133–41

Competition:

sinks prices to cost of production, I, 387, II, 24–5, 38, V, 189, VI, 24, VIII, 277, see also I, 12, 91, III, 390

domestic, and export prices, II, 153, IX, 96, 98

of capitals, and profits, III, 92, 143, 165, see also I, 62, IV, 24, VII, 69, 77

of employers for labour, I, 163, 220–1

fairest for public contracts, V, 59, for wages, I, 105, VIII, 316

see also I, 342, VI, 25, 129, 203

Complete Peerage, V, xv n.

Comte, Charles, VI, xxvii

Condorcet, *Life of Turgot*, VII, 365, 382, X, 399

Coningham, William, III, 370

Constable, Archibald, bookseller, IV, 145, VII, 316 n.

Constancio, Francisco Solano, translator of *Principles* into French, VII, 361 n., VIII, 161, 225 n., X, 374–6, 379

Constantinides, N. P., X, 355

Consumers, taxes on commodities fall on, I, 157, 159–60, 205, 252–4, 256–7, IV, 33–4 n., 240, V, 74, 136–7, VI, 173, VII, 94; see also II, 405–6

Consumption:

limited only by production, I, 151 n., II, 305–6, IV, 178, V, 435, VI, 164, VIII, 181, IX, 13; Malthus's

Consumption (*cont.*)

contrary view, II, 307, VIII, 216, IX, 16, 20–1; see also V, 111, 219

effect on, of taxes on food, I, 237 n.

unproductive consumption, no more stimulating than a fire, II, 421; discussions with Malthus on, II, 421–5, 433–6, VIII, 185, 301, 311, IX, 10–11, 15–17, 19–26; by labourers, or by employers, different effects (Malthus), IX, 22; see also I, 150–1 & n., IX, 27 n.

Continental Merchant, see 'Mr ——'

Continental tour of Ricardo, with his brother in 1817, VII, 160–5, 167–8, 178, X, 343, 347; with his family in 1822, IX, 208–51, X, 175–352

Continuation, see Time bargains

Cooke, Edward, *Address to the Public*, 1819, V, 365 & n.

Cooke, W. H., *History of the County of Hereford*, X, 98

Cooper, C. H., *Annals of Cambridge*, VI, 31

Coplestone, Edward, *Second Letter to Peel*, 1819, X, 391; article 'State of the Currency', 1822, IX, 249

Copley, J. S., V, 250 n.; see *Administration of the Affairs of Great Britain*

Copper, IV, 374, VI, xxxiii n., X, 388

Coppet, visit to Duc de Broglie at, IX, 218, 235–6, 242–3, 248, X, 269, 277–80

Corn:

whether a better standard of value than gold, V, 164, 166–7, 210–13, 237–9, 313

imports of, effect on profits, II, 222, IV, 22–3, 26–7, VIII, 208–9, 357–8, on rents, I, 421 n., 427–8, IV, 35, 38–9, 41

corn that pays no rent, VII, 379, see also II, 73, 166, 182–3, IV, 240, VIII, 194

see also Agriculture, Food, Raw produce

Corn, price of:

regulated on land that pays no rent, I, 74, 110, 156, 176, 225, 329, II, 70, 73

and rate of profits, I, 113–14, 120, 132, II, 125, 217–18, IV, 26, 37, 237, V, 50, VI, 168, 194, 210, 291

price of, and value of, distinguished, IV, 235–6

real labour, or natural, value of, I, 323

natural price of, I, 301; see also under Natural price

high price, and difficulty of growing, I, 113, 145–6, 312, IV, 19, 265, V, 167, VI, 220, VIII, 209; and scarcity of fertile land, VI, 181

advantages of high price (Malthus), VI, 231, 236, 255–6; disputed, IV, 212–13, VI, 233–4, 241, 269; advantages of low price, I, 270, 424–6, II, 412–13, IV, 239

cheap corn, and ability to pay taxes, I, 8, 421–4, IV, 39–40, VII, 104; Ricardo's riddle, V, 83, 88–9

whether all prices regulated by, IV, 21 n.; see also under Price

rise in, increases the whole surplus (Malthus), VI, 185; see Surplus

at various periods, V, 167–8, 212–13, 521, see also VIII, 374 & n.

rise of, in 1814–15, IV, 40, not due to taxation, VI, 181

unnaturally low, in 1815–16, V, 318, VI, 303–4, 344, VII, 16; in 1821–2, IV, 259–61, V, 72, 89, 108, 233–4, 241, IX, 152, 157–60, 199–200

Corn laws:

true principles of, V, 256

evils of, IV, 250, V, 55, 79, 151, 170–2; diminish production, IX, 197–8; drive capital to cultivation of poorer land, IV, 247, 263; lower profits, V, 33, 38; send capital abroad, VIII, 357–8, 364–5; sudden opening of ports ruinous to home-grower, IV, 242

Corn laws (cont.)

withdrawal of protection proposed, IV, 263–6, V, 156–9, 172–3, 180–4, VIII, 359; countervailing duty allowed, IV, 217–19, V, 82, 87, 151–2, 159, 257–8, VIII, 356–7

Report on, 1814, IV, 3, 29 n.

corn law, 1815, IV, 3–4, 249–51, V, 48, 52; petitions and riots against, IV, 70, VI, 180 & n., 183 & n., 184; see also VI, 158, VIII, 97, 101, IX, 165 n., 176

corn law, 1822, V, xxv; speeches on, V, 155–9, 170–86, 195–7, 256–8; see Agricultural committee 1822

see also under Protecting duties, Restrictions on importation

Corn-ratio theory of profits, I, xxxi–xxxii, xlviii–xlix, VI, 204; renders theory of distribution independent of value, VIII, 194, 297, 337

Corn trade:

true principle of, V, 87–8

committee on, IV, 3

tables of quantities and prices, IV, 270–1, IX, 166 & n., 181

project of loans to speculators in, IV, 253–5, see also V, 85, 90

cost of sending corn from country to London, II, 368–9, from Poland or Prussia, VIII, 374, from interior of America, IX, 98

see also V, 101–2, and under Free trade in corn

Coronation of George IV, V, 69; a harlequinade (Mill), IX, 7; 'the mighty Corronation' (Trower), IX, 30 & n.

Correggio, price of a picture, X, 312

Corrie, Mr, XI, xii

Cossa, Luigi, X, 355

Cost of production:

made up of wages and profits, VIII, 279, IX, 75, see also II, 369, IV, 36; nearly in proportion to quantity of labour, II, 35, 79

the regulator of price, I, 73 n., II, 25, 48–9, IV, 20 n., V, 300, of value, V, 212

Cost of production (*cont.*)
cost and value distinguished, I, 47 n.,
II, 34–5, 101
word 'cost' used ambiguously by
Malthus, II, 273, IX, 4
see also Difficulty of production,
Diminishing returns, Natural price
Cost price, IX, 81, 100
Cotton:
Arkwright's machine, IV, 33
cotton goods, manufacture of, II,
153, IV, 251–2, 374; export of,
II, 363
cotton-trade, V, 482
weavers, distress of, V, 68–9
see also I, 117, 317, V, 30, 31 n.,
214
Coulson, Walter, VIII, 186 n., see
also 10 n.
Counter-commodities, glut due to
lack of (Say and Torrens), VIII,
227, 260
Countervailing duties:
principle of, VIII, 356, see also IV,
246, V, 47–8
for taxes peculiar to one commodity,
IV, 243–4, 264, V, 45, 53, 82, 87,
151–2, VI, 206, IX, 8
correct view taken in Agricultural
Report, 1821, IV, 251–2
on corn, Ricardo's proposal, V, 82;
see under Corn laws
Country banks:
their notes and Bank of England
notes, III, 87–8, 227–35, 340, V,
375–6, 384, 389–90, VIII, 85–6;
guarantee for notes, IV, 72–3
their deposits in London, III, 295–6
failures in 1815, IV, 73, VI, 328,
343, see also VI, 268, VII, 16
under plan for a national bank, IV,
287–9, 292, 294–5, 300; under
ingot plan, V, 380
see also III, 151, 368, V, 156 notes,
VI, 116, IX, 176, 201–2
Country gentlemen:
a compact body to oppose reforms,
IX, 180, 194; Ricardo a mark for,
IX, 249

Country gentlemen (*cont.*)
attitudes to the poor, VIII, 43, 307,
and cp. VII, 142
pursuits of (Trower on), VI, 326, VII,
173, 268, 308–9, VIII, 322, IX, 312
Ricardo not half a country gentleman,
VII, 207
County meetings, see Gloucester-
shire, Hereford, Norfolk, Surrey
Courier, see Shuman
Courier newspaper, reports of speeches
V, 74, 76, 81, 118–20, 281, 308,
VII, 283 n., VIII, 352–4, IX, 181 n.
Courtenay, Thomas Peregrine, M.P.
for Totnes, IX, 198, 267 n.
Courtney, Leonard H., VI, xviii n.
Courtney, W. P., *The King of Clubs*,
VI, 87 n.
'Memoir of Whishaw', VI, 66 n.
Coutts & Co., bankers, III, 380, X,
68 n.
Cowell, John, his remedy for agri-
cultural distress, IX, 199–200
Cowell, John, jun., letter to, IX, 199–
200 & n.; met on the Continent,
IX, 218–19, 223, 228, X, 277 & n.,
301; see also VIII, 367 n., IX, 191
Cowes, VII, 279
Cowper, Lord, IX, 94
Cox, James, of the Museum, X, 173
Craig, John, *Remarks on . . . Political
Economy*, 1821, VIII, 378 & n.
Craufurd, Lt.-Gen. Sir Charles Gre-
gan, letters in Ricardo Papers, X,
388
Credit: transfers, does not create,
capital, V, 436–8; see also I,
249 n., 299–300 n., IV, 254–5
Crisp, theatre-manager, X, 389
Crombie, Alexander, letter to Ricardo,
VII, 31–2 & n.
Letters on the Agricultural Interest,
1816, VII, 31 n.
Letter to D. Ricardo Esq., 1817, VII,
32 n., 149
see also VI, 219
Cromwell, Oliver, his head, X, 167,
172–4
Cropper, Benson & Co., IX, 182 n.

Crops: secret method of estimating, VIII, 370 & n.; alternation of good and bad, IX, 314–15; rotation of crops, I, 80

Crosse, Thomas, Ricardo's solicitor, X, 390
letters from, quoted, V, xvi n., xviii, VII, 293 n., VIII, 319 n.
see also VII, 217, 232, X, 104 n.

Crown debtors, V, 281

Cumberland, George, father of Sydney, X, 143–59

Cumberland, George, jun., X, 143, 147

Cumberland, Richard, vicar of Driffield, X, 143–4, 146–7

Cumberland, Sydney, accused of enticing Mrs Ricardo's maid, X, 143–59

Curious effect of rise of wages (lowers some prices), VII, 82–3, see also I, 61–3, II, 60

Currency:
perfect, defined, IV, 55, V, 379, see also I, 361, IV, 66
theory of price and, VI, 348
excess of, III, 56–7, 61, 92 n., 94, 142, VI, 75; criterion of, V, 448–9; use of term, III, 147–9, 228–30, 248 & n.; see also I, 354–5
void in, III, 24, 60–1
proportion between currencies and commodities of nations, VI, 40, 65, IX, 81
restoration of, to original standard, effect on taxes, III, 137–8
Western's motion on the altered state of, 1822, V, 223–31; Ricardo's speech on, 231–45; see also Resumption of cash payments
Sinclair's proposal to increase, VIII, 186, 386
see also Depreciation, Money, Redundancy

Curries, Raikes & Co., bankers, X, 277 n.

Curtis, Sir William, M.P. for the City of London, VIII, 163 & n.

Curwen, John Christian, M.P. for Cumberland:
on taxes on agriculture, V, 74
frauds in corn imports, V, 78
gluts of corn, V, 88
moves repeal of agricultural horses tax, V, 101
duties on tallow and candles, V, 146, 291
on fair protecting price for corn, V, 174
moves repeal of salt duty, V, 194–5
his notion of a countervailing duty, VIII, 356
see also I, 108 n., V, 57, 85, 87, 90, 257–8

Customs and excise, IV, 190, V, 268, 511, see also VII, 303, X, 170, 262

Da Costa, Daniel, X, 206 n.

Da Costa, Isaac, Dutch poet, X, 207–8, 211–12, see also X, 17

Da Costa, Mrs, wife of the poet, X, 211–12

Da Costa, Isaac, author of *Israel and the Gentiles*, 1850, X, 19 n.

Da Costa, Rebecca, *née* Ricardo (D.R.'s cousin), X, 19, 30, 206–7, 211–12

Daily Worker, VI, 250 n.

Dalchurst, Manor of, or Hadlow Place, bought by Ricardo, X, 96–7, 105

Dalrymple, Col. A. J., M.P. for Appleby, X, 226, 305, 317

Dalton family, VI, 35 n., VIII, 349

Damer, Hon. Mrs, V, xviii

Damiens, tortures of, VII, 319

Dansey, Dansey Richard, X, 98

Danvers, F. C., *Memorials of old Haileybury College*, VI, xix n.

Darmstadt, X, 226–7

Darn, speech by, III, 179 n.

Darton and Harvey, Map of London, 1805, X, 47 n.

Davenport, Davies, M.P. for Cheshire, V, 323

Davies, Colonel Thomas Henry, M.P. for Worcester, V, 138, 185, 274, VIII, 16 n.

Davies, Mr, project of a review, VIII, 16

Davison, T., printer, VII, 13–14

Day and New Times, newspaper, I, xix

Dead capital, proportions of, V, 177–8

Dead stock, gold as, I, 229, 232, V, 408, 434

Dearth, VII, 194, 200

Death duties, I, 153; legacy duty, V, 315; transfer of property at death, V, 291; probate duty, V, 315, X, 103

Debyser, C., X, 355, XI, xxx

De Castro, Orobio, X, 203

Decker, Sir Matthew, *Essay on the Decline of Foreign Trade*, 1744, I, 234

De Crespigny, Sir William Champion, M.P. for Southampton, his motion on Robert Owen's plan, V, 30; see also VIII, 46

Deerhurst, Lord, M.P. for Worcester, VII, 102 & n.

De Leon, Mr, X, 208

Delessert & Co., Ricardo's bankers in Paris, X, 99–101, 341–2, 390

Delessert, Benjamin, letter to Ricardo quoted, V, 466 & n.; see also IX, 144, 203–4, 236, X, 100, 351

De Lolme, J. L., *The Constitution of England*, X, 397

Del Sarto, Andrea, X, 316

Delvalle, Abigail (D.R.'s mother), see Ricardo, Abigail

Delvalle, Abraham (D.R.'s great-great-grandfather), X, 26

Delvalle, Abraham (D.R.'s grand-father), X, 21, 27–8

Delvalle, Abraham (D.R.'s uncle), X, 28–9; letter to, as wine merchant, X, 141–3

Delvalle, Daniel (D.R.'s great-great-uncle), X, 26

Delvalle, Esther (D.R.'s aunt), wife of Isaac Lindo, X, 29, 106

Delvalle, Isaac (D.R.'s great-grand-father), X, 26–7, 28

Delvalle, Isaac (D.R.'s uncle), X, 22, 28, 106

Delvalle, Joseph (D.R.'s uncle), X, 28, 106

Delvalle, Leah (D.R.'s aunt), X, 28–9, 106

Delvalle, Rebecca (D.R.'s grand-mother), *née* Sequeira, X, 27

Delvalle, Rebecca (D.R.'s aunt), wife of Wilson Lowry, X, 29

Delvalle, Sarah (D.R.'s aunt), wife of Abraham Nunes, X, 29, 106

Demand:

a desire to possess with the power of purchasing, VI, 56, 58

where the power exists the will exists too, II, 311, 314, IV, 343–4, VI, 108; Malthus's contrary view, II, 36–7, 307, VI, 112, 123, 131–2, 155–6

limited only by production, I, 290, II, 365, IV, 178–9, V, 435, VI, 163–4, VII, 203, VIII, 258; Malthus disagrees, II, 377–9, VI, 168, 225, 229, VII, 214, VIII, 159–60, 216, IX, 13

lacking only if commodities are unsuitable, II, 304–5, VI, 164, IX, 26

occasioned by accumulation as much as by consumption, VI, 133–5, 141

effect of price on, I, 193; different for luxuries and for necessaries, VIII, 272, IX, 19, see also I, 293–4, 387; slight for bread, I, 385, great for gold and silver ware, VI, 91–2

influence of income on, VIII, 274–5

tax on corn, effect on demand, I, 237 & n.

effective (effectual) demand, I, 291, II, 234, III, 25, 53, VI, 114, 120, 133, 148–9, 164, VII, 125, 131, VIII, 216, 259; Malthus, VI, 117, 131, IX, 10; Adam Smith, VI, 58, 142

difference with Malthus on importance of, II, 370–1, VII, 57, 70, 77–8, IX, 80, XI, x–xi

see also VI, 129, IX, 27 n.

Demand and supply:
effect on price, I, 382–5, see also I, 119–20, 164–5, II, 224–5, VIII, 272, 279, 286, 302
contingent supply and demand, VIII, 196
increase of demand linked with increase of supply, I, 130, 163
see also Price, natural and market
Demanders, whether corn raises demanders (Malthus), or demanders raise corn (Ricardo), I, 400, 405 n., 406, 409, II, 107–9, 142; discussion with Trower, VIII, 219, 235–6, 248, 255–8, 273
Denison, William Joseph, M.P. for Surrey:
advocates an 'amicable arrangement' for the public debt, V, 251
suggests taxing malt instead of beer, 294
see also V, 185, VII, 267
Denman, Thomas, M.P., Solicitor-General to Queen Caroline, VIII, 243–4, IX, 12
Denmark, corn imported by fraud from, V, 78
Denmark, Crown Prince of, proposed visit to Ricardo, IX, 192, 195–6
Depreciation of currency:
distinguished from diminution of value, IV, 330–1, V, 166, 203–4, 310–11, 393–4
injustice of, III, 123, 133; enriches one class at expense of another, III, 136–7, 271, IV, 229–31, VI, 233–4, IX, 72–3, 246
two tests of, III, 75
measured by excess of market over mint price of gold, III, 29, 79, 99, 175, 187, V, 392, VI, 6
no standard to judge whether gold has risen or paper fallen, II, 6–7, III, 80, V, 373–4, IX, 276
actual and relative, VIII, 92–3; real, III, 56
of paper currency from over-issue, I, 209, 371, III, 51, 63, 78, V, 143, 208–9; gradual decrease of, as

Depreciation (cont.)
remedy, III, 17–18, 21, 94–5, V, 2–3, VI, 44–5
no effect on rate of interest, III, 137
unfavourable foreign exchanges as proof of, III, 18, 72, 83, 199, VI, 39
effect of, on prices of taxed commodities, I, 209–10
of paper compared with debased coinage, III, 97–8, see also 74–5, 78
of money by discovery of American mines, III, 362, 376–7, see also I, 86
proposal for preventing, without depriving merchants of accommodation, VI, 67–8
money incomes and depreciation, IV, 63–4
Depression:
of agriculture, IV, 230, V, 47, 73, 89, 125, 132, X, 321
of coin or paper, III, 197 & n.
of commodities, V, 400
of the Exchange, V, 448
of price, III, 100–1, V, 399; depressed price of corn, IV, 228, V, 241
De Quincey, Thomas, 'Dialogues of Three Templars', I, xxii n.
Dermody, Thomas, Irish poet, X, 44 n.
Destutt de Tracy, A. L. C., met in Paris, IX, 248
Elémens d'idéologie, 1804–15, I, 284–5
Dick, Thomas, Edinburgh police commissioner, IX, 162–3, 164, 177
Dickinson, William, M.P. for Somerset, V, 86, VII, 232
Diehl, Karl, X, 377–8
Dietz, A., Frankfurter Handelsgeschichte, X, 223 n.
Difficulty of production:
or cost of production, VI, 247–8, 271
limits population, I, 373, VI, 140
raises prices, I, 191, VI, 233, 241, and wages, I, 146, 218, 296, VII, 57, 80–1

Difficulty or facility of production, regulates price, I, 73, 158, VII, 3, 250, IX, 239, and value, I, 193, 273, 277, 280–1, 363, IV, 19; see also VII, 333, IX, 94–7

see also Facility of production, and under Rent

Diminishing returns from land:
early statement, III, 287
and theory of profits, IV, 13 & n., 14, VI, 197, 204, 207, 209–10, 213–14, 216–18, 220–2, see also I, 125–6; table showing progress of rent and profits, IV, 17
and cost of production, I, 156, V, 167–8, VI, 294
and population, I, 98–9
and rent, I, 70–2, 75, 83

Disagreeables: of negotiating a seat in parliament, VII, 269; of travelling VII, 56, X, 345

Discourses on parliamentary reform, V, 487–512, VII, 301–2

D'Israeli, Isaac, VII, 10 n.

Distress: due to reduction of circulation, 1817, VII, 151; general distress, 1819–20, V, 37–41, 133, 492 n., VIII, 103, 139, 150–1 n., 152–3 n.; see also Agricultural distress, Labouring classes, Manufacturers

Distribution:
of circulating medium, and national wealth, III, 120
good and faulty, of produce, II, 366, IX, 16–17, 24–6, 83 (Ricardo); II, 415, IX, 10, 15 (Malthus), of funds of society, I, 314; of capital (McCulloch), VIII, 353
of labour, I, 132–3, 152 n.
of net income, I, 425
of produce from the land, VI, 199, 203
of property, and alterations in value of money, V, 107; results of unequal distribution of property (Sismondi), IX, 243–4

Distribution (or division) of the whole produce by proportions:
between the three classes, I, 5, 49–51, II, 195 n., VIII, 194, 278, 337; see also I, 64, 270, 347, VI, 172, 315–16, VII, 24, 71, 78, IX, 20, 22
between profits and wages, II, 194–5, 258–9, 290, 304, 344–5, IV, 366, VIII, 130, 194–5, IX, 16–17, 21, 25, on no-rent land, II, 196–7, 198 n., 278, 284, 336, the same in manufactures as in agriculture, II, 322–4, V, 177–8; see also I, 226, II, 306, 363, IV, 408
rent as share of the produce, I, 83–4 & notes, 332–4, 402–3 & notes, II, 195–8 & notes, IV, 18 & n., IX, 40, see also IV, 13
division of surplus between rent and profits, II, 223, see also VI, 203–4, 213–14
division by proportions not essentially connected with value, VIII, 194, see also 297, 337

Dividends:
on National Debt, plan to avoid disturbance to money market, IV, 74–6, VI, 286, 299, 305, 312–13, VII, 22; proposal to adjust to price of corn, I, 425–6 & notes
should be taxed directly, I, 160–1
see also Bank of England, dividend

Division of labour, I, 94, 412, II, 395, IV, 25

Dixon, S., V, 476

Docks, I, 152, VIII, 155

Doctrinaires, VIII, 224

Dolby's Parliamentary Register, 1819, V, xxix n.

Domodossola, IX, 221, X, 288

Dorking, VI, xvi, IX, 326, 331–3

Dorrien, George, Governor of the Bank, V, 353, 363–4

Double standard of gold and silver, V, 92, 93 n.
inconvenience of, I, 366–9, III, 65, IV, 63, V, 426–8
more variable than gold standard, V, 40, 390

Double standard (*cont.*)

Baring's proposal, 1819, V, 46, 71, 74 n., 75–8, 92–5, 105–6, VIII, 346–7, 349–50; revived in 1823, IX, 270

in France, III, 178, V, 76, 106

gold made the only legal tender from 1817, V, 16 & n., see also I, 369, 371 n., IV, 67, VIII, 3

Douglas, William Robert Keith, M.P. for Dumfries, V, 299

Dover, VII, 168, 186

Drawback on exportation, IV, 217–19, 264, of corn, IV, 243–4

Dublin, V, 219, VI, 244

Dublin Morning Post, V, 528

Dublin rioters trial, IX, 274 & n.

Duboulay, F. N., VI, 112 n.

Ducie, Lord, V, 469–70, VII, 187 n., VIII, 330, X, 187 n.

Duckworth family, X, 309

Dugdale, Dugdale Stratford, M.P. for Warwickshire, V, 71

Duguid, C., *The Story of the Stock Exchange*, X, 73 n.

Dumont, Étienne, VI, 18 & n., 19–21

his translation of Bentham's *Alarm* (*Sur les prix*), III, 259–341; discussions on, VI, 13–18

at Geneva, IX, 215–20, 242–3, 248, X, 267, 270–2

excursion to Chamonix, IX, 215–17, 244, X, 273–7

his dinner party, IX, 219–20, X, 281–2

sides with Ricardo against Sismondi, IX, 235, X, 278

his MSS at Geneva, III, 263–4, VI, 20 n.

see also III, 11 n., VI, 90, 180, VII, 74, 188, VIII, 40 n., X, 303, 399

Traité des preuves judiciaires, 1823, X, 277

'*Des présomptions anté-judiciaires*', IX, 245 & n.

Dunbar, C. F., 'Ricardo's Use of Facts', I, xx

Dundas, William, M.P. for Edinburgh, IX, 162

Dundonald, Earl of, *Autobiography of a Seaman*, VI, 107. See Cochrane, Lord

Dunn, William, letter quoted, VIII, 338 n.

Dupont de Nemours, widow of, quoted on Ricardo, VIII, 224 n.

Duval, M., singer, X, 339

East, Sir Edward Hyde, M.P. for Winchester, V, 283

East India College, Haileybury:

Malthus professor at, VI, xix, 159 n., VII, 51, 213

Ricardo's visits to, VI, 60–1, 72, 94, 135 n., 176, 211

student troubles, VI, 77 & n., 336 & n., 341, VII, 26, 119, 121, 130–2, 135–8, 251 n., IX, 251 & n.

see also VI, 240, 346, VII, 167–8 & notes, 263 n., 264

East India Company:

Ricardo's speeches at General Court, V, 475–8

directorship suggested, VIII, 250–4, 262–3, 281–2, 292

Mill's appointment at, VIII, 40 & n., 47, 162, IX, 180, 279 n., 280 & n.

exports of silver, III, 172, 173 n., 249

sales of tea, IX, 330 & n., 342

see also IV, 97 n., V, 466–7, VI, 343 n., VIII, 53, IX, 97

East India stock, IV, 115, 117, V, 301

East Indies, III, 249, V, 297, 300, VII, 109, 273 n.; muslins from, VI, 55; see also India, Sugar

Easton Grey, Thomas Smith's home, VI, 135 n., VII, 52, 139, VIII, 276, IX, 232–3, 251, XI, xii n.; conversations at, VIII, 61–3, 75

Ebel's *Manuel du voyageur en Suisse*, X, 179

Ebrington, Lord, X, 182

Eckersall, Mrs Malthus's family, VI, xix, 135 n., VII, 311, VIII, 64, IX, 9

Eckersall, George, VII, 51, 56, 68, 253

Eckersall, Lucy, VI, 322, VII, 52, 56, 71

Economic situation of the country:
stagnation after the war (1815), VI,
303–5, 328, 344–5
revival (1816–17), VII, 16–17, 174,
185–6, 192
distress (1819), VIII, 103, 129, 139
unnatural depression (1821), V, 91,
VIII, 369, 371, and cp. IX, 13, 40
on the whole flourishing (1822–3),
IX, 158, 160; except for agriculture,
V, 321, X, 349
Économistes (physiocrats), IV, 37,
178, VI, 187
Economists, VIII, 38, 139, 321, 341,
382. See Political economists
Ede, J., *Gold and Silver Coins*, 1808,
III, 183 n.
Edgeworth, Fanny, IX, 137, 295, X,
167–71, 174
Edgeworth, Harriet, IX, 137, 230,
295, X, 167–71
Edgeworth, Honora, X, 167–9
Edgeworth, Lovell, X, 167, 169
Edgeworth, Maria, VI, xxxii–xxxiii
the potatoe question in Ireland, IX,
230–2, 237–9, 252–5, 257–61
visit to Gatcomb, IX, 104, X, 167–74
advice on her investments, IX, 203–4,
261–2
list of letters, IX, 393; other letters
quoted, VIII, 56 n., X, 32–3 & n.
see also VII, 312, IX, 242 n., X, 102,
179, XI, xxvii
Rosamund and the Purple Jar, X,
33 n.
Life and Letters, see Hare, Augustus
Edgeworth, Mrs, *Memoir of Maria
Edgeworth*, VI, xxxii n., VIII,
56 n., X, 167
Edgeworth, Packenham, X, 167, 169
Edgeworth, Sophy, IX, 295
Edinburgh:
few converts to Ricardo in, VII, 295,
316 n.
Police bill, IX, 161–3, 179, see also
137
relief works in, VII, 116 n.
society lampooned, VIII, 112–13
see also VII, 110

Edinburgh Annual Register, II, xiv,
IV, 358 n., V, 289 n., X, 39,
369
Edinburgh Magazine, 1818, IV, 306,
VII, 179 n., 315–16 & n., 324, 326,
332, 338, 354, 360, 362, 376, VIII,
8, X, 397
Edinburgh Review:
early articles on political economy,
VII, 246
Horner on its mercenary troops, III,
9 & n.
no rough handling of clergy, VIII,
222
number withdrawn, at news of
Waterloo, VI, 280, 316
adopts Ricardo's system, VIII, 376
see also III, 434, IV, 307 n., VI, 255,
313, VII, 245 n., VIII, 17, 28 n.,
44, 205 n., 242, IX, 139, 147, 150 n.,
155, 206 n., 312
Edinburgh Review, articles:
1802, Thornton's *Paper Credit* (Horner), III, 64
1803, Lord King's *Restriction of
Payments* (Horner), III, 73, 83
1804, Bounty on corn (Horner), I,
302, 307, 315
1808, Thomas Smith's *Essay on
Money* (Mill), III, 9 n.
1809, Burdett's plan of reform
(Jeffrey), X, 397
1811, Bullion (Malthus), III, 10–11,
99 & n., VI, 24–5, 38, 82
(Feb.); III, 12, VI, 31, 41, 47, 66
(Aug.)
1813, Grimm on Voltaire, IX, 375
1818, *Economical and Secure Currency*
(MᶜCulloch on), IV, 47, VII, 354,
383, VIII, 1–2, 5, 6, 10, 20, 23–4
Principles (MᶜCulloch on), VII,
179 n., 278–9, 280–2, 285–9, 291,
295–7, 309, 316 n.
Madame de Staël (Jeffrey on), X,
397
parliamentary reform (Mackintosh),
VII, 263 n.
1818, 1819, Fellenberg's school
(Simond), X, 262 n.

Edinburgh Review, articles in (*cont.*)
1819, Owen's plan (Torrens), VIII, 82 n., 159, 164, 376 & n.
trade with France (McCulloch), VIII, 82, 127
1820, foreign commerce (McCulloch), VIII, 190, 197
taxation and the corn laws (McCulloch), VIII, 164–6, 168–74, 176–7
tithes (McCulloch), VIII, 203, 214, 222, 229, 237, 262
parliamentary reform (Mackintosh), VIII, 327–8 & n.
1821, Scottish juries (Cockburn), IX, 136, 142
Mushet on gains and losses to fundholders (McCulloch), VII, 93 n., VIII, 392, 396, IX, 7 n., 15
machinery (McCulloch), VIII, 325, 338, 351–2, 366, 373, 378, 383, IX, 9, 18
Godwin on population (Malthus), IX, 84, 89–90, 94, 101, 154
1822, taxes (McCulloch), IX, 160, 185
Ireland (McCulloch), IX, 186
corn laws (McCulloch), IX, 186, 188, 192, 197
1823, funding system (McCulloch), VIII, 222–3 n.
East and West India sugars (McCulloch), IX, 273, 277
periodical press (Hazlitt), V, xxvii n., VI, xxii, VII, 28 n., VIII, 186 n.
1824, combination laws (McCulloch), VIII, 313 n., 338
profits (McCulloch), IX, 179 n.
East India Company (McCulloch), IX, 330 n.
1827, taxation (McCulloch), VIII, 238 n., IX, 342, 345, 362
1830, commerce in Holland (McCulloch), IX, 135 n.
1837, life of Malthus (Empson), VI, xx, VII, 2 n., 201 n.
Edinburgh, University of: Mill at, VII, 213 n.; McCulloch and Chair at, VIII, 204–5 & n.

Education of the lower orders in the Metropolis, Report on, 1816, VII, 150 & n.
Education of the lower orders, Brougham's committee on, 1816, 1818, VII, 304 n.; report, X, 262 n.; see also Schools
Education of the poor, committee on, 1819, VII, 45 n.; see also VII, 276, 357 n.
Edwards, Mr, of Ross, VI, 13
Ehrenberg, R., *Das Haus Parish in Hamburg*, III, 431–4 notes
Ehrenbreitstein, fortifications of, IX, 211, X, 218–20
Elasticity of demand, see Demand, effect of price on
Elections:
general, 1818, VII, 264–7, 269–70, 272, 275–6, VIII, 17 n., XI, xi–xii; 1820, VIII, 156, 162–3
contested, disgusting spectacles at, V, 504–5, 508–9, VII, 272–3
triennial, VII, 261, 267, 273 & n.
see also V, 473, VIII, 164, 210–11 and under Ballot, Parliament, seat in, Westminster election
Electors' Remembrancer, V, xxii n., xxiii n., X, 267 n.
Eliason, Daniel, VI, 8–9
Eliot, F. B., *On the Fallacy of the Supposed Depreciation*, 1811, X, 401
Elizabeth, la belle batelière, X, 255
Elizabeth, Princess, X, 224
Ellenborough, Lord Chief Justice, VI, 106, VIII, 288
Ellice, Edward, M.P. for Coventry:
his amendment to Peel's bill, V, 8, 11, 206
supports colonial trade bill, V, 188
on Spitalfields Acts, V, 295–6
see also V, 222, IX, 194
Ellis, Charles Rose, M.P. for Seaford:
Bank of Ireland and Irish exchange, V, 98
protection to West India sugar, V, 297
Ellis, T. F., stockbroker, VII, 14
Ellis and Tucker, loan contractors, X, 82, 85

Ellman, John, farmer, IX, 67 & n.

Elphinstone, William, East India director, VII, 136–7

Elwin, H.: and savings banks, VII, 47–8 & n., 63, 153, 173; visits Gatcomb, IX, 46; see also VII, 155, 162, VIII, 33

Emigration:
of artisans, restrictions on, V, xx, xxiv, 296, 332, IX, 55 & n.
to America, VII, 257, 259–60, IX, 61
to Canada, Horton's plan for, XI, xv–xvi
see also V, 21, VII, 142

Employment of labour:
relation to quantity of capital, V, 501; and to distribution of capital, I, 349, 395, IV, 35
full employment, necessary for increase of wages, II, 412
in 1821, IX, 13, 40
want of employment, whether due to faulty distribution of product, IX, 10–11, 16, 20, 24–5
in change from war to peace, I, 265
unexampled scarcity of work, 1816, VII, 62, 66–7
want of demand for labourers in 1817, VII, 150; labourers unemployed, VII, 194
see also V, 113–14, 224–5, VII, 248, and under Labour, Wages

Empson, William, article on Malthus, 1837, VI, xx, VII, 2 n., 201 n.

Encyclopaedia Britannica, VIII, 66, X, 370. *Supplement* to eds. 4–6 (1814–24), IV, 145, articles in:
Cold (John Leslie), IV, 249 n.
Colonies (Mill), VII, 183, 195
Corn Laws (McCulloch), I, 267 n., 318, VII, 295, 337, 354, VIII, 159
Cottage System (McCulloch), VII, 295, 337
Exchange (McCulloch), VII, 384, VIII, 81, 85–93
Funding System (Ricardo), IV, 143–200, VIII, 72, 78, 127, 144, 240, 262. See also under Ricardo

Encyclopaedia (cont.)
Government (Mill), VIII, 211, 240 n., 291, IX, 154 n.
Interest (McCulloch), VIII, 313, 341
Jurisprudence (Mill), VIII, 290, 296, IX, 5, 154
Liberty of the Press (Mill), IX, 5, 154 & n.
Money (McCulloch), IX, 134, 149, 157, 159
Political Economy (McCulloch), IX, 206, 271, 275, includes value, VIII, 189 & n., 214, IX, 313 & n., 334 & n.
Prison Discipline (Mill), IX, 280
other articles projected: Lottery, IV, 147–8, National Debt, VIII, 222–3, 238, Value, VIII, 189 & n.; see also IV, 147 n.

England:
still in the progressive state, IV, 34, VII, 17, 185–6, 192; confidence in, keeps capital at home, V, 32
must be manufacturing as well as agricultural, V, 180
exaggerated idea of her wealth beside the Dutch, X, 197
as enemy of all liberal principles, IX, 217, and cp. VI, 321
Englishmen endure abuses too long, V, 486

Ensor, George, *Population of Nations*, 1818, I, li, 100 n., VII, 334, 349

Epictetus, VI, 271–2

Equality, increase of population and of food under a system of, IX, 49–50; unequal distribution of property, IX, 243

Equilibrium:
of currencies, I, 141–2, 145, III, 55, 170, VIII, 127
between agriculture and manufactures, VIII, 101–2
of imports and exports, III, 245, VII, 43
of prices, V, 21, 304
of profits, II, 289; between profits and wages, I, 226

Erasmus, X, 233

Erskine, Lord: *Armata: a Fragment*, 1817 (anon.), VII, 142; *Second Part of Armata*, VII, 173, X, 395; his speeches on Reform, X, 396

Espinoza, Michael d', Spinoza's father, X, 32

Essex, Lord, VIII, 28 n., X, 50, see also VII, 252 n.

Essex-street Unitarian Chapel, VII, 171 n., X, 39–40

Estcourt, T., VII, 304

Esterhazy, M., X, 383

Eton, Mortimer Ricardo at, X, 63, 389; see also VII, 138, IX, 199 n.

Eton College Tables, V, 226, 238

Euclid, V, 38

Evans, Thomas, the Spencean, VII, 307–8

Evans, William, M.P., V, 185

Evelyn, John, *Silva*, VI, 237

Everas, Ricardo's estate, X, 97

Evil, the problem of, VII, 206, 212

Examiner, X, xxii

Excess of currency defined, III, 147–9. See Currency

Exchange, Foreign, I, 146–9
  nominal and real, III, 420, IV, 336–7, 353, V, 448, VI, 23, 41, VIII, 88, 90–3, 126, 141
  principles of calculating, III, 174–5, 178–9
  par of exchange, I, 229–32, III, 109–10; with America, III, 182–3, with France, 176–80, with Hamburg, 417–18, VI, 8–10, between gold and silver currencies, III, 166–75
  real par of, III, 167–8, 185, 247, V, 391, VI, 8; whether to include expenses of transmission, III, 174, VIII, 89 & n., 92, 140–1, 178–80, 184
  unfavourable, caused by redundant currency, III, 20–1, 64 n., 75 n., 83, 100, 107, 140, 169, 194–5, 356–8, 372–3, VI, 7, VIII, 93; whether the only cause, VI, 62–5, 74–8, 82–3, 87–9, 119; whether it measures depreciation, VI, 30, 39, 83

Exchange, Foreign (*cont.*)
  whether it tends to right itself, VI, 34, 39, 75, 77, 83, VIII, 91 & n. 5
  natural limits to rise and fall of, III, 19–20, 71–2, 161, V, 448, VII, 43–4, VIII, 2
  effect of foreign subsidies on, VI, 39, 41, 73–8, 83, 89; of government foreign expenditure on, IX, 272, 276–7, 285–6, see also IV, 327–56
  in turbulent times, VI, 78–81
  effects of peace on, VI, 116, 119, 122
  recovery of, after resumption of cash payments, VIII, 44, 70, 79
  McCulloch on, criticised, VIII, 85–93, 126–7, 140–1
Exchange, with America, IX, 272, 277, 301, 362, see also III, 182–3
  with Amsterdam, III, 73–4, VI, 97–9, 298–9
  with the Continent, VI, 78–9
  with Hamburg, I, 148–9, III, 80–1, 116, 118–21, 163–75, 185–6, 247, VI, 7, 86, 100–1, VIII, 91
  Irish, III, 399, V, 70, 98–100, VIII, 24
  with Jamaica, VI, 23, 28, 31–3, 35, 40–1
  between London and the country, VIII, 85–6
  with Paris, III, 164, 176–82, V, 186–7, VI, 119 n.
  with Rio de Janeiro, VIII, 92
  with Russia, VI, 79
  between Spain and her colonies, III, 171, VIII, 89, 126, 141
  with Sweden, III, 183–4
Exchangeable value, I, 11–66, IV, 361–412. See Value
Exchequer bills: not paper money, III, 290–3, 298, see also IV, 108; interest on, I, 297–9, IV, 102, V, 115, VIII, 135, IX, 262, X, 86; see also III, 233, IV, 91–2 n., 277, V, 59
Excise Duties bill, V, 23–7
Export duty on manufactures, as substitute for import duty on corn, II, 153–5

Exports:
no exports without imports, I, 263, VI, 108–9
bounties on exports, of corn, I, 301–11, of manufactures, 312–16
flourishing in 1823, V, 246
Exports and imports:
balance of, in 1810, III, 63 & n.
equilibrium of, III, 245, VII, 43
nominal and real value of, III, 133–4, 141, VI, 93
see also Balance of trade, Foreign trade
External commodities, IX, 65–6, 75–7
Extra post, V, 148
Extravagance, public, II, 307, IV, 339, VI, 120

Fabrikant, N. V., X, 381
Facility of production:
defined, VI, 292
relation of, to profits and wages, VI, 289–94, 296–7, 303–4, 319, VII, 52, 57, 69, 77–8, 80–1, VIII, 194–5, 215–16, IX, 99–101; to profits, IV, 26, VI, 140, 144–5, to wages, I, 292, VI, 224–7, VII, 80
diminishes value, adds to riches, I, 274, 281, IX, 170–1, see also IV, 407–8
see also Difficulty of production
Fair Circassian, V, 368 & n.
Fallesen, Ludvig Sophus, X, 380
Famine, I, 99, 101; in Europe, 1817, X, 184; in Ireland, 1822, V, 234–5, IX, 231–2, 254
Farmers:
profits of, regulate all profits, VI, 104. See Profits
interests of, contrasted with commercial classes, IV, 255; analogy with manufacturers, II, 200; see also IV, 229–31
mistake their own interests on protection, VIII, 337, 369–70, 374, IX, 67
distress of, V, 150, 157, 181, VII, 38, 87, X, 349

Farmers (cont.)
gentleman-farmers, VI, 149, 158, 279, 326, VII, 268, VIII, 109, 132, IX, 264; Ricardo as, VI, 150, VII, 170, 207, VIII, 307
Fashion, influence on price, I, 90, 119, 194, see also I, 263, VIII, 275
Fearon, H. B., Narrative of a Journey through...America, 1818, VIII, 16 & n.
Fellenberg, P. E. von, his school at Hofwyl, X, 262
'Fellow of University College', see West, Edward
Ferrara, X, 310–11
Ferrara, Francesco, X, 380
Ferrier, Rotterdam banker, X, 195–6
Fertility of the soil:
rent the result of diminishing, I, 69–70, 74–7, 402–4, II, 112, 116, 211, 213, VI, 292–4, 301–2
price of raw produce increases as fertility decreases, I, 72, 120, see also IV, 27
and accumulation of capital, I, 98, 126, II, 321
and profits, I, 120, 125–6, II, 132, 255, 336, 446–7, VI, 152, 162, 168, VII, 69, 78
Fetter, F. W., 'Editions of the Bullion Report', XI, xxxi
Fictitious capital, no stimulus to production, V, 445–6
Field, G., Ricardo's clerk, X, 74
Fielding, Henry, Tom Jones, VII, 303
Finance, Report on, 1819, IV, 193, V, 64–6; see also IV, 305 n.
Financial situation of the country, 1823, V, 248–51. See Budget
Finnerty, Peter, reporter, V, xxviii
Fire balloon at Coblentz, IX, 212, X, 218
Fisher, P. H., Notes and Recollections of Stroud, X, 168 n.
Fishing, at Gatcomb, VIII, 49, 283, IX, 327–8, 335; see also V, 122
Fiske, Mrs, X, 158
Fitzwilliam, Lord, VIII, 50, 111 & n., 134

Fixed capital, I, 31–2, 52, 150, 266, IV, 305–6, 311–12. See Capital, fixed, Machinery

Flogging, vote on, V, xxii

Florence, visit to, X, 312–21, see also IX, 219, 224, 247

Fluctuations in prices: injurious to farmers, IV, 238, 246, V, 88, and to landlords, IV, 266; inevitable under corn laws, IV, 240–2, 249–50

Foligny, M. de, VII, 168 & n.

Folkestone, Viscount, M.P. for Salisbury:
on raising the standard price of gold, V, 93, 254–5
proposes 'equitable adjustment', V, 322
on Mill's article 'Government', VIII, 213
a staunch reformer, IX, 268
see also V, 154 n., VI, 277 n.

Fontainebleau, X, 346–7

Fonteyraud, Alcide, French translator of Ricardo, X, 31 n., 375–6, 380

Food:
cheap food and profits, I, 119, 126, 132, 289, 296, II, 221–2, IV, 11, 22, 25–6, 347, V, 50, VI, 104
increased supply of, and increase of population, I, 292, 295, 373, II, 161, IV, 179, X, 408–9
whether food creates its own demand, I, 406, II, 111, VII, 201, VIII, 258, IX, 56–7; limit to demand for, I, 293, 387, VIII, 274–5, IX, 19
dependence on foreign food, IV, 265–6; increased production of food, during French war, VI, 94–5; see also IX, 50
consequences of cheap food in Ireland, I, 100 n., IX, 56
Adam Smith's notion that food production always yields a surplus, I, 327–9, 332–3
see also Corn, Necessaries, Potatoes

Forbach, X, 231–2

Forbes, C., V, 475, 478–9

Forced abundance of silver, low value from, I, 229; forced circulation of

Forced (cont.)
money, I, 231, III, 214–15, 336, 362, 364, of paper in America and France, III, 98; forced exportation of gold, III, 393, see also 220; forced value of gold coin, III, 40

Ford Abbey, Bentham's summer residence, VI, 124–7, 136, 317, VII, 76, 169; Ricardo's visit with J. B. Say, VI, 156–7, 161

Foreign Enlistment bill, V, xxii

Foreign exchange, I, 146–9. See Exchange, foreign

Foreign trade, I, 128–49
principles of, in terms of barter, I, 133–6, in terms of money, I, 137–49; finally a trade of barter, I, 228, II, 154, IV, 214, VI, 109
increases mass of commodities but not amount of value, I, 128, 319–20, II, 403, 407, V, 435, VI, 163, 167–8, 170–1, see also II, 436, III, 331, VII, 99
does not raise rate of profits, I, 128–9, 132–3, 345–6, II, 363–4, 408, IV, 25–6
and general rise or fall of home prices, I, 168–72, 228–9, 310–11, II, 154–6
between manufacturing and corn-producing countries, II, 288–91
sudden changes in channels of, I, 263–8
state of, in 1812, VI, 80; expansion of, during war, VI, 93
see also IX, 114 n., 127–8, 130, and under Commerce, Exports and imports, Trade

Foreign Trade committees, 1820: Commons', VIII, 197 & n., Lords', IX, 104 n.

Foreign vessels, reciprocity of duties, V, 305

Forgery of bank notes, IV, 292, V, 96–7, VI, 282, VIII, 350; executions for, IV, 225–7, V, 201, 279

Forster, Lubbock, & Co., Ricardo's bankers, X, 55 n., 68 & n.

Fortescue, George Mathew, X, 182 n.

Forty-shilling freeholder, V, 506

Foster, John, M.P. for County Louth, VII, 347–8, see also V, 58

Foster, John Leslie, *Essay on the Principle of Commercial Exchanges*, 1804, VII, 348 & n.

Foster, Peter le Neve, letter to, IX, 173–4

Foster, Thomas, X, 40–1

Fox, Charles James: on universal suffrage, V, 485; Mill on his India policy, VII, 238, 249; see also VIII, 6 n., X, 396–7

Fox Bourne, H. R., *English Merchants*, X, 90 n.

Foxwell, Herbert Somerton, I, vii, VI, xx n., 139 n., X, 401, XI, xxvii

France:

in 1815, VI, 246–7, 255, 321; prosperity in 1822, X, 184; nobility miserably poor, X, 281–2

inheritance law in, II, 386–7, see also VIII, 225, 377

political economy in, VIII, 224–5, 227, IX, 191, 244–5, 248–9

trade with, VIII, 82, 127, 190, 197, see also IV, 30

visits to, in 1817, VII, 160, 164, 167–8, 178, 224; in 1822, IX, 227, 236, 244–6, 248, X, 339–52

see also I, 134, III, 98, V, 76–7, 106, IX, 268, X, 396, and under Bonaparte, French, Paris

Franchise, extension of, V, 498–503, VII, 368–70, see also V, 112, 473, 506, VII, 273 & n.

Francis, John, *Chronicles of the Stock Exchange*, X, 58 n., 79, 123 n.

Francis, Sir Philip, X, 118; letter to, VI, 10–13

Reflections on the Abundance of Paper in Circulation, 1810, VI, 10 n., 11 n.

Frankfort, visit in 1817, VII, 160, 164–5; in 1822, X, 222–6; theatre at, X, 223–4, 258

Franking of letters by M.P.s, VI, xxxix, 257, IX, 47 n., 163 & n., see also VI, xxxii, VII, 364, 371, 378, IX, 63, X, 261

Franklin, Benjamin, his bust, IX, 228 & n.; see also VII, 378

Free discussion of religious opinions, V, 277–80, 324–31, IX, 277–80, 288 & n., X, 397, XI, xxiv

Free trade, I, 133–4, 317–18 & n., 343, IV, 70–2, 252, V, 34, 188–90, 432, VII, 161, VIII, 228, 275, 353, 359, IX, 4, 77, 80–2

merchants' petition for, V, 42–4, VIII, 164, 178 & n., 183

Free trade in corn:

argument for, IV, 32–3, 36, V, 82, 87, 256, 258, VII, 271, VIII, 359, see also I, 126, 428, II, 203–5; misrepresented by Malthus, VIII, 208–9; no allowance to be made for loss of rent, VI, 173

dangers of dependence on foreign supply considered, IV, 27–30, 264–6, V, 54–5

increases ability to pay taxes (Ricardo's 'riddle'), V, 83, 88, and cp. I, 8, 421–4

lowers rate of profits in exporting countries, VI, 171

see also Corn Laws, Protecting duties, Restrictions

Freiburg, X, 232–3

French funds, VII, 230, IX, 144, 203–4, 229, 236, 256, 261–2, X, 185; loan of 1823, X, 57, 341

French Revolution, VI, 94–5, VII, 273–4, VIII, 108, 385, IX, 210, 218, 220, 274, X, 192

Frend, William, VI, xix; letter quoted, X, 34 & n.

'Friend to Bank Notes', see Trower, Hutches

'Friends of the People' (1792), VIII, 62–3

Fromowitz, Dr Wilhelm, X, 378–9

Fubini, R., X, 355

Fuchs, Major, a Swiss in the English service, X, 247–8

Fund for the maintenance of labour: and extension of market, I, 132; and immoderate savings, I, 292–3, IX, 24; and increase of money, III,

Fund for...labour (*cont.*)
302; and loss of capital, I, 222, VII, 75; and machinery, I, 286; and population, I, 78, 108–9, 218–20, 289; and price of corn, I, 270, 306; and taxation, I, 153, 196, 221–2, 225–6, V, 27; and wages, I, 164–5, 219, VIII, 258; and war, I, 265, VII, 67; see also Revenue, gross and net

Fundholders:
gains and losses of, IV, 229–31, V, 236–9, 252–3, 314, 320, VI, 178, VII, 37–8, 93 n., VIII, 396–8, IX, 39, see also I, 419–20, 425–6, II, 162–3
'landed estates mortgaged to', V, 126–7, 132, VIII, 147, see also VII, 75, IX, 267 n.
see also V, 101 n.

Funding system, IV, 143–200. See Sinking fund, and under Ricardo, David, Works

Funds:
price of, regulated by rate of interest, III, 93–4, but not a steady criterion of rate, I, 298; price of, and value of currency, V, 214–15
compared with land, as investment, VII, 187 n., 230
see also National Debt, Stocks

Fusina, X, 310

Galileos's tomb, X, 317
Gallois, J.-A. G., IX, 248
'Galovegian Stot' (McCulloch), VIII, 205 n., 'Galloway Stot', IX, 205 n.
Gamage Hall, Ricardo's estate, X, 97
Ganilh, Charles: *Inquiry into the Various Systems of Political Economy*, 1812, X, 399, see also II, 16 n.; *Des systèmes d'économie politique*, ed. 2, 1821, IX, 245 n.
Garnier, Germain, his notes to the *Wealth of Nations*, VIII, 224–5, IX, 244–5, 249; *Mémoire sur la valeur des monnaies*, 1817, X, 393
Garrett, John, X, 98

Garrow, Sir William, judge, VII, 283 & n., 290, 293
Gas-lighting, V, 179, X, 56 & n.
Gaster, M., *History of the Ancient Synagogue in Bevis Marks*, X, 20 n., 27 n.
Gatcomb Park, VII, facing p. 1
purchase of, VI, 100, X, 95–6
move to, VI, 113–15, 128, 130
Ricardo on, VII, 170, 305, VIII, 231, IX, 263
Hume's description, VI, 158
Maria Edgeworth on, IX, 230, X, 167–71
visitors: George Basevi, VI, 312, 325, VII, 306, 308, 317, 324; Malthus, VII, 48, 52, 56, 361, 368–9, 370–2, VIII, 331, 334, 336; Mill, VII, 285, 292, 299, 302–3, VIII, 229, 231–2, 241, see also VI, 136–7, IX, 329, 333–4, 377, 391; Say, VI, 156–61, 273
visitors a distraction, VI, 312, 314–15, 325, 335, 340, 349, VII, 54, 262, 306, VIII, 55, 58, 77–8, IX, 328
improvements at, VIII, 282–3, 293, IX, 12, 104, 326–7
boating, VII, 55–6, 68, 71, 76; fishing, VIII, 49, IX, 327–8; riding, VI, 267, VIII, 48, 78, IX, 44–5
see also VI, 244, VIII, 230, X, 105, 295
Gatty, C. T., *Mary Davies and the Manor of Ebury*, X, 48 n.
Gaubey, Clavet, agent de change, X, 101
Gautier, Madame, IX, 236
Gelders, IX, 211, X, 213
Gell, Sir William, VIII, 276
Geneva: visit to, IX, 214–20, 234, 244 n., X, 269–73, 277–82, watchmaker, X, 270; see also VII, 61, IX, 245
Genoa: visit to, X, 328, 330–4; road from Pisa, IX, 225–6, X, 324–30; see also VII, 192
Gentleman's Magazine, V, xv, VII, 155 n., VIII, 165 n., IX, 135 n.

Gentz, Friedrich von, *Briefe*, III, 434 & n.

Geological Society of London, Ricardo a member, X, 6, 49–50; other members, VI, 90 n., 180 n., 205–6 & notes, VII, 185 n., 191 n., 269 n., 275 n., VIII, 160 n., X, 144; see also VI, xxx, VII, 119 n.

History of, see Woodward, H. B.

George III, V, xviii, 41, VII, 218, 276; death of, VIII, 156

George IV (before 1820 see Wales, Prince of, and Regent):

his Coronation, V, 69, IX, 6; the Queen barred from, IX, 12 n., 30 & n.

and Canning, IX, 115

see also V, xxiii, 28, 64 n., VIII, 200, 221 n., 230, 294, X, 111 n.

Gernsbach, X, 231

Ghent, VII, 160, IX, 211

Gibbon, Edward, his house at Lausanne, X, 264, 269; see also VI, 279

Giessbach waterfall, X, 254, 257

Gil Blas, VII, 303, X, 290

Gilchrist, Ebenezer, banker, III, 228, 231

Glasgow Herald, V, xxiv n.

Globe and Traveller, IV, 7, IX, 301 n.; see also *Traveller*

Gloucester:

assizes, confusion at, VII, 283 & n., 290, 293; see also VII, 258–9, 277, 296, 300, 309, VIII, 56, 134, 212

Bishop of, VI, 310

theatre, X, 389

Gloucester, Duke of ('Silly Billy'), on Ricardo's plan, X, 187 n.; see also VI, 31 n.

Gloucestershire:

Ricardo Sheriff of, VII, 223–4; see also under Ricardo

clothiers, petition against corn bill, IV, 70–1 & n.; their bad wage system, VIII, 316; see also VIII, 70, X, 168–9

Gloucestershire (*cont.*)

Commission of the Peace, Ricardo not placed on, VIII, 157 & n.

constituency of, VIII, 156, 162–3

county meetings: Ricardo presides at (1818), VII, 268, 272, 372, 381–2; Ricardo's speech at, for the Queen (1820), V, 469–70, VIII, 330–1

mode of harnessing oxen, X, 231

Glut:

general, impossible, III, 108; extreme case of, I, 292–3

difference with Malthus on, II, 308, 312, VIII, 257, 285, 300–1, IX, 9–10, 25; with Trower, VIII, 257, 272, 289

glut of particular commodities, IV, 178–9; from miscalculation, II, 304–5, 413, IV, 344–5; due to lack of counter-commodities (Say and Torrens), VIII, 227–8, 260–1; see also I, 89, IX, 131

of corn, IV, 254, 263–4, 266, V, 88, 235, 304, in Europe, X, 184

of money, III, 383

glut in the foreign market, III, 101, VI, 38

see also Stagnation

Godalming, VII, 23 n.

Godwin, William, VI, 158 n., VIII, 114 n.

Of Population,...an Answer to Mr. Malthus, 1820, VIII, 291 n.; criticised by Mill, VIII, 292, by McCulloch, 326, by Trower, 361–2, by Ricardo, 368, by Malthus, 376; reviewed in *Quarterly*, IX, 147, 154, in *Edinburgh Review* (by Malthus), 84, 89–90, 94, 101; see also VIII, 290, 296, 307, 323, IX, 49 n., 59–60

Gold:

price of gold, Ricardo's letters to *Morning Chronicle* on, 1809, III, 15–46

high price of, caused by excess of paper, VI, 1–2, 5; other causes, V, 273–4

Gold (*cont.*)

value of, in terms of goods, III, 16, 28, V, 374; in terms of corn, different in different countries, I, 144–5, 377–8, II, 86

paper, not gold, altered in value (1810), III, 80

no criterion whether gold has risen or paper fallen (1819), II, 6–7; dispute with Blake (1823), IV, 328–9, 353–5, IX, 276, 284–7, 289

value and money price of, distinguished, III, 393, VI, 5–7, see also V, 392

less required under ingot plan, V, 383, 453, IX, 123; necessary reserve estimated, V, 424

gradual reduction of price proposed (1819), V, 381–2, 439–41, 450–1

unnecessary purchases by Bank from 1819, V, 165–6, 199–200, 205, 209, 311–12, 519

below mint price in 1820, V, 61

gold as a commodity, I, 44–5, 104, 168–9, 200, 352, 376–7, III, 52, 103–4, 142, VI, 21–2, 247–8, VIII, 2

as a measure of value, IV, 371–3, 382, 386–7, 389, 400–1, 406; assumed to be invariable, I, 87 & n., II, 83; Malthus's objections to, II, 82–3, 86

picked up in a day on the sea-shore, Malthus's measure of value, II, 81, IV, 365, VIII, 343

high value of, on Continent (1822) due to England's demand, X, 192–3, 195–6, see also V, 133–4

Gold mines, I, 195–200, III, 54, 111, see also I, 86–7, III, 216–17

Gold standard: whether the effective standard, III, 41, 66–70, 85 n., 255–6, VI, 2, 5–7

inconvenience of, while other countries have silver, V, 390–1, 427–8

a variable standard, III, 391, V, 94, 212, 374, 442, 517; but the least variable known, I, 45–6, 149, III, 65 n., IV, 62–3, V, 205–6, 388, 426–7, VII, 43

Gold token, V, 92, 96

Gold and Silver:

invariability of precious metals assumed in theory of value, VI, 348–9

distributed by competition among countries, I, 137–41, 343, III, 52–4, 65, 87, VI, 74–5

free trade in, I, 229–30

value regulated by difficulty of production, I, 193, 352, V, 444

as measures of value, I, 14, 86–7, II, 29

as general medium of circulation, I, 137

natural price of, I, 86

relative value of, III, 42–5, 67–70, 84, 178, V, 75–6, 94–5, 106, 378–9, 386–7, 426–7, VI, 2–4, 6–7

their variability underrated by bullionists, IV, 62, V, 205–6, VI, 344

new uses for, if price falls, VI, 90–2

improvements in production of, no advantage to England, III, 305–6

part of capital, but yield no revenue, I, 232, III, 55, 220, IV, 276, 298

unusual demand for, 1797–8, III, 171–2

quantity coined, 1816–19, VIII, 27 & n.

see also Bullion, Coin, Double standard, Hoarding, Silver

Goldau ruins, X, 246

Goldsmid, Aaron Asher, bullion broker, III, 350, V, 462, VI, 85

Goldsmid, Abraham: evidence to Bullion committee, III, 163, 198 n., 358–9; as loan contractor, X, 80, 92–4

Goldsmid, Benjamin & Abraham, III, 395–6, X, 80, 91, 125

Goldsmid, Sir Francis Henry, *Memoir* of, IX, 277–8 notes

Goldsmid, Isaac Lyon, bullion broker, VI, 85 n.; letter to, IX, 277–8

Goldsmith, Oliver, *The Traveller*, VI, 184, 327

Goldsmiths' Library, University of London, III, 380 n., V, 128 n., 250 n., 522 n., VI, 139 n., VII, 31 n., 93 n., IX, 154 n.; Ricardo Tracts in, X, 400, 402

Gonner, E. C. K., his edition of Ricardo's *Principles*, X, 364–5, of *Essays*, 371; tables of corresponding pages in various editions, I, 443–7, III, 435–7, IV, 419–22

Gooch, Thomas Sherlock, M.P. for Suffolk, Chairman of Agricultural committee 1821, V, xxiv, 81, 86–7, 148; see also IV, 203, VII, 45

Gordon, Mrs, '*Christopher North*', a *Memoir of John Wilson*, VIII, 205 n.

Gordon, Robert, M.P. for Cricklade, V, 109

Gordon, Viscount, V, 351

Gorton, John, *General Biographical Dictionary*, 1826–8, X, 38 n., 39 n.

Goulburn, Henry, Chief Secretary for Ireland, V, 304, IX, 124 n.

Government, checks on, V, 495, VIII, 133; free press as, V, 497, VII, 323

Government expenditure:
effects of, I, 246, IV, 348, 355–6, VIII, 171, 174, IX, 272, 276, 287 & n., see also I, 106, 153, VIII, 155
Ricardo accused of encouraging, VII, 280–1, 286, 337–8, 353, and cp. I, 151–2 & n., 242
Malthus's peculiar opinions on, II, 433, 447, 450
see also Public expenditure, Public works

Government interference, when justified, IV, 71–2, VIII, 133

Government, opinions on, in Holland, IX, 213, in Geneva, 217

Government paper money, Say's plan, VI, 165–6

Grade, Mr, V, 186

Graham, Earl, V, 351

Graham, Sir James, *Corn and Currency*, 1827, VII, 93 n.

Grain, Lords' Report on, 1814, VI, 130, 132

Grand St Bernard, IX, 220, X, 283, 285–7

Grant, Charles, founder of the East India College, VII, 130 n.

Grant, Charles, jun., East India Director, VII, 110

Grant, James, *The Great Metropolis* and *The Newspaper Press*, V, xxvii n., xxviii n., X, 73 n.

Grant, John Peter, M.P. for Tavistock, V, 16, 110

Grant, Robert, on East India College, VII, 130–2

Granville, and house at Brighton in 1795, X, 109–10

Granville, Viscount, V, 351

Gravitation, principle of, I, 108, VI, 204; of profits, I, 120

Gray, Simon, *The Happiness of States*, 1815, VIII, 38 n. For other works see under Purves, George

Greek loan, X, 58 & n.

Greeks, defeat in 1822, X, 278, see also IX, 39

Greenland, George, bookseller, VIII, 378 n.

Greenough, George Bellas, VI, 206 n. his geological map, VII, 118–19 & n. *Critical Examination of . . . Principles of Geology*, 1819, VIII, 43 see also VI, xxiv, X, 49

Green Park, walks in, VIII, 191

Greffulhe, John Louis, his evidence to Bullion committee, III, 163, 178, 182, 197–8, 360–1, 429 n.

Gregory, T. E., II, xv, X, 373

Grellier, J. J., *History of the National Debt*, 1810, X, 70 n.
The Terms of all the Loans, 1812, X, 75 n.

Grenfell, Pascoe, M.P. for Great Marlow till 1820, then for Penrhyn, VI, xxxiii

resolutions on the Bank, 1815, IV, 51 n., 54, 76–7, 86, 136–7, VI, 242, 278, VII, 25–6, X, 9; other references to the Bank, V, 20, 62, 193, 247, VI, 257 n., 267–8, VII, 252 n.

Grenfell, Pascoe (*cont.*)
on Bank of Ireland, V, 70, 98
on using sinking fund to diminish
borrowing, IV, 171–3, V, 4, 18,
21–2, 58, 62, 193, 243, X, 81–2,
85
and resumption of cash payments,
V, 350, 352, 354, 356, VIII, 19
on proposed tax on capital, V, 270
on loan contractors, V, 4
and *Economical Currency*, IV, 45–6,
95 n., VI, 241–2, 265, 267–8,
285–6, 295, 305, 313, X, 9
Mallet on, VIII, 152 n.
list of letters, IX, 393–4
see also I, lx, IV, 82, 97 n., V, 23, 26,
37, 59 n., 65, 67, 277, VI, 284 n.,
VII, 15, 19 n., 22, 25 n., 189, 347,
VIII, 18, 77
Speech on applying the Sinking Fund,
1817, V, 22 n., see also 4 n.
Grenside, John, IX, 166 n.
Grenville, Lord, VII, 220 & n.
letter from, VIII, 150–1
studies *Principles*, VII, 189, 220,
259
on free trade, IV, 250–1
and resumption of cash payments, V,
351–4, 356, 365, VIII, 19 & n.
see also III, 413 n., IV, 71 n., VII,
17, 262, 267, IX, 270
Grey, Earl, hollow speech on reform,
VIII, 6, 8–9, Ricardo's lost paper
on, 6 n., 8; see also VI, 183 n.,
VII, 142, VIII, 11, 68 n., 335
Griffin, C. S., editor, X, 383
Grillparzer, Franz, *Die Ahnfrau*, X,
223–4 & n., 258
Grimm, F. M., *Correspondence littér-
aire*, IX, 375
Grindelwald, X, 256
Grote, George, VI, xxxiii
extracts from his diary, VI, xxxiv
MS on foreign trade, VI, xxxiv
letter to, IX, 288
Question of Parliamentary Reform
(anon.), 1821, VIII, 328 n.
Posthumous Papers, 1874, IX, 288 n.,
301–2

Grote, Mrs, letters quoted, IX, 288 n.,
301–2; *The Personal Life of
George Grote*, VI, xxxii n., xxxiv,
IX, 288 n.
Grote and Prescott, bankers, VI, xxxiii
Ground rent, I, 201–4
Guardian Insurance Company, IX,
104 & n.
Guido d'Arezzo, X, 312, 316
Guildford, VII, 62, 267
Guineas, I, 369–70, III, 18, 24, 32,
40–1, 69–70, 82–3, 141, 322, VI, 2, 7
Guinness, Arthur, Governor of the
Bank of Ireland, V, 99
Guise, Sir B. W., M.P. for Gloucester-
shire, VII, 272 n., VIII, 156 n.
Gurney, Hudson, M.P. for Newton,
Hants., V, 161, 202, 217–18

Haarlem, X, 204
Hadlow Place, or Dalchurst, Manor of,
Ricardo's property, X, 96–7, 105
Hague, The, X, 197–203; the much-
travelled waiter, IX, 213–14, X,
199–200; story of a pair of shoes,
X, 32–3
Haileybury College, VI, xix. See
East India College
Haldimand, William, M.P. for Ips-
wich, Director of Bank of England,
VIII, 163 & n.
on effects of resumption, V, 198–200
his evidence, V, 352–4, VIII, 21 & n.
see also V, 185
Halévy, Elie: *La Formation du Radi-
calisme philosophique*, VI, 157 n.,
161 n.; *History of the English
People in 1815*, X, 39
Half-share tenancy in Italy, Malthus
puzzled by, VIII, 377
Hall, Francis, *Travels in Canada and
the United States*, 1818, X, 395
Hall, Mrs, boat-builder, VII, 51, 68, 71
Hallam, Henry, *Europe during the
Middle Ages*, 1818, X, 397
Hamburg, see Bank of, Exchange with
Hamilton, Alexander, professor at
East India College, VI, 66, VII,
167

Hamilton, Robert, *Inquiry concerning the National Debt*, ed. 3, 1818, IV, 149–51, 156–7, 167, 171–2, 174, 184, 199–200, 351, VII, 23 n., VIII, 61, 64, 67, 76, 78, 123–5, 320, X, 69 n., 75–8 notes

Hammersley & Co., bankers, their circular Exchange Notes, X, 192, 195, 223, 244

Hammond, George, III, 432

Hammond, William, VI, 113 n.

Hancock, C. H., stockbroker, VII, 15; letters in Ricardo Papers, X, 388; see also X, 123–4 & n., 126–8

Hand weavers' petition, V, 302; see also V, 68

Hansard's Parliamentary History, I, 107 n., X, 77 n., 396–8

Hansard, T. C., *Parliamentary Debates* (referred to as *Hansard*), V, xxix–xxxii, XI, xxv

Hansard, T. C., jun., V, xxix n.

Happiness:
whether more in a large than in a small population, I, 349 n., Ricardo non-committal, II, 382, VII, 379

as much from idleness as from consumption, VII, 185, see also I, 99–100 & notes, VII, 48–9, IX, 261

depends on abundance, not value, II, 21, 203, 365, see also IV, 248–9, VI, 236

of the people, and government, I, 99, VII, 299, 366, IX, 213; and education, VI, 264, VII, 204

Ricardo's motto, IX, 239

England could be the happiest country, V, 55

Hardcastle, Daniel (pseudonym of Richard Page), *Letters on the Bank Restriction*, 1819, V, 361 n., VIII, 3 n.

Hardenhuish, home of the Clutterbucks, IX, 296, X, 62, 315; Ricardo's tomb at, X, 12

Hardware, I, 134, 406, II, 390–1, IV, 251, V, 102

Hare, Augustus, *Life and Letters of Maria Edgeworth*, VI, xxxii n., VII, 264 n., IX, 143 n., 230, 295 n., X, 167

Harman, Jeremiah, Governor of the Bank of England, his evidence in 1810, III, 363, 372–7, IV, 68 n.; in 1819, V, 10 & n., 353, 363

Harrow School, VII, 138, X, 267

Harrowby, Earl of, V, 351, 354, 365, 416, 439

Hartley, David, IX, 332

Harvests, bad:
and foreign exchange, III, 106–7, VI, 37

and wage regulation, I, 162

in 1816, VII, 61, 66, 87, 90

see also Abundance

Harvey, Robert Crytoft, evidence on agriculture, IV, 210, 239–40

Hashizume, Akeo, X, 384

Hastings, Warren, VII, 237, 249

Haultain, Mr, X, 147

Haygarth, John, *Provident Institution at Bath*, 1816, VII, 130

Hazlitt, William, 'Periodical Press', in *Edinburgh Review*, 1823, V, xxvii n., VI, xxii, VII, 28 n., VIII, 185–6 n.

Heaphy, Thomas, portrait of Ricardo, VIII, facing p. 1, X, 51, 53

Heathfield, Richard, letter to, VIII, 143–5

Plan for the Liquidation of the Public Debt, 1819, VIII, 143 n.

Heidelberg, visit in 1817, VII, 160, 164, 167; in 1822, X, 227–8

Henriques de Castro, D., *De Synagoge der Portugeesch-Israelietische Gemeente*, X, 18 n.

Hereford:
celebration for Joseph Hume (1821), IX, 113, 118–19, 121, 141 & n., Ricardo's speech at, V, 471–4, 515

County meetings: in support of income tax (1822), IX, 247; Cobbett attacks Ricardo at (1823), IX, 266–7 & n.

see also VII, 299, X, 98

Hertford, VI, 60–1. See East India College
Heygate, Alderman William, M.P. for Sudbury, IV, 232 n., V, 17, 61–2, 203, 295
Hibbert, X, 309, 310
Hicks, H., VII, 293, 304, 336, IX, 13
Hill, J., *Life and Writings of Hugh Blair*, 1807, VI, 326
Hills, Mrs Eustace, unpublished life of Richard Sharp, VI, xxxvi–xxxvii, VII, 291 n., XI, xxvii
Himes, N. E., 'The place of J. S. Mill and Robert Owen in Neo-Malthusianism', VIII, 72 n.
Hindus, civilisation of, VII, 223, 228, 249; metaphysics, VII, 235 n.; see also VI, 96 n.
Hitchings, James, tutor of Ricardo's children, VI, 240 & n., VII, 51, 71, 144, X, 62, 63, 389; his obituary of Ricardo, VI, xxxv
Hitzigrath, H., *Merchant Adventurers in Hamburg*, III, 430
Hoarding of gold: in banks, VI, 289, 300–1; by timid people, III, 172, 322; incitement to, by Cobbett, IX, 167 & n., 176
Hoare, P. R., *Examination of Sir John Sinclair's Observations*, 1811, X, 402; *On National Bankruptcy*, 1811, X, 400
Hoare's Bank, VI, 116
Hobhouse, Sir Benjamin, VII, 109–10, 113
Hobhouse, Edward, X, 273, 275
Hobhouse, John Cam:
  and the Westminster election, VII, 357 & n., 360, 372
  on Ricardo first reading Adam Smith, X, 36
  Mill on, VII, 363, VIII, 59
  see also V, 484, VII, 131 n., VIII, 56, 300, IX, 268, X, 58 n., 227–8, 236 and under Broughton, Lord
Hobhouse, Miss, VIII, 56, 59, 75
Hodges, John, stockbroker, VI, 112 n., X, 126–8
Hodges, William, VI, 112 n.

Hodgetts, T., engraver, X, 52
Hodgson, David, corn merchant:
  his method of forecasting crops, VIII, 370 & n., 371–2
  invites Ricardo to stand for election at Liverpool, IX, 182, XI, xiv
Hofwyl, X, 262
Holl, William, engraver, X, 52, 369
Holland:
  Ricardo's ancestors in, X, 17–21
  visits to, when young, X, 3–4, 30–3; in 1822, IX, 209–11, 213, X, 193–213
  low rate of profits and interest in, I, 290 n., IX, 160
  commerce in, article by McCulloch, IX, 135 & n., 139
  see also I, 148, IV, 32, VI, 97, IX, 222, and under Amsterdam
Holland, Dr Henry, VII, 269
  Recollections of Past Life, VII, 269 n.
Holland House, VII, 54 n., 114, IX, 94, 101; Ricardo's visit, VII, 144 n.
Holland, Lady, IX, 94
  Memoir of Sydney Smith, IX, 89 n., 108 n.
Holland, Lord, VII, 54 n., VIII, 28 n., 335, IX, 94, X, 50, 396
  Memoirs of the Whig Party, 1807–21, VII, 222 n.
Holland, Swinton, supports ingot plan, V, 355–6; see also VIII, 367 n., IX, 173 n., 208
Hollander, Jacob H.:
  The Economic Library of, III, 5 n.
  David Ricardo, A Centenary Estimate, I, xxii n., IV, 203 n., X, 17 n., 18 & n., 20 & n., 21 n., 29, 37 n., 81 n.
  'Development of Ricardo's Theory of Value,' I, xxxvii, xl n.
  see also II, xv, III, 406, VII, 155 n., VIII, 136 n., X, 371–3, 387
Holroyd, Justice, VII, 293
Holte, Lady, X, 169
Homburg, X, 224–5
Hone, William, parodies of the Church Catechism, etc., 1817, prosecution for, V, 325 & n.
Hope, Mr, IX, 208

Hope, Sir Alexander, VII, 313 n.

Hopkins, T., *Bank notes*, Ricardo's comments on, X, 402

Hori, Tsuneo, X, 384

Horner, Francis, VI, xxxiv–xxxv
and the bullion question, III, 9–10, 413–14, VI, 1–7, X, 8, 14–15, 92
and foreign exchanges, III, 12, VI, 8–10, 78–81
on price of corn regulating all other prices, I, 302–3
motion for resumption of cash payments in 1816, IV, 51, VII, 28, 30
on Locke's good temper in argument, VII, 206, 212
his last illness, VII, 85, 89–90; tomb at Leghorn, IX, 227–8, X, 322
letters to, VI, 1–10, 78–81; Malthus's letter to, VI, 186–8
see also V, xiv, VI, 23, 66, 127, 159 n., VII, 193, VIII, 160, IX, 123 n., X, 49, 50, 388, XI, xxvii
articles in *Edinburgh Review*: on Thornton's *Paper Credit*, 1802, III, 64; on Lord King's pamphlet, 1803, III, 73, 83; on a bounty on the exportation of corn, 1804, I, 302, 307, 315
Memoirs and Correspondence, VI, 127 n.; ed. 2, III, 9–10 & n.

Horner, Leonard, VIII, 160; see also III, 10 n., VI, xxxv, 187

Horses:
substitution of, for labour of men, I, 394–5, II, 335; and vice-versa, II, 237–9 & n.
employed in husbandry, I, 82
ill-treatment of horses bill, V, 122
Lord John Russell's horse, IV, 258 & n.
ploughing with horses in the Netherlands, X, 188
tax on, I, 205, 242, 251, V, 101
horses at Gatcomb, VI, 130–1, 267, VII, 361, 365, VIII, 48, 78, 231–2, IX, 44–5, X, 168; 'Old Consul', X, 348, see also 342
on the Continent, VII, 163–4, X, 177, 183, 216, 222, 234, 237, 251, 260, 310–11, 313, 324, 343

Horton, John Robert Wilmot, letter to, XI, xv
Outline of a Plan of Emigration to Upper Canada, 1823, and *Causes and Remedies of Pauperism*, 1829, XI, xv notes

Horwood, R., *Plan of London*, 1799, X, 29 n.

House of Commons:
interests controlling it, V, 284, 286, 288, 470, 478, 496, VII, 49, 323, VIII, 163, 304, 330, IX, 4, 158, 198
its ministerial compliance, V, 269
Mill on venality of members, VI, 253, 263, 307, 310–11
see also Parliament, Reform

Household suffrage, V, 473, 485, VII, 273 & n.

Houses, taxes on, I, 201–4; house and window duties, V, 79, 84 n.

Hudson, John, Trinity College Tutor, X, 136, 139

Hughan, T., III, 429 n.

Humboldt, Alexander von, IX, 219
Essai Politique sur la Nouvelle Espagne, 1811, II, 28, 337–44, VII, 184, 189; English translation, X, 394; see also IX, 252, X, 293 n.

Hume, David:
on magic effect of rise of prices, IV, 36, V, 524
and *Wealth of Nations*, I, vii, XI, xxvii
Essays and Treatises, VII, 197, X, 399
Natural History of Religion, X, 395
Political Discourses, Of Interest, III, 90, V, 12 & n.; Of Money, IV, 36–7, V, 524, VI, 34
see also III, 163, VII, 227, 229

Hume, David, judge, XI, xxvii

Hume, Joseph, M.P. for Aberdeen and Montrose, VI, 138 & n., VIII, 209–10 & n.
his description of Gatcomb, VI, 158
reads *Principles*, VII, 364–5, 373
tribute to Ricardo, V, 332
presents petition from Mary Ann Carlile, V, 277

Hume, Joseph (*cont.*)
  motion against combination laws in
    1824, Ricardo's promised support
    for, V, xx, 332
  on free discussion of religious
    opinions, V, 324, 330 & n., XI,
    xxii
  sinking fund and pensions scheme,
    V, 161, 191–4
  Spitalfields Acts, V, 295
  his activity in parliament, VIII, 202,
    209–10, IX, 45–6
  his 'phalanx', V, xxii n.
  speech in honour of, V, 471–4, IX,
    141 n., see also IX, 113, 118–22,
    141, 144–5
  Ricardo's letter to, XI, ix, see also
    X, 388
  see also V, 138, 185, 278 n., 281, 467,
    476, VI, 107, 127, 310, 313, 325,
    332, VII, 141, 303, 314, 336, 358 n.,
    361, 371, VIII, 8, 72, 296, 323–4,
    IX, 41–2, 123, 153–4, 186, 194, 228,
    X, 13, 58, 267 n., 388, XI, xvii, xx
  Proceedings in Herefordshire, 1822,
    V, 471 n.
  *Account of the Provident Institution
    for Savings*, 1816, VII, 34 n., 47 n.
Hume, Mrs Joseph, XI, ix n., x
Humphrey Carvick & Co., III, 430
Humphrys, Mr, VII, 327
Hunt, Henry, VII, 270 n., VIII, 66, 99,
  129, IX, 120
Hunting and shooting, V, 122, VI,
  300, VII, 308–9, 318–19, 335,
  VIII, 360 n., X, 162, 336
Huskisson, William, M.P. for Chichester, later for Liverpool, IX,
  182 n., President of the Board of
  Trade, 1823, IX, 270 n.
  his liberal principles, V, xx, 305
  tribute to Ricardo, V, 332
  joint author of Bullion Report, III,
    413 n.
  his singular argument for lowering
    bank rate, IV, 234 & n.
  on the standard of currency, V, 198,
    216–18
  on unrestricted issue of paper, V, 316

Huskisson (*cont.*)
  in committee on resumption of cash
    payments, V, 351, 353–4, 356,
    VIII, 19
  defends sinking fund, V, 79
  in agricultural committee, 1821, V,
    xxiv–xxv, 86, IX, 37, 197; draws
    up report, IV, 203, VIII, 390;
    declines attending 1822 committee,
    IX, 177
  resolutions on corn importation, V,
    159, 169, 172, 175, IX, 197
  differs from Ricardo on desirable
    extent of agriculture, IX, 7–8
  merchant vessels apprenticeship, V,
    273, 283
  East and West India sugars, V, 301
  reciprocity of duties on shipping, V,
    305
  for repeal of Spitalfields Acts, V, 292,
    308–9, IX, 318
  see also V, xxi, 136, 223, 256, 282,
    321, 335, 461, VII, 153, VIII, 374,
    IX, 176
  Depreciation of our Currency, 1810,
    III, 11, 111–12, 171 n., 177 n.,
    209–10, 227, 252–4, VI, 34, IX,
    270 n.; passages on which Ricardo
    differs, X, 400 & n.; Ricardo's lost
    remarks on, X, 400 n.
  Speech on the State of the Finance,
    1813, IV, 154, 166–7, 200
  Speeches, 1831, IX, 177 n., 270 n., with
    biography by E. Leeves, XI, xxix
  William Huskisson, by A. Brady, III,
    427
Hutcheson, Archibald, *Proposal for
  Payment of the Publick Debts*
  (1714), anticipates Ricardo's plan,
  V, 40, 41 n., see also I, 248 n.
Hutchinson, Christopher Hely-, M.P.
  for Cork, V, 474
Hyamson, A. M., *The Sephardim of
  England*, X, 18 n., 23 n., 27 n.
Hyde, Osman Ricardo's residence,
  VII, 182, 186 & n., see also VII,
  171, VIII, 48
Hyde Park, walks in, VI, xxviii n.,
  VII, 277

Ice machine, IV, 249
Idleness, luxury of, VII, 70, 184–5.
    See Indolence
Impey, Mr, VII, 132
Import duties:
    on butter, V, 218–19; candles, V,
        146; cheese, V, 146; tallow, V,
        146–7, 291, 294; timber, V, 102–4,
        110–11; wool, V, 42
    reciprocity of, V, 305–6
    see also Countervailing duties, Pro-
        tecting duties, Sugar
Improvements in agriculture:
    two kinds of, I, 80–4
    effect on profits, I, 120, II, 140–1, IV,
        11 & n., 19 n., VI, 94–5, 145, 162,
        339
    effect on rent, I, 79–80, II, 135–6, IV,
        19 n., 41, VI, 172, 190, 293–4; long
        and short term effects, I, 81 n., 412,
        II, 112–13, 118, 185, 198, VI, 302,
        VII, 282–3, VIII, 182, 184, 208
    see also II, 161, IV, 346, V, 94, 211,
        VI, 104, 194, and under Leases
Inclosure bills, VII, 299, X, 98
Income, gross and net, I, 420–5
    net income increased by machinery,
        gross income diminished, I, 388–9,
        see also 396
    country enriched only by net in-
        come, II, 235; labouring class
        affected by how it is spent, I,
        392–3
    all taxes paid from net income, I, 178
    net real income (rent and profits), I,
        348
    see also Revenue
Income tax:
    no effect on prices, III, 241, IV,
        216–17, VIII, 153
    and tax on capital, I, 152–3
    prying into every man's concerns, I,
        160–1, and cp. VIII, 154
    began 1798, VI, 282; raised to 10%,
        VI, 275; ended 1816, VII, 25 n.;
        proposed revival, 1819, VIII, 135,
        190, 196
    see also III, 138, IX, 246–7, and
        under Tax on property

India:
    government of, by correspondence,
        VIII, 40 n.; see also IX, 116, and
        under Mill, James, History of
        India
    labour in, IX, 305, 322, 337, 347–9
    see also East India Company
India bonds, III, 291, 295, 298, IX,
    262
Indies, see East Indies, West Indies
Indolence:
    preferred to riches, II, 313–15, 338,
        VII, 70
    easily obtained food and, II, 87, 334,
        339–41, VII, 184–5, IX, 56; in
        Ireland, I, 100 n., IX, 231; in
        South America, II, 337, VIII, 216
'Ingenious calculator' (William Mor-
    gan), IV, 415–18; see also III,
    358 n., IV, 99, 279, VI, 275
Ingliss, Stewart, IX, 184, 187, 194
Ingot plan:
    paying bank notes in bullion, IV,
        65–70
    savings from, V, 433–4, 444–5
    circulation of gold coin compatible
        with, V, 429–31
    first suggested 1811, III, 124–7; pro-
        posed to Perceval, VI, 43–6, 70, to
        Tierney, VI, 67–71
    submitted to 1819 committees, V,
        354–64, VIII, 20–1, 23; Ricardo's
        evidence: Commons', V, 379–90,
        405–6, 409–15, Lords', 422–33,
        439–44, 450–6; his speech, V,
        9–17
    supported by Baring, V, 91–2, 352 n.,
        356, 358–61, by the Governor of
        the Bank, V, 363–4; as a temporary
        measure, by Tooke, V, 361–2, by
        Samuel Thornton, V, 363
    opposed by Rothschild, V, 357, by
        Harman, V, 363
    adopted till 1823, V, 7–8 & n., 367–8;
        with deviations, VIII, 26–7, 31–2,
        35–7, 39; whether to be made
        permanent, V, 40, 46, 70, 92, 135
    danger of forgery of small notes, V,
        96–7

Ingot plan (*cont.*)
  Grenfell on, VI, 286; Malthus, VI, 41 & n., 298–9; McCulloch, VIII, 36, X, 370; Torrens opposed to, VIII, 82–3; attacked by Cobbett, VIII, 74 & n., IX, 176 & n.
  ingots called 'Ricardoes', V, 368–9; few demanded, V, 76, 311–12; see also IX, 176 n.
  not fairly tried, IV, 224–5, V, 165, 312, 518, IX, 123, 141
  see also I, 356–61, II, 48–9, IV, 104, V, xix, xxxiii, 71, 73, 204, 516–17, VI, 165, 300–1, VII, 353, VIII, 5, 6, 134, 361, IX, 201
Inquiry into . . . the Nature of Demand, 1821 (anon.), IX, 27 & n.
Insurance, I, 263, III, 19, 71, 161, 183, VI, 284 & n., IX, 104 & n.
Intellectual attainments, demand and supply of, VII, 131
Interest, see Rate of interest
Interests:
  of the individual and of the community, I, 133–4, 349–50 n., III, 56
  of landlords, contrasted with those of farmers or manufacturers, I, 312–13, II, 199–200, V, 158 n., and with those of consumers, I, 335–6, II, 117–18, V, 87; opposed to interests of every other class, IV, 21, VII, 17, VIII, 182, 207–8, see also II, 198, V, 314
  of master and workmen, opposite regarding machinery, I, 388, 392, IX, 194
  see also V, 53
Interlaken, X, 253–4, 258
Inventions, destroy capital but this no reason for suppression, I, 271, IV, 33; see also V, 179, and under Machinery
Inverarity MS, VI, 159 n.
Ionian Islands, vote on, V, xxii
Ireland:
  bank failures, V, 70, 99
  Catholic emancipation, V, xxii–xxiii, VIII, 50, 350–1, 369, see also V, 329–30

Ireland (*cont.*)
  corn imports from, IV, 259–60, V, 94, 108, 125, VIII, 369, IX, 158
  currency, III, 398–9
  curse of small farms, IX, 145–6, 153, 314, 372
  indolence and low profits, II, 344–9, VII, 184 & n.
  Insurrection bill, V, xxii
  labouring poor, Ricardo member of committee on, V, xxvi–xxvii, 331 n., IX, 313 & n., 314, 316, 372
  Lord-lieutenancy, motion for abolition of, V, xxii; see also IX, 145
  Malthus's tour of, VII, 168, 174–6, 184
  misrule in, IX, 153, 295–6, see also V, 99
  potato famine in 1822, V, 234–5, IX, 231–2, 254
  protecting duties, V, 57–8, 104, 218–19
  remedies for evils of, I, 100 n., VII, 48, 334
  taxation in, IX, 160 & n, 185 & n.
  tithes composition bill, V, 304; see also IX, 153, 186
  see also IV, 32 n., 408, V, 36, VI, 244, IX, 239–40, 274, Bank of Ireland and Exchange, Irish
Irving, John, M.P. for Bramber, V, 37 & n., 98
Isle of Wight, VII, 279, 283
Islington, VI, 49, 56, X, 25
Isola Bella, X, 291
Israel, early family name of the Ricardos, X, 18 & n. 4
Israel, Hannah, wife of Joseph Israel Ricardo, X, 19, XI, xxix
Italy, visit to, IX, 221–8, X, 291–339
Iveson, John, IV, 210–11, 260

Jackson, Randle, spokesman for Bank of England on Bullion report, III, 9 n., 145–53, 358–9
  opposes increasing dividend, V, 466–7
  on East India College, VII, 130 n., 131, 135–6, 138

Jackson, Sir T., & Co., loan contractors, X, 85

Jacob, William, witness before agricultural committee, V, xxiv, IX, 67, 87

Letter to Samuel Whitbread, 1815, I, 268 n., VI, 180, 186, 190

Jacobs, Mr, his piety, X, 389

Jamaica, I, 339, III, 350, X, 350 n.; see also Exchange

James, J. T., *Journal of a Tour in Germany*, 1816, X, 395

James, William, letter in Ricardo Papers, X, 388

Jannaccone, P., VIII, 375 n.

Jefferson, Thomas, on Ricardo's *Principles*, X, 372

Jeffrey, Francis, editor of *Edinburgh Review*:

articles by, X, 397; in *Scotsman*, VIII, 82

vetoes MᶜCulloch's reviewing of Malthus, VIII, 139, 189, 325

his 'mercenary troops', III, 9

see also VII, 353, VIII, 166, 205, 351, IX, 206 n., 218, 342, X, 50, 272

Jeffrey, Mrs (*née* Charlotte Wilkes), VIII, 205, X, 272 & n.

Jenks, L. H., *The Migration of British Capital to 1875*, X, 58 n.

Jenner, Dr, given the palm over Napoleon, X, 211

Jesus College, Cambridge, VI, xix, xx n.

Jew brokers, X, 22, 56–7, see also IX, 267 n.

Jewish Historical Society of England, *Transactions*, IX, 278 n.; *Miscellanies*, X, 22 n., 57 n., 60 n.

Jewish origin of Ricardo, X, 16–33, 37–9

Jews, letter on disabilities of, IX, 277–8

Jobbers, Stock-Exchange, X, 69–70; Ricardo a jobber, X, 70–3

Joel, Jacob de, X, 26

John Bull, newspaper, IX, 136, 204

Johnson, J. M., III, 432–3

Johnstone, A., *London Commercial Guide*, 1817, VI, 284 n.

Johnstone, A. Cochrane, and the Stock Exchange hoax, VI, 105–7

Johnstone, George, *Speech on Lord Stanhope's bill*, 1811, X, 400

Jonas, J., X, 383

Jonathan, D., X, 336 n.

Jones, Inigo, his work at Ford Abbey, VI, 125

Jungfrau, X, 254

Junius, VI, 10 n.

Kaltenbrunn, X, 239

Kay-Shuttleworth, Nina, see Hills, Mrs Eustace

Keelmen, strike of, VIII, 99

Kegan Paul, C., *William Godwin*, VIII, 114 n.

Kelly, Patrick, III, 168, 186
The Universal Cambist, IX, 183–4 & n.

Kemble, John Philip, X, 268–9

Kennington, Ricardo's homes at, X, 46, 110–11

Kensington Gardens, see Walks

Kent, Duke of, takes chair at meeting on Owen's plan, V, 467 & n.; persuades Ricardo to join committee, VIII, 45–6; see also VII, 346

Keynes, J. M., 'Robert Malthus', in *Essays in Biography*, VI, xiii, 35 n.

Keyser, Isaac (D.R.'s brother-in-law), VII, 15, 240, X, 56–7

Keyser, Rebecca (D.R.'s sister), see Ricardo, Rebecca

Kiddington, X, 36 n., 64

King, Lord:
demands his rents in gold, 1811, V, 316

scheme for resumption, V, 353

suggests stopping Bank dividends while gold at a premium, VII, 262–3

and *Principles*, VII, 250–1

see also V, 351, 354, 356, VI, 231, VII, 173, VIII, 19, 164, IX, 123 n.

Thoughts on the Restriction of Payments [1803], III, 4, 51, VI, 9, VII, 250 n.; Horner on, III, 73, 83

Thoughts on the Effects of the Bank Restrictions, 1804, III, 51, 173, VI, 9

King of Clubs, VI, 87 n., X, 50; see
    also VI, 91, 171, 180, 196, 198,
    220, VII, 8, 18, 20, 136, 138, 262,
    291 n., VIII, 18, IX, 151, 157
Kinnaird, Douglas, on East India
    College, VII, 131–2; see also IX,
    41–2
Kinoshita, Akira, X, 385
Kirkcudbright, IX, 135 n., 302 & n.
Kirkland, Nugent, and Portarlington
    seat, V, xvi, VII, 216, 232, 346–7
Kirkpatrick & Co., III, 430
Knatchbull, Sir Edward, M.P. for
    Kent, V, 81, 86, 90
Knotty point on fixed value and
    changing profits (Malthus), IX,
    65–6, 74–85, 90–101, 111–13; other
    knotty points, IX, 158 & n.
Knyvett, his concert, VI, 90; at
    Gatcomb, VIII, 282
Koch, Christian Friedrich, hock mer-
    chant at Frankfort, X, 223 & n., 226
Koe, John Herbert, Bentham's aman-
    uensis, VI, 161 n., VII, 74, 336, 351
Koizumi, Shinzo, X, 384
Kolthammer, F. W., X, 365
Kotzebue, A., his play 'The Stranger',
    X, 199
Kunatt, Stanislaw, young Pole met on
    the Simplon, X, 289–90 & n., 301,
    see also IX, 223–4; translator of
    Ricardo, X, 379

Labour:
    demand for, not the same as supply of
        necessaries, VIII, 236, 248, 258 n.;
        depends on circulating, not on
        fixed, capital, II, 234 & n., see also
        I, 395–6 n.; diminished by taxation,
        I, 233, VIII, 177
    economy in the use of, I, 25–6,
        36, 44, 51, 65 n., 80, 133; see
        also Machinery
    estimation of different qualities of, I,
        20–2
    immediate and accumulated, IV,
        379–80, 386, IX, 307, 338–9, 365,
        see also I, 34, 410, VII, 316 n.,
        IX, 323, 343, 385

Labour (cont.)
    natural and market price of, I, 93–7,
        II, 227–8, 268; commodity price of,
        II, 371; see also Wages, natural
        price of
    quantity of, in a day's work, dif-
        ferent in different countries, II, 87,
        IX, 305, 309–10, 319, 322, 337,
        347–9
    quantity of, as measure of value, I,
        12–13, 15, 17 & n., 85–6, 88, IV,
        381–6, 397; not a perfect, but a
        tolerable one, II, 66–7, IV, 405
    labour bestowed on a commodity
        (Ricardo), I, 13–14, 24–5, 37,
        46–7, 73, II, 34–5, 101–2, IV,
        387, IX, 348; and on machines, II,
        87
    labour commanded (Malthus), II,
        29–30, 383, 410–11, IX, 348, see
        also I, 18–19, IX, 1–3
    see also Employment, Value, measure
        of, Wages
Labour of horses, I, 394, II, 335; of
    machines, VIII, 138, IX, 325 n.,
    369; of nature, I, 76 n.
Labourers:
    real condition of, II, 249–50
    their situation in a general glut, II,
        308
    benefit from rise in value of money
        (Cobbett), IX, 166, and cp. IX, 40
    their taste for enjoyments should be
        stimulated, I, 100 & n., see also II,
        373, VI, 147, VIII, 275
Labouring classes:
    cannot contribute to taxation, I, 159,
        235, and cp. 347–8 & n.
    distress of, 1819–20, V, 47, 224–5,
        VIII, 103
    fully employed in agriculture and in
        manufactures, 1821, IX, 13, 40
    see also Classes, working, Manufac-
        turing classes
Laing, John, VII, 244–5
    Account of a Voyage to Spitzbergen,
        VII, 245 n.
Lamb, George, M.P. for Dungarvan,
    V, 185, VII, 363 n.

Lamb, William, M.P. for Hertford-
shire (afterwards Lord Melbourne),
V, xiv, xxiii, 24, 185, 350
Lambeth, Ricardo's marriage at, X,
38; his homes in, 46
Lambton, John George, M.P. for
Durham, motion for the reform of
parliament, V, 112, VIII, 367 n.;
see also X, 36
Lancaster, Joseph, educational reformer, letter in Ricardo Papers,
X, 388; see also VI, 112 n., VII,
45 n., 155 n., X, 402
Lancaster, Joseph, stockbroker, *The
Bank – The Stock Exchange...
An Exposé* [anon.], 1821, X,
93–4 & notes, 95 n., 123–4 & n.
Lancey, Miss, governess, IX, 241, X,
177, 197–8, 209, 220, 235, 237–8,
305, 327
Land:
appropriation of, and value of commodities, I, 23 n., 67, 77–8
that pays no rent, I, 74, exists in every
country, I, 328, not necessary for
theory of rent, I, 412–13 n., VII,
372, 379, VIII, 4, 57, 149–50; see
also I, 83 n., 113, 157, 181, 225,
VI, 173
supposition of fertile tract added to
island, IV, 18, VI, 162, 217–18,
220–2, see also I, 15
neat surplus from, defined, VIII, 311
land as a machine, I, 408, II, 118,
185, IV, 24 n., 34, VIII, 208
see also Diminishing returns, Fertility, Rent
Land tax redemption plan, V, 248,
250, 259–60
Landaff, Bishop of, see Watson, R.
Landed gentlemen, hostility to Ricardo, VIII, 147, IX, 262, 266, X, 349
Landlords:
their interests opposed to those of
every other class, I, 335–6, II,
116–17, 198
their interest in protection permanent,
that of manufacturers temporary, I,
312–13, II, 199–200

Landlords (*cont.*)
relinquishing their rents would not
lower price of corn, I, 74–5, II,
118, 182–3, IV, 21
make the laws, VIII, 182, IX, 158,
see also V, 81, 291, VIII, 158, 348,
350, IX, 37
Ricardo misrepresented as enemy of,
II, 117–19, VIII, 207–8
Lang, A., *Life of Lockhart*, VIII,
205 n.
Lang, L., X, 383
Langman, Lady, VI, xxxv, XI, xxvii
Langston, James Haughton, M.P. for
Woodstock, V, 185
Language:
new and unusual, accusations of, I,
19, II, 190–4, IX, 283
meaning of terms, I, 47 n., II, 322–3,
III, 228–9, 247–8, V, 166, VI, 22,
25–6, 34–7, 41–2, VII, 81, 145
disputes about words, II, 35, 224–5,
250, 259, VIII, 121–2, 149, 228–9,
311, IX, 10
Verbal Disputes in Political Economy,
IX, 27 & n., 38
Lansdowne, Lady, V, 17 n.
Lansdowne, Marquis of, VII, 284 n.
member of Lords' committee on re-
sumption, V, 351, 354, 356, 364–5,
VIII, 19–20, IX, 270
Ricardo's visit to Bowood, VII,
198 n.
see also VII, 284, 291, 356, X, 37 n.,
and under Petty, Lord Henry
Laputa: tailors, VII, 122; philosopher,
VIII, 114
La Rochefoucauld, VII, 168
Larpent, George, VIII, 367 n.
Lasteyrie-Dusaillant, Comte de, IX,
231, 253, 273
Lauderdale, Earl of:
on supply and demand, I, 384–5
and monopoly of the home market,
VI, 169–70
gold and silver payments by the
Bank, I, 371 n., VIII, 3
silver as standard of value, VIII,
45 & n.

Lauderdale, Earl of (*cont.*)
member of committee on resumption, V, 351, 354, 365
see also VII, 142, 265, 267, VIII, 29 n.
Inquiry into . . . Public Wealth, 1804, I, 276, 384
The Depreciation of the Paper Currency, 1812, VI, 81
Letter on the Corn Laws, 1814, VI, 169–70, 186, 189, 192
Three Letters . . . of An Old Merchant, 1819, V, 17 & n., VIII, 45 n.

Laurence, Charles, stockbroker, VII, 14

Lausanne, IX, 218, X, 264, 268–9

Lauterbrunnen, X, 257

Lavater, Johann Kaspar, his tomb, X, 238

Laveno, X, 291–2

Law Merchant, committee on, 1823, Ricardo a member, V, xxvi, 293; Report, IV, 280

Law proceedings, tax on, V, 147

Leases, and improvements in agriculture, I, 269 n., II, 142–3, 202, VI, 140, 145, 174–5, 177

Le Bas, C. W., professor of mathematics at East India College, VII, 168, 253

Ledbury, IX, 121 n.

Leeves, E., biography of Huskisson, XI, xxix

Lefevre, John George Shaw, IX, 224, X, 289 & n.

Legacy duty, I, 153, V, 315

Legal tender: silver and gold as, I, 366–72; gold only, V, 16 & n., VIII, 3; bank notes as (1811), V, 316, VI, 45, 68

Leghorn, see Livorno

Leicester Fields, ground for school, VII, 190, 198, see also VI, xxix

Leonardo da Vinci, X, 301

Le Roy, Arnaud Jacques, see Saint-Arnaud, Comte de

Le Sage, A. R., *Gil Blas*, VII, 303, X, 290

Leser, Dr E., X, 378

Leslie, John, VIII, 28 & n.; his ice machine, IV, 249

Lethbridge, Sir Thomas Buckler, M.P. for Somerset:
on pressure of taxation, V, 101 n.
on 'the abominable theories of political economists', V, 169
on absentee residents abroad, V, 186
Russian tallow, V, 291, 294
see also V, 195, IX, 265–6
Letter to the King, by a Commoner, 1820, VIII, 144 n.
Letters to the Proprietors of Bank Stock, by an Old Proprietor, 1816, VI, 276, 278, 283, 288

Levi, guide at Haarlem, X, 204

Levick, George, IX, 181 n.

Levy, Harriet, wife of Jacob Ricardo, X, 58

Lewis, Thomas Frankland, M.P. for Beaumaris, V, 351, 354, 356, VIII, 19

Leycester, Ralph, M.P. for Shaftesbury, V, 198, 202

Leyden, IX, 211, X, 204

Liberal principles of trade, IV, 70–1, IX, 269, see also V, 44, VIII, 164, 381

Library, Ricardo's, X, 399–402

Liddes, X, 285–8

Liesse, André, *Un professeur d'Économie politique sous la restauration, J.-B. Say*, IX, 192 n.

Life annuities, see Annuities

Lille (Lisle), VII, 160, X, 185–6, 188

Limitation of currency, principle of, I, 353–4, II, 48, III, 357, 373, IV, 64–5, VII, 353, VIII, 186

Lincolnshire, Malthus's visits to, VI, 34–5 & n., 40–1, VII, 193, VIII, 226, 349; see also V, 304

Lindo, Esther, *née* Delvalle (D.R.'s aunt), X, 29, 106

Lindo, Isaac, X, 29

Lindo, Miriam, wife of Benjamin Ricardo, X, 59

Lindsay, Dr James, Unitarian minister, VIII, 84, X, 40–1; robbery at his house, X, 118 & n.; see also IX, 60

Linen, duties on, I, 317, V, 57–8, 104, 290; see also IV, 374

Lisbon, VI, 85

Littleton, Edward John, M.P. for Staffordshire, V, 74, 218, 351

Liverpool election, Ricardo declines standing for, V, xix, IX, 182–3, XI, xiv

Liverpool, 1st Earl of, *Treatise on the Coins of the Realm*, 1805, I, 369 n., III, 7, 30, 31 n., 32, 41–2, 65–7, 81, 176, 189 n., 203, VII, 21, X, 390

Liverpool, 2nd Earl of, First Lord of the Treasury:
and resumption of cash payments, V, 351, 353, 365, VIII, 134, X, 90 n.
wants Canning in his Cabinet, IX, 115
see also IV, 251, V, 84 & n., VIII, 200 n., 287, 294, IX, 269–70, X, 78 n., 86, 88

Livorno, Ricardo's ancestors in, X, 18 & n.; visit to, X, 321; Horner's grave, IX, 227–8, X, 322; see also IX, 234, 242, X, 323

Lloyd, Lewis, on ingot plan, V, 357–8

Loans:
method of issuing, X, 75–9; discount on prompt payment, V, 343–4
whether in 3 or 5 % stock, IV, 184–5, V, 67, VIII, 320, 332
for Great Britain, table of, X, 80–1
loans bid for by Ricardo, 1806–1819, X, 75–94, see also 57–8
in 1807, X, 80; tribute from subscribers, X, 125–8
in 1811, X, 80; anxiety of friends, VI, 48–9 & n., 52
in 1815, X, 82–4; and Waterloo, VI, 229, 231 & n., 233, 237–8, 245, 249, 251, 262; Malthus sells too soon, VI, 231 & n.; see also VI, 230, X, 78 n.
in 1819, X, 84–91; and sinking fund, IV, 173, V, 18–19, VIII, 30–1, 33; speech on, V, 21–2 & n.; see also X, 78 n.
in 1820, speech on, V, 58–60
Report on negotiation of loan, 1796, X, 75–8 notes

Loans and taxes for war compared, I, 244–7, IV, 185–90, VIII, 170, 172

Lobatto, Rehuel Cohen, X, 18

Lobb, Charlotte, wife of Ralph Ricardo, VIII, 22 n., X, 59

Locke, John:
favours silver as the only standard, III, 65–6, 81, 202
corn less variable than gold, V, 210–11
his tolerant spirit, VII, 205–6
see also VII, 227, 229
Essay concerning Human Understanding, VII, 197, 205–6, 211–12
The Reasonableness of Christianity, X, 395
Some Considerations of . . . Raising the Value of Money, III, 65, 81, 188, 202
Further Considerations, I, 369, X, 390

Lockhart, John Gibson, VIII, 204, 205 n.
Life of Scott, IX, 136 n., 187 n.
Peter's Letters to his Kinsfolk, 1819, VIII, 25 & n., 112, 134

Lockhart, John Ingram, M.P. for Oxford:
on Ricardo's riddle, V, 83, 88–9
on delay of agricultural report, V, 114
Ricardo's propositions 'destructive', V, 173, though not intentionally so, 175–6, 180

Lombardy, plains of, X, 302

London Institution, VI, 281 & n., X, 49 & n.

Londonderry, Marquis of (up to 1821 see Castlereagh, Viscount):
on sinking fund, V, 25
concurs with Ricardo on taxation and agriculture, V, 127 n., 154, 155
chairman of agricultural committee, 1822, IV, 203–5, prepares report, IX, 180
on measures for the relief of agriculture, V, 155–9, 169, 182, 185–6, 195, 197
Mallet on, V, xxv
his suicide, IX, 214–15, X, 241, 243
see also V, 124, 129, 145, 174, 335

Longman, T. N., publisher, IX, 116 & n.

Lotteries, IV, 147–8, V, 3

Louis XVIII, VI, 235

Lowenthal, E., X, 372

Lowless and Crosse, Ricardo's solicitors, X, 390. See also Bleasdale, Lowless and Cross

Lowndes, Mr, V, 476

Lowry, Rebecca, *née* Delvalle (D.R.'s aunt), X, 29

Lowry, Wilson, X, 29, 49

Lubbock & Forster, Ricardo's bankers, X, 55 n., 68

Lucca, X, 324

Lucerne, X, 249; Lake of, 245–8

Luddites, V, 302 n., VIII, 385

Luneville, VII, 167

Lungern, X, 251

Lushington, Stephen Rumbold, and balance-sheet form of accounts, V, 100, 145; see also VI, 149

Luxuries:

whether taste for, essential for net revenue, VIII, 285, 300–1, 309, see also II, 312–15, III, 276, 278, VII, 70

expenditure on, and employment, I, 392–4, II, 332–3

fall in price of, does not affect rate of profits, I, 132

spending on, distinguished from prodigality, III, 284–5

of the labourer, V, 26, see also II, 347

luxury of the Grand Duke of Baden's palaces, VII, 165

taxes on, I, 205, 233, 235–6, 241–4, VIII, 177, 189–90, 195–6

Lyne, Charles, *Letter to George Rose*, 1810, X, 401

Lyons, IX, 229, X, 341–3

Lyttelton, William Henry, M.P. for Worcestershire, V, 3, 26–7

Maberly, John, M.P. for Abingdon, IX, 288 & n.

motion on retrenchment, V, 79

public accounts, V, 145

Maberly (*cont.*)

redemption of land tax, V, 248, 250, 259

malt and beer tax, V, 301

see also V, 35, 143, 185

McColluch, J., innkeeper, VII, 37 n.

McCulloch, John Ramsay, VI, xxi–xxiii, IX, 312

adherence to Ricardo's doctrines, VI, xxii, VIII, 376 & n.; later modified, X, 370

reviews *Principles*, VII, 282, 291, 296–7; alterations in ed. 2 due to: on taxation, I, 152, 242, VII, 280–1, 286, 334, 349, 353, on currency, I, 354, 356–61, VII, 353, VIII, 4–5, on corn trade, I, 267, 318, VII, 354; in ed. 3, VIII, 341–2

and article 'Funding System', VIII, 137–8, 141

and Notes on Malthus, VIII, 296–9, 312, 315, 318, 325, 333–4, 338–40, XI, xiii

on Ricardo's concession that some prices rise with a rise of wages, VIII, 339–40, 343, 352

early views on machinery, VIII, 171 n.; reverses his opinion, VIII, 366 n.; shocked by Ricardo's change of view, VIII, 381–6, 391–2, IX, 9, 13–14, 18–19

accumulated profits regarded as labour, IX, 358, see also IV, 377–8, 410–11

on 'labour of machines', IX, 369, see also VIII, 138, IX, 325 n., 343, 354 n., 358–9

joins in discussions on absolute and exchangeable value, IX, 301–3, 309, 312–13, 353, 358, 363, 366–9, 375, 377, see also 324–5

his measure of value, IV, 376–9, 410–12; goes further than Ricardo, IX, 178, 185. See also Value, measure of

on tampering with the standard of currency, VIII, 392, 396, IX, 15

MᶜCulloch, J. R. (*cont.*)

suggests reducing interest on national debt, I, 426 n., VII, 93; too violent for Ricardo, VII, 37–8, 102–6; later disowns, VII, 93 n.; suppresses Ricardo's revealing note, I, 426 n.; see also VIII, 378 n.

his proposal for paying off national debt, VIII, 157–8 & n., see also VII, 351–2, VIII, 4

attacks corn laws, IX, 160, 186, 197

disagrees with Blake on depreciation, IX, 271–2, 275–7, 284–7, 289, 302, 312

on Malthus as an economist, VIII, 139, 167, 312, 378; not allowed to review him in *Edinburgh Review*, VIII, 189, 325; meets him in London, IX, 312

holds private class in political economy, VIII, 365–6, IX, 134 & n., 155; his public course, IX, 272 & n., 277, 301; sends lectures to Ricardo for comment, IX, 134–5, 139, 178–9, 184–5, 192–4

visit to London, IX, 275, 284, 290–1, 301–2, 312

resents John Wilson's election as professor, VIII, 204–5 & n., IX, 205 n.

abused by Scottish tories, VIII, 205 n., IX, 205–6 & n.

Ricardo memorial lectures, IX, 301 n., 391 & n.

list of letters, IX, 394–5

see also II, viii–xi, 64 n., 353 n., 452 n., IV, 146, 375 n., VII, 245 n., 259, 307, 339, X, 35 n., 59, 372, 387

ARTICLES IN *Edinburgh Review*

1818: on Ricardo's *Principles*, VII, 179 n., 278–9, 280–2, 285–9, 291, 295–7, 309, 316 n., 319

on *Economical and Secure Currency*, IV, 47, VII, 353–4, 383, VIII, 1–2, 5–6, 10, 20, 23–4

1819: Trade with France, VIII, 82, 127

Articles in *Edinburgh Review* (*cont.*)

1820: Taxation and the Corn Laws, I, lviii, VIII, 164–6, 168–74, 176–7

Foreign Commerce, VIII, 190, 197

Tithes, VIII, 203, 214, 222, 229, 237, 262

1821: Effects of Machinery, I, lviii, VIII, 325, 338, 351–2, 366 & n., 373, 378, 383, IX, 9, 18

Degrading the Standard of Money, VII, 93 n., VIII, 392, 396, IX, 7 n., 15

1822: High and Low Taxes, IX, 160, 185

Corn Laws, IX, 186, 188, 192, 197

Ireland, IX, 186

1823: Funding System, VIII, 223

East and West India Sugars, IX, 273, 277

1824: Combination Laws, VIII, 313 n., 338

Rise and Fall of Profits, IX, 179 n.

East India Company, IX, 330

1827: Taxation, VIII, 238 n., IX, 342, 345, 362

1830: Commerce in Holland, IX, 135 n.

ARTICLES IN *Scotsman*

1818: on Ricardo's *Principles*, VII, 219–20, 222, 256

1819: Importation of Foreign Corn, VIII, 28

1820: Ricardo's plan for paying off national debt, VIII, 157

Merchants' Petition, VIII, 178 n.

Malthus's *Principles*, VIII, 178, 185

Corn Laws, VIII, 197

Translation of Say's *Traité*, VIII, 315, 374

1821: Reduction of the Standard, VIII, 378 & n., IX, 15

Agricultural Report, IX, 7–8

Evidence in Political Economy, IX, 162 n.

High and Low Taxation, IX, 185 n.

Articles in *Scotsman* (*cont.*)
1822: Money, V, 515, IX, 140 n.
Peel's bill, IX, 149 & n.
County Meetings, IX, 159 & n.
Standard of National Prosperity, IX, 179
Rate of Profit, IX, 179
Protection to Agriculture, IX, 183 n.
Cost of Production, IX, 206 n.
Progress of Commercial Science, IX, 187 n.
1823: Blake's *Observations on Expenditure*, IV, 326, IX, 284–5, 286 n., 289, 301 & n.
Combination Laws, VIII, 313 n.
Obituary of Ricardo, X, 369
1824: Exchangeable value, IX, 366 n.

ARTICLES IN *Supplement to Encyclopaedia Britannica*

Corn Laws and Trade, I, 267 n.,' 318 n., VII, 295, 337, 354, VIII, 22, 37, 159
Cottage System, VII, 295, 337, IX, 231
Exchange, VII, 384, VIII, 2–3, 37, 81, 85–93, 126, 128, 131, 139, 140–1
Interest, VIII, 313, 316, 338, 341, 345
Money, IX, 134, 140, 149, 157, 159
Political Economy, VIII, 189 n., IX, 187 n., 206, 271, 275, 330–1
Value, VIII, 189 & n., 203, 214, 226, 229, IX, 313 n., 334

OTHER WORKS

article on value in *Edinburgh Magazine*, 1818, IV, 307, VII, 315–16 n., 324, 326, 354, 362, 364, 376
Essay on a Reduction of the Interest on the National Debt, 1816, VII, 37–8, 93 n.; enlarged version, 1816, I, 426 n., VII, 93, 102–5, X, 399
Progress of Commercial Science, 1822, IX, 186–7 & n.
Rise of Political Economy, 1824, IX, 134 n., 162 n., 178 n.
Principles of Political Economy, 1825, IX, 275 n., 325 n.

McCulloch, Other Works (*cont.*)
Literature of Political Economy, 1845, II, xiv n., III, 6, VI, xxii, VII, 93 n., VIII, 337 n., IX, 135 n., 277 n.
Early English Tracts on Commerce, 1856, IX, 150 n.
Treatises and Essays, 1859, VI, xxii, X, 370
Note on Rent, IV, 6–7 & n.
his edition of Ricardo's *Works*, II, xiv, V, 488, VI, xxii, X, 368–70, see also VII, 93 n., X, 377, 381; table of corresponding pages in other editions of *Principles*, I, 443–7, of Pamphlets, III, 435–7, IV, 419–22
publishes Ricardo's papers on parliamentary reform, V, 489–90, 494, X, 368
Life and Writings of Ricardo, successive versions, X, 369–70, see also I, xix, II, xiv, III, 6 & n., IV, 8 n., 358, V, xx n., VI, xxii, X, 14, 29, 35 n., 38–9, 53, 375
Letters to David Ricardo, VI, xxiii
Macculloch, Dr John, geologist, VII, 309 & n., 319
McCulloch, William, Examiner of India Correspondence, VIII, 251 & n., 252, 254, 262–3; see also VIII, 241, IX, 333, 373
Macdonagh, Michael, *The Reporters' Gallery*, V, xxvii n., xxviii n., xxxi n.
Macdonald, Captain D., letter in Ricardo Papers, X, 388
McDonnell, Alexander, VIII, 57 & n., 62, 75, 152 n.
Machiavelli's tomb, X, 317
Machinery, I, 386–97
early view: beneficial to labourers, I, 386–8; raises wages, IV, 35; employs no less labour, II, 351–3, V, 30, 31 n., VII, 157–9, VIII, 171, 215; see also II, 365, VI, 228
transitional view, II, 234–9
later view, injurious to labourers, I, 388–92, V, 302–3; Barton's view found correct, I, 395–6 n.

Machinery (*cont.*)

Ricardo's change of view discussed, I, lvii–lx, 386, VIII, 373 & n.; earliest statement of, VIII, 377; McCulloch shocked, VIII, 381–6, 391–2, IX, 14–15, 18, answer to, VIII, 386–90, 398–400; labouring-class opinion, IX, 18 & n., and cp. VIII, 384–5; discussion at Political Economy Club, IX, 9 & n., 158 n., 159

increases net revenue, but may diminish gross, I, 389–92, VIII, 387, IX, 13, 14, 23, see also VI, 294

always the product of less labour than it displaces, I, 42, 62; in constant competition with labour, I, 395

effects of, on the relative value of commodities, I, 30–8, 59–63, II, 361–2, III, 303

adds to riches, not to value, I, 286 & n., 287, see also III, 334

and rate of profit, I, 131–3, 387, see also I, 62, II, 408

no cause of unequal distribution of property, IX, 243–4

difference with Malthus on, defined, VIII, 387, see also II, 361, 365

old countries impelled to employ, I, 41 n.

should not be discouraged, I, 396–7, V, 303

restrictions on export of, opposed, V, xx, 332

Cobbett defends use of, V, 302–3 & n.

manual weavers and, V, 68, 302–3

land as a machine, II, 118, 185, IV, 24 n., 34, VIII, 208

workmen regarded as (McCulloch), IX, 343

labour of (McCulloch's notion), VIII, 138, IX, 325 n., 369; questioned by Ricardo, IX, 358–9

employed in agriculture, I, 15, 82, II, 335 n.; in cotton manufacture, IV, 33, V, 68; in mining, I, 14, V, 93 n., 391 & n., 427, VIII, 3

wear and tear of, I, 39

Machinery (*cont.*)

see also I, 16, 25, 266, 271, V, 55, 290, 450, IX, 193, and under Capital, fixed, Steam engines, Thrashing machine

Machlup, Dr Fritz, X, 378–9

Mackenzie, Alexander, *Voyages from Montreal*, 1801, VII, 189, X, 394

Mackintosh, Sir James, M.P. for Knaresborough:

appointed to East India College, VII, 251 & n.

his eloquence, VIII, 148

on *Essay on Profits*, VI, 182

on *Principles*, VII, 280

on Reform, VII, 263 & n., VIII, 68 n., 327–8

unlucky article on eve of Waterloo, VI, 280

see also V, xxi, xxii, 128, 335, 351, VI, 87 n., VII, 111, 253–4, 284, VIII, 22, 25 n., 107, 375, X, 50

articles on Parliamentary Reform in *Edinburgh Review*, 1818, VII, 263 n., 1820, VIII, 327–8 & n.

Vindiciae Gallicae, 1791, X, 398

Letter to Pitt on his Apostacy from Reform (anon.), 1792, VIII, 63, 68, 77, 84, 148

MacMinn, N., and others, *Bibliography of J. S. Mill*, IV, 7 n., IX, 385 n.

McNiven, Mrs Charles, X, 272–3 & n.

Macon, X, 342

Macrae, and the Stock Exchange hoax, VI, 106

McVickar, John, *Outlines of Political Economy*, 1825, IV, 147 n.

Maggiore, Lake, X, 291

Mahomed Reza Khan, VII, 237

Maitland, Charles Fox, X, 139

Malines, X, 191

Mallet, Sir Bernard, I, xi

Mallet, John Lewis, diarist:

first meeting with Ricardo, VII, 50 n.

on Ricardo's physical appearance, X, 51; his personality, VIII, 152–3 n., X, 51; his Stock Exchange activity, X, 73

Mallet, J. L. (*cont.*)

and Moses Ricardo, X, 16–17

glimpse of the agricultural committee, V, xxv

impact of Ricardo's speech on resumption, V, 17 n.

Ricardo cheered by Ministers, V, 127 n.

Robert Owen incident, V, 331 n.

inner workings of resumption committees, V, 352–4, 365–6, VIII, 18 n., 19 n.

on plan to pay off national debt, VIII, 147 n.

on machinery, I, lix–lx

rotten boroughs, VII, 254 n.

on Huskisson, IX, 270 n.

on 'Silly Billy', X, 187 n.

visits to Gloucestershire, VII, 187 & n., 189, VIII, 157 n.

correspondence with, XI, xvii–xxi and cp. X, 389

see also VI, xxxv, VII, 220 n., 252, 275 n., VIII, 21 n., 367 n., X, 32 n., 67, 95, 314 n., 370

Mallet du Pan, XI, xvii n.

Mallory, Harriett, see Ricardo, Harriett

Mallory, Henry (Harriett's brother), X, 242–3, 254, 264–5, 318, 343

Mallory, Miss, X, 265, 344, 351

Mallory, Mrs, X, 264–5

Mallory, Robert Harvey, VIII, 284, X, 61

Malthus, Charles, VIII, 308 n., 318

Malthus, Henry, VI, xx n., 298 & n.

Malthus, Mrs, VI, 29, 60–1, 87, 298, VII, 175 n., 265, VIII, 107, 308

Malthus, Robert, I, xi, VI, xx

Malthus, Sydenham, brother of T. R. Malthus, VI, xx, 295, VIII, 308 n., 318

Malthus, Col. Sydenham, VI, xx

Malthus, Thomas Robert, VI, xviii–xxi

professor at East India College, VI, 77, 159, 240, 336, 341, 346, VII, 26, 51, 119, 130–2, 135–8, 213–14, IX, 251

Malthus (*cont.*)

his living at Walesby, VI, 35 n., 40–1, VII, 193, VIII, 226, 349; 'Parson Malthus', VIII, 74 n., VII, 212–13; tours Ireland, VII, 174–6, 184; visits Paris, VIII, 224–7

friendship with Ricardo, VIII, 41, 101, 178, 380, IX, 111–13, 382; Ricardo's visits to, VI, 322, 325, VIII, 173; visits to Ricardo, in London, VII, 24, 26–7, 29, 35, VIII, 47, 64, at Gatcomb, VII, 48, 51–2, 56, 361, 365, 368–9, 370–2, VIII, 314–15, 317–18, 331, 334, 336; bequest to, X, 105

loan of 1814, VI, 107–8, 110, 116, 119, 122; of 1815, sells on eve of Waterloo, VI, 229, 231 & n., 233, 235, X, 84

his library at Jesus College, Cambridge, VI, xx n.

location of his MSS, II, xiii, VI, xx, X, 386–7

list of letters, IX, 395–7, see also XI, x

other letters: to Horner, VI, 186–8, to Sismondi, VIII, 375–7; letters quoted, to Prévost, I, liv, to Horner, VI, 159 n., to Cadell and Davies, VI, 160 n.; see also, to Place, VII, 2 n., to Napier, IX, 302 n.

ON RICARDO'S WORKS

on Ricardo's *Principles*, VII, 176, 179; alterations due to him: in ed. 2, I, li, on rent, I, 412–13, VII, 282–3, on importation of corn, I, 428–9, VII, 271; in ed. 3, on effects of rise of wages, I, xliii–xliv, 35 n., 43 n., II, 64, IX, 178, on improvements in agriculture, I, 81 n., 335 n., II, 118, on cost and value, I, 47 n., II, 34, 101, on rent as proportion, I, 49 n., 83 n., 402, II, 196–8, on rent and fertility, I, 404 n., II, 121–3; see also I, 18–19

on *Economical and Secure Currency*, VI, 298–9, 300, 313, 315, VII, 10, 19–20

On Ricardo's Works (*cont.*)

on *Essay on Profits*, VI, 186, 188, 190–1, 216–18, 221–3

ON ECONOMIC SUBJECTS

accumulation, effective demand restricted by, VI, 142, 149; not true of France, VIII, 225–6; see also II, 310–11, 321, 325

arena for employment of capital, VI, 103–4 & n., see also II, 140, 293

on bounties, VI, 289, 314, 346, VII, 2, 68

foreign trade, whether profits from are clear gain, II, 401–2, 405–9, see also VI, 167–8, VIII, 182–3

machinery, II, 351–2, 357, 360–1; relation to Ricardo's views on, VIII, 382, 387, IX, 23

motives to produce, IX, 9–10, 13, 15–16, 19–21, 24–6

his measure of value, see Value, Malthus's measure of

population: wages the great regulator of, I, 218–20, VI, 155, see also II, 249

on corn raising demanders, I, 400, 405 n., II, 107–9, 142, VIII, 236; whether food or population precedes, VII, 201–2 & n.

and facility of producing food, VI, 140

artificial checks to, VII, 63, 218–19, VIII, 71, 80–1

price: natural, regulated by supply and demand, II, 46–7, 52–3, VII, 250–1, see also VIII, 201, 207; 'real price', I, 414–16, VII, 145, see also I, 413 n.

depressing effect of fall in, IV, 36–7

three causes of high price, I, 400–1

price of corn: regulated by last additions, VI, 195, 198, 200; regulates all prices, VI, 203, 212, VII, 105

startling conclusion that rise in price of, increases surplus, VI, 185,

On Economic Subjects (*cont.*)

187, 190–2, 194–6, 199; qualified, VI, 201–2, 207–8; controverted, VI, 189–90, 192–4, 196–8, 203–5, 209–10

advantages of high price, VI, 231, 236, 255, increases employment, VI, 200, 204; low price not advantageous to lower classes, IV, 35

profits: denies that profits of farmer regulate all profits, VI, 104, 117–18, 152–3, 155, 167, 182–3, 207, VII, 176

and facility of production, VI, 140, 224–6, 289–91, 296–7, 303–4, 318–19, VII, 52, 176, VIII, 194–5

and diminishing returns from the land, VI, 207, 209, 216–18, 220–3, and demand and supply, VII, 52, 68–9, 77, 80

public works, XI, x–xi

rent: his theory of, I, 398–429, see also I, 5–6, IV, 9–10

alters opinion on no-rent land, VII, 371–2, 379

supposes rent a creation of riches, I, 398, II, 116, 166, VI, 173–5, VII, 120, see also VIII, 209

misrepresents Ricardo on landlords, II, 117, VIII, 182, 184, 208, see also IV, 35

restrictions on importation of corn: effects of, IV, 27, 30, 32–3, 35–6, VI, 110, 116–17; throws off impartiality, VI, 177–8, 205; his dangerous heresy, VIII, 142

taxation of necessaries, IV, 33–4 n., VI, 173, 176; taxes as remedy for distress, II, 379, 432–3, VIII, 181

wages: real, II, 249–50, VII, 81 & n., 214

rise of, effect on prices, I, lxiii, 35 n., 43 n., II, 64

and rent, II, 132–3

and price of corn, II, 243–4

OPINIONS ON HIM

always for merchant against consumer, VIII, 215, see also II, 40ç

Opinions on him (*cont.*)
a friend to moderate reform, VIII, 107; too moderate, VIII, 129; no real wish for, VII, 263, 266, 368–9; his reform no reform, VII, 372, 374, see also VII, 380
accused of inconsistency, II, 64–5, VI, 38–9, VIII, 209, 232–3, 331, IX, 329, 347, 350, 378; of fallacies, II, 96, VIII, 233–4, IX, 287; of using 'a new language', I, 19, IX, 283; his replies, VI, 202, IX, 365
aversion to controversy, VII, 247; socratic method used on, VII, 378
McCulloch on his poisonous nostrums, VIII, 366; thinks him over-rated as an economist, VIII, 139; on his trick of book-making, VII, 383, VIII, 341
see also I, xlviii, l, lv, IV, 3, 349, VI, 249, 270 n., 274, VII, 15, 34 n., 177, 257, 264, 316 n., 357, VIII, 96–7, 99, 385, 391, IX, 30, 31, 155, 218, 242 n., 261, 265, 268, 342, X, 35, 50, 83, 90, 141, 179, 375–6, 405

WORKS

articles on Bullion in *Edinburgh Review*: Feb. 1811, III, 10–12, 99–123, VI, 21–30, 33–42, 47, 82, see also VI, xviii n.; Aug. 1811, VI, 47–8 & n., Ricardo's lost notes on, VI, 66 & n., references to the notes, VI, 73–8, 82–3, 87–92; see also III, 12, VI, 31 n., 41
review of Godwin on Population, 1821, IX, 84, 89–90, 154; keeps authorship secret, IX, 94, 101
Essay on Population, I, 398, VII, 126–8, 194, 201–3, 214, IX, 51–5, 62; ed. 1, 1798, VII, 2, 212 n.; ed. 2, 1803, VII, 2–3 & n.; ed. 3, 1806, I, 218–19; ed. 4, 1807, I, 106, 162; ed. 5, 1817, with Additions, VII, 123–4 & n., Sumner's review, VII, 247, Say on, VII, 168, IX, 36, alterations to meet Ricardo's objections, VI, 289, 314, 336, 346, VII,

Works (*cont.*)
2–3 & n., 26–7; French translation, X, 270 n.; see also VI, xix, 103 n., 295, 317, 341, VII, 8, 21, 24, 30, 46 & n., 68, 383 & n., VIII, 323, 341 n., 361–2, IX, 147, 232, X, 399 and under Godwin, *Reply to Malthus*, Place, *Reply to Godwin*
Grounds of an Opinion, 1815, IV, 4–5, VI, 176 n.; Ricardo on, I, 414–15, 419–20, 427, II, 61, IV, 9, 32–9, VI, 177–8; Torrens on, VI, 205 n.; see also I, 429, IV, 30, VI, 182, 186, 201 & n., 211
Inquiry into Rent, 1815, IV, 5, VI, 167, 172 n.; Ricardo on, I, 5, 398–429, IV, 9, 11–12, 15 n., 38, VI, 172–3, 176–8, VII, 120; Malthus replies, VI, 174–6, VII, 123; see also I, 74, II, 71, 73, 118, IV, 22, 24, 27 n., 33, VI, 182, 183, 211, VII, 379, X, 382, 399
Measure of Value, 1823, II, xii, IX, 280 n., 280–3, 287, 309, 318–19; his table of the invariable value of labour, IX, 281 & n.; McCulloch on, 290; Trower on, 292–3; reviewed by J. S. Mill, 385 n.; see also I, xxxix, IV, 358, IX, 302 n., 317, 334, 370, X, 392
Observations on the Corn Laws, 1814, VI, 109, 167 & n., 205; ed. 3, 1815, I, 408–9, 414, 416, IV, 32, VI, 167 & n., 177, VII, 120
Principles of Political Economy, ed. 1, 1820, II, vii–viii; planned as answer to Ricardo, II, 11–12, VII, 215, 221, 247, VIII, 65–6; Ricardo on, VII, 284, 371–2, 379–80, VIII, 79–80, 130, 132–3, 179–85; deserves rough handling (McCulloch), VIII, 138–9, 167, 189; Trower on, VIII, 201, 218–20, 320–2; dull sales, VIII, 298, 312; reviewed by Torrens, VIII, 185, by McCulloch, 178 & n., 185; revision for new ed., II, xii–xiv, VIII, 285, 298, 308, 341 & n., 373, 377–8, IX, 249; French translation, VIII,

Works (*cont.*)
225 n.; see also I, lvi, VII, 194, 257, 312, 329, 370, VIII, 22, 41, 47, 64, 74, 109, 142, 160 n., 173, 222, 261, 325, IX, 239, XI, xiii
Ricardo's *Notes*, see under Ricardo, David
Statements respecting the East India College, 1817, VII, 114, 119, 121, 136
proposed edition of *Wealth of Nations* forestalled, VI, 159 n.; notes for, VI, 159–60, 169
article on Malthus, by W. Empson, VI, xx, VII, 2 n., 201 n.
essay on, by J. M. Keynes, VI, xiii, 35 n.
Malvern, visits to, VII, 66, 70, 84, VIII, 231, IX, 90, 104, 108
Man, Isle of, corn shipments through by fraud, V, 78
Manchester massacre, 1819, VIII, 54 n., 56–8, 66, 70, 80, 107, 111–12 & n., 129, see also V, xxii
Manicheism, VII, 196, 206 & n., 212
Manning, William, M.P. for Lymington, Bank director, V, 8, 14, 201, 351, 365
Mansfield, Sir James, IV, 112–13
Mansfield, John, M.P. for Leicester, V, 20
Manufacturers:
greatest gainers from cheap corn, IV, 35–6
distress of, V, 133, 492 n., see also V, 315
Manufactures:
improvements in, I, 141, IV, 374, VI, 194, VIII, 171–2
protecting duties on, opposed, IV, 250–2
manufactured necessaries, I, 224–5; taxes on, I, 243
see also II, 291, V, 184 and under Inventions, Machinery
Manufactures and agriculture:
comparative advantages of, VII, 270–1, 279; whether either is more productive, VIII, 102–3

Manufactures, agriculture (*cont.*)
transfer of capital between, I, 306–7, V, 83
prices of, move in opposite directions, VIII, 232–3
proportions of wages and profits in, V, 177–8, see also II, 380
profits of manufacturers and farmers compared, I, 110–17, 122
Manufacturing classes, V, 296, VII, 220
Manufacturing country:
England as, V, 180
population of, better informed than agricultural, IX, 192–3, and cp. IX, 67
see also V, 408–9
Manuscripts, Ricardo's, X, 386–98
Marcet, Dr Alexander, V, 352, VIII, 19 n., X, 49
Marcet, Mrs (Jane), V, 353, VIII, 56 n., 163, X, 172
Conversations on Political Economy, 1816, advice for second edition, VII, 140 & n.; ed. 4, 1821, IX, 122; see also IX, 118, X, 270 n.
Marengo, plain of, IX, 222, X, 335
Marginal contents, Mill on, VI, 324, 329 & n., VII, 7, 97, 107, X, 391
Marginal theory, IV, 6 n. 3
Marjoribanks, Stewart, M.P., V, 185
Mark Lane, quantities of corn sold in, IV, 261, IX, 181, see also table IV, 270
Market, extending the, I, 93, 132, II, 360–3, 420, VI, 93, 104–5, 225, 228–9
Market price, I, 88–92; see also Natural and market price
Marks, Jeanette, *The Family of the Barrett*, X, 267 n., 350 n.
Marlow, Bucks., VI, xvi, IX, 5, 11, 41, 43, 48
Marnell, Mr, VII, 254–5
Marryat, Joseph, M.P. for Sandwich, on price of bullion and foreign exchange, VI, 7; see also III, 80 n., V, 102 n., 111, 144, 298 301

Marshall, Alfred, *Principles of Economics*, I, xx, lii
Martigny, IX, 220–1, X, 283–4, 288
Martin, Richard, M.P. for Galway ('Humanity Martin'), V, 122; on the 'member for Portarlington', V, 289
Martinique sugar, V, 298, VI, 93
Marx, Karl, *Theorien über den Mehrwort*, I, xxii n., IV, 306, IX, 27 n.
Mary Ann, Miss, letter to, X, 164–6; see Bayley, Mary Ann
Mass of commodities, I, 128, 132, 134, 274, 278, 421 n., 423, II, 371, 373, 383, 390; money value of, IV, 39; rent estimated in, II, 137; as measure of value, IV, 59, VI, 22, 170–1, of absolute value, IV, 374, 400; see also VI, 42, 153, 163, IX, 361, 363
Mass: of corn, VI, 191, of gold and silver, III, 303, of prices (Bentham), III, 299, 301, of revenue, III, 281, of wealth, III, 332; general mass of circulation, III, 328, of production, I, 179
Massani, Tommaso, valet de place, X, 321
Masses, the, VIII, 111; the mass of the people, IX, 126
Matthews, William, *Historical Sketch of the Origin of Gas-lighting*, 1827, X, 56 n.
Maunoir, Dr Jean-Pierre and Mrs, X, 272 & n.
Maximum price, for corn, VIII, 158–9, for provisions, VII, 203 & n.
Maxwell, Captain and Mrs, X, 264, 266–8, 334
Maxwell, John, M.P. for Renfrewshire, on handweavers, V, 68; see also V, 56 n., 158 n.
Maxwell, Sir Murray, VII, 270 n., 273 & n., 357
May, Thomas Erskine, *Constitutional History of England*, V, xiv n., xxi n.
Mayence, VII, 165, X, 221
Mayor, Mr, Brook Street house bought from, VII, 17

Meade, Catherine, wife of Mortimer Ricardo, X, 64
Meade, Gen. Robert, X, 64
Mechanics Institute, Chichester, VII, 155 n.
Meetings of the people in 1819, VIII, 57, 59, 80, 110–11, 133, 146–7, 328; right to hold, V, 28–9, VII, 368; see also Manchester massacre
Meetings, county, see County meetings
Meilen, X, 243
Meillerie, Rocks of, IX, 220, X, 282
Meiringen (Meyringen), X, 252
Melbourne, Lord, see Lamb, William
Mellish, William, M.P. for Middlesex, Governor of the Bank, IV, 86–8 & n., 138–41, V, 20, 26, 464–5, VI, 276, 305
Melon, J. F., *Essai politique sur le commerce*, 1761, I, 244
Melville, Hon. R. S. L., X, 136, 138–40
Melville, Lord, VIII, 204
Memel, V, 182
Menial servants, see Servants
Mer de Glace, IX, 216, X, 275
Mercantile system, I, 316–17, III, 111, 118, V, 219, VIII, 164
Mercator's letters on bullion in *Morning Chronicle*, III, 27 & n.
Merchant vessels apprenticeship, V, 273–4, 276–7, 282–3
Merchants:
loans to, IV, 278–81
profits of, II, 393–4, 401
Malthus always for, II, 409, VIII, 215
see also II, 26–7, 376–7, X, 163
Merchants' petitions:
on commercial distress, 1819, V, 37
for free trade, 1820, V, 42–6, VIII, 164, 178, 183 & n.
protest against Reports of 1819, VIII, 29 n.
Merle, William, III, 345, 351
Mestre, X, 310
Methodism, V, 330 n., VIII, 118
Metternich, Prince, III, 432 n., 433
Michelangelo's tomb, X, 317

Middle class, see Classes
Middleton, Conyers, *Examination of the Bishop of London's Discourses*, 1750, X, 398
Midleton, Lord, VII, 23
Mieville, V. A., VI, 112 n.
Miklashevsky, A., X, 382
Milan, visit to, X, 298–301; Bonaparte's unfinished gate, IX, 221–2, X, 300; see also IX, 228
Mildmay, Lady, X, 333–4
Mile End, Ricardo's house at, VI, xix, 47, 53 & n., X, 47, 118
Mill, Henry (son of James), VIII, 211 n.
Mill, James, VI, xv–xviii
  educated to be a priest, VII, 213 & n.; his large family, VI, 137; and Sir John Stuart, VIII, 105 & n.; and John Black, IX, 201 & n.
  dependence on Bentham, VI, 136, VII, 181–2 & n.; Chrestomathic school, VI, xxix, xxxi, 112 & n., VII, 182 n., VIII, 197–9; at Ford Abbey, VI, 124–6, 254, 309–10, 322, VII, 169, 181–2; proposed radical review, VIII, 16–17 & n.
  appointment at East India House, VIII, 40 & n., 47, 51, 72, 162, IX, 180; promotion, IX, 280 & n.
  friendship with Ricardo, VII, 73–4, 246, X, 8–10; walks with, VI, xxxiv, VII, 263, 266, 268, 273, 275, VIII, 7–8, 10, 162, X, 264; Ricardo's 'schoolmaster', VI, 321, 324, 329–30, 338–40, VII, 7, 59–60, 66, 73, 107, 111, 196, 199, 205, 301–2, 317–18, VIII, 58, 60
  visits Ricardo, at Mile-end, VI, 47, at Brighton, VIII, 211–12, at Gatcomb, VI, 137, VII, 277, 285, 292, 299, 302–3, 305–6, VIII, 51, 229, 231–2, 241–2, IX, 329, 332–4, 377; reckoned 'immoderate' by Mrs Ricardo, VII, 303
  arranges visit to Bentham, VI, 156–7, 160, 161 & n.
  urges Ricardo to enter parliament, V, xiii–xvii, VI, 138, 252, VII, 85–6, 110, see also IX, 182 n.

Mill, James (*cont.*)
  suggests travel journal, IX, 208, 209, X, 178–9, 190, 198
  on Ricardo's last illness, IX, 390–1
  bequest to, X, 105
  and *Economical Currency*, IV, 46–7, 93, VI, 313, 320–1, 324–5, 329–32, 335, 337–8, VII, 4–5
  and *Essay on Profits*, IV, 8, VI, 249, 338–9
  and *Funding System*, IV, 145–8, VIII, 54–5, 57–61, 66–7, 78, 83, 105–6; on payment for, VIII, 240, 242–3 & n.; see also VIII, 72–3, 123, 141
  and *Notes on Malthus*, II, ix–xii, xvi, VIII, 292–3, 296, 333, 346
  and *Plan for a National Bank*, IV, 274, 359, XI, xxvi
  and *Principles*, I, xiii–xxvi, l, lii, liii, comments on draft, VII, 60, 66, 86–8, 97–101, 106–8, 111–12; see also X, 10
  and Ricardo's posthumous works, XI, xxvi
  and Bentham's *Alarm*, III, 261, 263, 265–6, VI, 13–14, 18–20
  on Godwin's answer to Malthus, VIII, 291–2, 307, see also 323; on Place's reply to Godwin, IX, 47–8, 59, 103, 115–16
  on Say's notes on *Principles*, VII, 375, VIII, 5, 10
  his measure of value, quantity of labour worked up, IV, 375 6; 'labour of machines' included, IX, 325 n.
  supply can never exceed demand, IV, 178, VI, 56, 132, 134, 141–2, 148, 149, see also II, 311
  year as turnover period, I, xlii
  parliamentary reform, V, 113 n., VI, 252–4, 308–9, VII, 198, 238, 301, 303, VIII, 52–3, 58–9, 291; on Ricardo's discourses, VII, 373–4, VIII, 8–10, 68
  on Whiggery, VIII, 8–9, 68, 106, 327–9
  on education, VII, 196–7, 313–14, 317–18, 356–7 & n.

Mill, James (*cont.*)
  on 'fashionable life', VI, 59, VII,
    364
  Horner on, III, 9–10 & notes; Wake-
    field on, VII, 182 n.; Mill on him-
    self, VII, 181–2
  list of letters, IX, 397–9; letters
    quoted: to Place, VI, 157 n., VIII,
    105 n., to Dumont, VIII, 40 n., to
    Napier, VIII, 59–60 n., 68 n.,
    243 n., IX, 6 n., 150 n.
  see also VI, 46 n., 51, 102, 270, 274,
    VII, 14, 28–9, 36, 132, 179, 180,
    255, XI, ix n.

WORKS

  articles: in *Edinburgh Review* on
    Th. Smith's *Theory of Money*, III,
    9 n.; in *The Philanthropist*, VI, 313
  articles in *Supplement to Encyclo-
    paedia Britannica*: Colonies, VII,
    183, 195, IX, 56
  Government, V, 113 n., VIII, 211,
    213, 240, 291, IX, 102, 148, 154 &
    n., 213
  Jurisprudence, VIII, 290–1, 296,
    IX, 5, 154
  Liberty of the Press, IX, 5, 6 n., 11,
    41, 44, 102–3, 154 & n.
  Prison discipline, IX, 280
  see also VII, 329
  Analysis of the Human Mind, 1829,
    IX, 332–3 & n., 374
  Commerce Defended, 1808, II, 360 n.,
    IV, 178, VI, xv, 132
  Elements of Political Economy, 1821,
    IX, 114–15; Ricardo's notes on, I,
    xliv, IX, 125–33; a school book,
    VIII, 327, 331, IX, 117–18;
    steers clear of value, VIII, 296–7,
    336–7; see also I, xlii, VIII, 229,
    262, 283, 362, 368–9, 375, 395, IX,
    6 n., 69, 87, 103, 122, 147, 154,
    159; ed. 2, IX, 325 n.
  History of British India, 1817: writing
    of, VI, 309, VII, 75–6, 182–3, 195;
    publication, VII, 197, 204, 207,
    210 & n.; Ricardo on, VII, 222–3,
    227–8, 231, 236–44, 249; reviewed

Mill, James (*cont.*)
  in *Edinburgh Review*, VIII, 10 & n.;
    see also I, xxi, xxiii, VI, xvi, 309,
    313, 317, VII, 111, 113, 186, 221,
    252, 253, 257, VIII, 50, 106
  lost paper on bullion, 1811, VI,
    49–50, 53–9, 60–2
  James Mill, by A. Bain, IX, 390 n.;
    see Bain
  'Life of', by John Morley, VI,
    xxxvi n.
Mill, John Stuart:
  Ricardo's early interest in, VI, xvii,
    IX, 44, 48, 60, 104, 115, 117; his
    paper on the measure of value,
    IX, 385–7
  his education, VI, xxxi, 329 n.;
    attends lectures at Bagshot, VII,
    313, astonishes professors, VII,
    314, 326; account of studies, VII,
    313 n., VIII, 198, XI, xxvii; classes
    at Montpellier, VIII, 293, returns
    grown up, IX, 43–4, 332
  appointment at India House, IX,
    280 & n.
  his library, IV, 326; his copy of
    Ricardo's *Principles*, VI, xviii n.
  see also III, 265, VI, 124, VII, 165,
    VIII, 297, IX, 107, 331 n.
  review of Malthus's *Measure of
    Value*, IX, 385 n.
  Autobiography, I, xix, VI, xvii,
    xxxiii n., 329 n., VII, 212 n., 213 n.
    292 n., VIII, 17, 186 n., 293 n., IX,
    107 n., 201 n., 280 n., 332 n.
  Dissertation on Rent, 1827, IV, 7 & n.
  Principles of Political Economy, VI,
    xv
  Bibliography of, by N. MacMinn and
    others, IV, 7 n.
  J. S. Mill, A Criticism, by A. Bain,
    VII, 313 n.; see Bain
Mill, Mary, IX, 334 n.
Mill, Mrs James, VI, 51, 53, 60, VII,
    55, 62, 314–15, 326, VIII, 210–11,
    IX, 334
Mill–Ricardo papers, VI, xliii, X, 386;
    contents of, X, 391–2; found in
    Ireland, I, ix–x

Millar, John:
Historical View of the English Government, 1787, VII, 197, 382, ed. 1803, X, 397
Origin of the Distinction of Ranks, 3rd ed. 1781, VII, 197 n., X, 399
Milligan, Joseph, publisher, X, 371–2
Mills, William, VII, 313 n.
Milton, Viscount, M.P., V, 42, 47
Minchinhampton: Ricardo's purchase of Manor of, X, 95–6, 105; schools established at, VII, 45 & n., IX, 328–9, X, 169; celebrations for the Queen, VIII, 296; coaches to, VII, 277, VIII, 310; see also X, 168, and under Gatcomb Park
Mines:
rent of, I, 85–7, 329–32; mines that pay no rent, I, 87, 192, 332
discovery of mines, and value of currency, III, 54, 269–270, 303, 362, 376–7, 391
tax on gold, effect on mining country, I, 195–9
improvements in machinery for mining silver, V, 93 n., 390–1 & n., 427, VIII, 3, see also I, 14, 146
see also Coal mines
Minimum wage regulation, VII, 142
Minster, Ricardo's estate at, X, 98, 105
Mitchell, Mr, VIII, 214, IX, 1
Mocatta and Goldsmid, bullion brokers, VI, 85, IX, 278 n.
Moerdyk ferry, X, 195, 197
Moggridge, Mr, V, 515–16, 519–20
Mombert, Paul, X, 378
Monarchy, VII, 380–1
Monbrion, M., *Principales banques de l'Europe*, 1805, III, 175 n.
Money, William Taylor, M.P. for St Michael, on Owen's disbelief in a future state, V, 330, 331 n.
Money, I, 352–72, III, 13–127, IV, 43–114
alterations in value of, I, 48, 141–5, effect on wages, I, 63–4, on foreign trade, I, 168–72, 228–9, 310–11, II, 154–6
no effect on relative prices, II, 396,

Money (*cont.*)
or on rate of profits, I, 50–1, 65, VII, 156, 159
gains and losses from alterations: fundholders, IV, 64, 229–30, V, 252–3, 320–1, 314, VII, 37–8, VIII, 396–8, IX, 39, landlords, III, 137, IV, 230–1, V, 313–14, farmers and manufacturers, III, 136–7, IV, 229–31, IX, 72–3, workers, IV, 257, IX, 166; see also V, 315–16
is not capital, III, 390, see also III, 92–3, 286–7; proportions between capital and money, III, 54
circulation of, admits of indefinite enlargement, III, 150, can never overflow, I, 352–3, is never saturated, III, 381–2, see also V, 71
circulation of notes and coin in 1822 estimated, IX, 201
money considered as a commodity, III, 103–4, 142, V, 346, VI, 24–5, 203; demand for, I, 193–4
as dead stock, I, 229, 232
degradation in the value of, I, 148, 310, V, 527, see also I, 228
depreciation of, see Depreciation
distribution of, through the world, I, 140, III, 87, VI, 74–5; world stock estimated, V, 209
economy in the use of, III, 86, 90, VI, 26, 93, between nations, III, 112–13, 242 n.; see also V, 420
an equivalent, not a pledge or security, VIII, 104
importance of, exaggerated in political economy, IX, 100, see also II, 180
perfect currency defined, I, 361, IV, 55, 66, V, 379
prices determined by quantity of, I, 105, III, 193 & n., 215–16, 230, VI, 93–4, by proportion between commodities and, III, 90, 106, 118, 311
whether prices raised by taxation require more money, I, 169 & n., 213–14 & n., III, 242–3, 385, IV, 321–2, discussed at Political Economy Club, IX, 158–9

Money *(cont.)*
principle of limitation of quantity, I, 353
quantity of, required to circulate commodities, III, 140–1, 238–9, 356–7, V, 417–18, IX, 101; reduced by density of population, V, 421
increase in quantity, lowers rate of interest temporarily, I, 298, V, 445, but not permanently, III, 374–6; can augment riches only at expense of wages, III, 318–19, VI, 16–17, see also III, 302, 334
relative price and relative value of, VI, 79
rise in value of, distinguished from fall in price of commodities, I, 47–51, 63–4, VII, 203 & n.
money and wealth distinguished, III, 108, 145
see also Bank notes, Circulating medium, Coin, Currency, Gold, Paper money, Rapidity of circulation, Silver
Money, standard of:
no invariable standard exists, I, 149, III, 65 n., 391, IV, 54–5, V, 209, VII, 42–3
gold the best standard, IV, 62–3, V, 388, 390–1, VII, 42–3; assumed to be invariable, I, xlii, 27–8, 46–7, 110 n., IV, 236, VI, 348–9; produced by same quantity of unassisted labour (ed. 1), I, 55, 63, 87 n.; by average proportions of fixed and circulating capitals (ed. 3), I, 45–6, 87, IV, 371, IX, 347
whether value of standard can be judged by the mass of commodities, IV, 59–61, V, 374, see also I, 377, III, 104–5
money without a standard, IV, 59, 62, 64, see also I, 354
Moneyed men, I, 89, III, 136, and cp. I, 123
Moniteur Universel, III, 179 n., X, 374
Monk, John Berkeley, M.P. for Reading, on sinking fund, V, 266

Monmouth, meeting at, V, 515, IX, 119, 121, 141 & n.; see also VII, 277
Monopoly:
natural monopolies, I, 404–5 & n.
and land, VI, 169–70, 175, 177; partial monopoly of land, I, 284, II, 114, VIII, 215, IX, 171, see also II, 104–5
of colony trade, I, 340–6
monopoly price, I, 249–51, 253, 384–5, II, 48–9, IX, 97–8, 100, see also I, 194, 197–8, 316–17 n.
see also I, 277, II, 260–1, 291, 409, V, 47, 88, 104, 111, 219, 301, VII, 202, VIII, 353
Montanvert, IX, 216, 235, X, 275
Mont Blanc, IX, 216, X, 257, 273, 275
Mont Cenis, X, 339; road, 340
Montesquieu: *Esprit des lois*, IV, 307 n., V, 288–9, VI, 308, 311, 332, VII, 383, X, 397; *Reflections on the . . . Roman Empire*, X, 398
Monthly Magazine, IV, 415–16
Monthly Review, on *Principles*, I, xxi
Monti, Vincenzo, Brougham reading the Italian poets with, VII, 74
Montrose Academy, VI, 138 n.
Moore, Daniel, VII, 254–5
Moore, Peter, M.P. for Coventry, V, xxvi, VIII, 324
Moore, Thomas, *Memoirs*: on Ricardo's quitting the Jewish faith, X, 37 n.; on Harriet Ricardo, X, 61
Morat, X, 263
Moravians, X, 213
Morellet, André, *Mémoires*, 1821, IX, 274
Morgan, John, loan contractor, X, 78
Morgan, William, F.R.S., the 'ingenious calculator', IV, 415–18, see also III, 358 n., IV, 99, 279, VI, 275
article on the finances of the Bank, 1797, IV, 415–16
View of the Public Finances, 1801, X, 78 n.
Morley, John, on Richard Sharp, VI, xxxvi n.

Morning Chronicle:
Ricardo's contributions to, III, 3–46, 129–53; see also III, 82 n., 88 n., X, 7, 14
Trower's letters to, III, 4, 22, 28, 81, 88
Mercator's letters to, III, 27 & n.
scale of discounts published in, IV, 416–18
parliamentary reports, V, xxvii–xxviii, 9, 49, 52, 138, 196–7, 250, 269, 293, 463 n., VI, 106, 335–6, IX, 291 n.
see also VI, 11 n., 78, VII, 218, 303, VIII, 221, IX, 201, 385 n.
Morning Herald, V, 121 n.
Morning Post, V, 463 n.
Morris, Dr, pseudonym of J. G. Lockhart, VIII, 25 n., 112
Morritt, Mr, IX, 232, 240
Mortimer, Thomas:
Every Man his own Broker, 1761, X, 77 n.
The Nefarious Practice of Stockjobbing, 1810, X, 77 n.
Moselle, X, 219–21
Mr ——, a Continental merchant: evidence before bullion committee, III, 163, 168 n., 185, 288, 352–6; identified as John Parish, jun., III, 427–34
Mullion, Hugh, pseudonym of John Wilson, skit on McCulloch in *Blackwood's Magazine*, 1819, IX, 205–6 n.
Mullion, Mordecai, pseudonym of John Wilson, *Illustrations of Mr McCulloch's Political Economy*, 1826, VIII, 205 n., see also IX, 205 n.
Murray, John, Ricardo's publisher, VI, xxxv
Principles, ed. 1, I, xix; ed. 2, VII, 162, 333, 337; ed. 3, VIII, 315, 341 n.
rejects Place's book, IX, 47–8, 57–9, 61, 64, 115–16; lukewarm on Torrens, VII, 141
knocked down by ruffians, VI, 230
records of firm, X, 87, 355–6, 358, 360, 368

Murray, John (*cont.*)
list of letters, IX, 399
see also IV, 273, VI, 211, VII, 1, 4, 8, 16, 24, 120, 207, 361, 364, 370, 375, 379, VIII, 4, 152 n., 298 n., IX, 107 & n., 183, XI, xxvi
Murray, Sir John, I, xi, IV, 273, VI, xxxv, X, x
Murray, John Archibald, reprint of Dudley North's *Discourses upon Trade*, IX, 150–1, 157; see also III, 10 n.
Mushet, Robert: evidence on Resumption, V, 13; letters in Ricardo Papers, X, 388; see also VI, 88, 91, VIII, 367 n.
Enquiry into the Effects produced by the Bank Restriction Bill, 1810, III, 116, 248 n., VI, 8–9, 14, 89, Ricardo's copy, X, 402; ed. 2, III, 166–70, 174–5, 185, 204, V, 426–7, VI, 9 n., 14 n.; ed. 3, III, 169 n., VII, 384, VIII, 3 & n.
Series of Tables exhibiting the Gain and Loss to the Fundholder, 1821, VII, 93 n., VIII, 390–1 & n., 392, 396–8; ed. 2, V, 138 n., 252–3, 314, VIII, 398 & n., IX, 7, 39, 133

Nabarro, J. N., X, x, 17 n., 19 n., 20 n., 24 n.
Namur, VII, 160, 167
Napier, Macvey, editor of *Supplement to the Encyclopaedia Britannica*, VIII, 188 n.
and Ricardo's article 'Funding System', VIII, 54, 58–60 & n., 72–3, 75–6, 78, 83, 144, 188; payment for, VIII, 240, 242–3; see also IV, 145–7, VIII, 64, 69, 137, 141
see also VIII, 189, IX, 5, 41, 150 n., 302 n.
Selections from the Correspondence of, VIII, 60 n., IX, 6 n.
Naples, revolution in 1821, V, xxii, VIII, 363 & n.
Napoleon, VI, 199 n., IX, 247 n., X, 211, 324, 335, 345–7, 374. See Bonaparte

Napoleon III, X, 325 n.

Nasmith, James, *The Duties of Over-seers of the Poor*, 1797, VII, 289 n.

National debt:
evils of, V, 33, 38, 54
whether cheap corn lightens burden of, IV, 39–40, VII, 104–5
management of, by Bank of England, IV, 51–4, 81–95, 98; table of charges, IV, 115–41; see also V, 100, VI, 275, 283–5, 333, 347–8
commissioners for, proposed, VI, 268, and cp. IV, 289–91
effects of annihilating, II, 451–2, on rate of interest, VIII, 145, on landowners and salary- and wage-earners, VIII, 238–9, on the middle classes, II, 444–5
McCulloch's early suggestion for reducing interest on, VII, 37–8, 103–5, 351–3, VIII, 4; later disowned, I, 426 & n., VII, 93 n.; see also VIII, 157–8, 378 n.
see also Dividends, Sinking fund

National debt, Ricardo's plan to pay off: by tax on capital, V, 38, 271, on 'mercantile, landed and funded property', V, 187, 472; to be paid off at market price (1819), V, 34–5, VIII, 144, 147, 157, at par (1822), IX, 173–4; first outlined in *Principles* (1817), I, 247–8, then in *Sinking Fund* (1820), IV, 146–7, 196–7
special checks to be issued, V, 39, or particular paper money, VIII, 239
criticised by Brougham, V, xxxiii, 40–1 & n., 268–9, by Baring, V, 270; Grenfell on 'Ricardo's crotchet', V, 270–1; opposed by both stockholders and landowners, VIII, 147; 'a wild sort of notion', VIII, 147 n.; an 'adjustment of property', V, 266
objections to plan answered, IV, 197, VIII, 238–9
similar proposals, I, 248 & n., V, 37 & n.; Hutcheson's and Watson's, V, 40–1 & n., Heathfield's,

National debt, R.'s plan (*cont.*)
VIII, 143–5, Sinclair's, VIII, 187, Trower's, IX, 174
see also V, xx, 20–1, 55, 86, 90, VI, 345, VIII, 33, 78–9, 152 n., 166 & n., 223, X, 187 n.

Natural agents, add to riches, not to value, I, 285–7; McCulloch on, IX, 342–3

Natural and market price, I, 88–92, 119, 191, 196, 217, 312–13, 317 n., 340–3, II, 83, 299, VIII, 255–6
of corn, I, 301–3, 312–13, 374–5, II, 227–8
of labour, I, 93–6, II, 228

Natural price, or cost of production, I, 385, II, 34–5, 38–9, 46–9, 224, VIII, 207, see also VII, 250–1; or money cost of production, I, 383; or real cost of production, I, 301; or necessary price, I, 120, 302, II, 52; synonymous with value, II, 35
natural price of corn, I, 120, 374–5, IV, 241, VI, 198, or necessary price, I, 415; and restrictions on importation of corn, II, 154–5

Natural value: defined, II, 35; or necessary value, I, 415; and exchangeable value, IV, 375; and absolute (Malthus), IX, 307–11, 364

Nature, gifts of, I, 76–7 n.
whether rent due to bounty of, (Malthus) or niggardliness of, (Ricardo), II, 210–12
see also I, 69, 75, 85, 126, 134, 159, II, 123

Navigation laws, V, 190, 197; and Navy, V, 305, IX, 269 n.; see also V, 51, 478, IX, 342

Navy bills, I, 297, III, 291–2, IV, 102, V, 140–1

Neat: produce, VIII, 311, revenue, II, 381, VIII, 285, 300, surplus from the land, II, 164, VIII, 309, 311. See Net

Necessaries:
price of, relation to wages, I, 93, 95, 118, 161, 165, IV, 236, see also I, 296, IV, 179, VII, 57, 72, 81; rises as population increases, I, 101

Necessaries (*cont.*)
demand for, limited, for luxuries unlimited, I, 292–4, 387, VIII, 272,
IX, 19
whether demand for labour is the
same as supply of necessaries, VIII,
220, 236, 245, 248, 258, 270, see
also II, 426
the labourer's necessaries, I, 20, 97,
104, 224, 234, 275, 306, 406, VIII,
275
manufactured necessaries, I, 243
see also Corn, Food, Provisions,
Raw produce, Taxes on necessaries
Necker, Jacques, X, 269, 279–80
Net revenue, and happiness of human
beings, I, 348–9 & notes, II,
381–2, VII, 378–9; see also under
Revenue
Net surplus from land, II, 164–5;
Malthus says impossible without
taste for luxuries, VIII, 285, 300–1,
309; his ambiguous use of term,
VIII, 311
Netherlands, IX, 309, X, 188
Neuss, IX, 211, X, 213
New Edinburgh Magazine, VII, 332.
See *Edinburgh Magazine*
New Gravel Pit Unitarian Chapel,
X, 40
New Grove, Ricardo's home at
Mile End, VI, 51, 53 & n., X, 47,
118
New Lanark, V, 218, 468
New Monthly Magazine, VIII, 249
New Times, The, V, xxvii n., 3, VIII,
29 n.
Newcastle, Duke of, IX, 105
Newland, Abraham, Principal Cashier
at the Bank of England, III, 188–90,
V, 462, X, 76 n.
Newnham, Glos., VIII, 231–2
Newport, Sir John, M.P. for Water-
ford, V, 138, 185, 281, 335, 351,
354, IX, 160–1, 163, 185, 194, X,
99
Newspaper stamp duties bill, VIII,
148

Newton, Rev. Benjamin, *Diary, 1816–
1818*, VII, 56 n.; MS diary, VIII,
334 n., X, 62 & n.
Newton, Isaac, on gold and silver
coins, III, 203
Nicholas de Flue, Saint, X, 252–3
Nicholl, Sir John, M.P. for Great
Bedwin, V, 351, 365–6
Nicoll, Walter, *The Planter's Kalendar*,
1812, VI, 237
Nimeguen, IX, 209, X, 213
No-rent land, see Land, that pays no
rent
'No Trafficker', letters on bullion in
The Pilot, III, 27 & n.
Noel, Sir Gerald, M.P., VIII, 324 & n.
Nominal, or money price, II, 67, 280;
and real price, II, 250
Nominal value, II, 26–7
Nominal wages, see Wages, nominal
and real
Norfolk County meeting (1823), Cob-
bett takes over, IX, 265 & n.
Norman, George Warde, X, 277 & n.,
301; see also VIII, 367 n., IX, 218–
19, 223, 288 n., 301
North, Dudley, *Discourses upon Trade*,
1691, IX, 150–1, 157
North, John Henry, IX, 274
Norwood, R. P., *History of Kidding-
ton*, X, 64 n.
Nugent, Lord, V, 475
Nuncomar, VII, 237
Nunes, Abraham, X, 29
Nunes, Sarah, *née* Delvalle (D.R.'s
aunt), X, 29, 106

Obata, Shigeo, X, 385
O'Connell, Daniel, V, xvii n.
O'Connor, Irma, *Edward Gibbon
Wakefield*, VII, 216 n.
O'Connor, M. J. L., *Origin of Aca-
demic Economics in the United
States*, X, 372
Old Proprietor's *Letters to Proprietors
of Bank Stock*, 1816, VI, 276 n.,
278, 283, 288
O'Meara, B. E., *Napoleon in Exile*,
1822, IX, 247

Omnium (scrip of government loans), X, 77 & n.; rising (1811), VI, 42, 48–9, rickety, 52; thriving (1812), 85 & n.; falling (1814), VI, 108, 110, 116, 119, a strange and sad business, 122, 128; rises with victory, VI, 231 & n., 233, 237; see also VI, 106, X, 80–4, 86, 89

Onslow, Arthur, Serjeant-at-law, M.P. for Guildford, moves repeal of usury laws, V, 109, 323, 335–7, VII, 46 n., VIII, 17 n.; see also VIII, 250

Oracle, Ricardo as the, V, 40 & n.

Orange, Prince of, *Proposals for . . . Trade*, 1751, IX, 135 n.

Ordnance bills, III, 292

Otaheite, VI, 290, 292–4, 296, 301

Otter, William, his edition of Malthus's *Political Economy*, 1836, II, xii, xiv

Overplus, proportion of, to capital, I, 91. See Surplus produce

Overstone Library (originally J. R. McCulloch's), IX, 302, X, 401

Overtrading, V, 397–8, 446–7

Owen, Robert:
  plan for employment of the poor, VII, 150 & n.; parliamentary committee to inquire into, V, xxvii, speech on, V, 30–1, VIII, 46 n.
  Duke of Kent's committee on, Ricardo a member, V, 467–8, VIII, 42–3, 45–7
  Torrens's speech on, VIII, 82, and article on, VIII, 82 n., 159 n., 164, 376 n.
  see also V, 7, IX, 50
  his model villages, VII, 177 & n., and cp. IV, 222
  provision system at his shop at New Lanark, V, 218
  infant school, VII, 356, see also VI, 112 n.
  his irreligion, V, 328, VII, 177 & n., VIII, 153 n.; complains of Ricardo's allusion to, V, 330–1 & n.
  and birth control, VIII, 71–2 & n., IX, 62
  see also VII, 247
  Life of, written by himself, V, 468

Oxen, in Germany, X, 231, in Lombardy, X, 302

Oxford, Lord, VII, 217, 232

Oxley, Charles, VII, 162

Padua, X, 310

Page, Richard, his evidence in 1819, V, 361
  Letters of Daniel Hardcastle, 1819, V, 361 n., VIII, 3 n.

Paget, Thomas, *Letter to David Ricardo on the Depreciation in the Currency*, 1822, IX, 250 & n.

Paine, Thomas, *The Age of Reason*, V, 325; *An Appendix to the Theological Works of Thomas Paine*, V, 277; see also X, 395

Paley, Dr, his test for a theorem, III, 251–2; his spirit of toleration, V, 324–5

Palma, painter, IX, 222

Palmella, Count, VII, 276

Palmer, Charles, *Speech on the State of the Nation*, 1832, VIII, 143 n.

Palmer, Mr, of India, VII, 110

Palmer, Mr, of Monmouth, on Ricardo and Peel's bill, V, 515–17, 519–20

Palmer, Mr, Trower's adoptive father, VI, xxiii

Palmerston, Viscount, M.P. for Cambridge University, V, xxvi

Pamphleteer, The, 1817, VII, 32 n., 151 n., 260 n.; 1823, V, xxi n.

Panics: banks have no security against, IV, 68, V, 394, 409–10, 456; panic of 1797, III, 364–5, V, 15, 400, VI, 44; on the Stock Exchange, 1819, VIII, 32 & n.

Paper money:
  provides a cheap currency, IV, 234, 276, 298, VII, 42, VIII, 295; other advantages of, IV, 57–8
  perfect currency consists wholly of, I, 361, V, 387, VII, 151, but exchangeable for bullion, I, 356, VI, 69, VIII, 186, ought to conform to value of gold, I, 105, 195, and cp. VII, 37

Paper money (*cont.*)

value maintained by limitation of quantity, I, 353–4, see also III, 138–9, 269–70

Bank of England's rule for issuing, IV, 68 & n., see also III, 363–4, V, 255

made legal tender in 1811, V, 316, VI, 45 & n., see also VI, 68

should be issued only by the State, I, 362–3; Ricardo's plan for independent commissioners, IV, 114, 282–97, VI, 268, IX, 329

see also III, 332–5, and under Bank notes, Depreciation, Money

Paper Money System, III, 135, VIII, 153 n.

Paraira, M. C., and da Silva, J. S., *Gendenkenschrift 300-jarig bestaan Ets Haïm*, X, 31 n.

Paris: proposed visit to, in 1803, X, 117; visit in 1817, VII, 160, 164, 167, 178, 224, 231; with family in 1822, IX, 234, 236, 244–5, 248, X, 346–52; see also V, 186, VI, xxv, 247, 250, IX, 233

Paris, Peace of, 1814, V, 350, VI, 119 & n.

Parish & Co., Hamburg merchants, III, 430–1

Parish, Charles, III, 431

Parish, John, III, 431

Parish, John, jun., 'Mr.—' of the Bullion Report, III, 427–34. See also Mr. —

Parish, Richard, III, 431

Parish relief, I, 108, VII, 304, XI, xv–xvi; see also Poor, the

Park, Mr and Mrs, X, 309

Park, Mungo, *Journal of a Mission to the Interior of Africa*, 1815, VI, 244–5 n.

Parliament:

a narrow oligarchy, VII, 273, 290; controlled by interested men, V, 288, 478, VII, 299, and country gentlemen, IX, 180, 194, 246, 249; aristocratical influence, V, 284, 286, 496; few enlightened com-

Parliament (*cont.*)

mercial men, VIII, 163; not moving in sympathy with the people, V, 269, 470, VIII, 330; an instrument of misgovernment (Mill), VI, 252, VIII, 329

Ricardo's seat in, V, xiii–xix, X, 11; Mill presses for, VI, 138, 252, 263, VII, 85–6, 110, 113, 190, 198, 300–2, 317, 349–50, 358, 364; search for uncontested seat, VII, 101–2, 110, 252, 254, 260, 264, 269, 272; settles for Portarlington, VII, 216–17, 232–3, 292–3, 300, 304–8, 311, 346–8, 355, 359, 362–3, 373, 382, VIII, 7, 10; takes his seat, VIII, 17 & n., 18–19, 21; re-elected 1820, VIII, 156, 162; tenure extended, VIII, 326–7, 330; refuses to contest Gloucestershire, VIII, 156, 162, or Liverpool, IX, 182–3, XI, xiv

price of a seat, V, xiv n., VII, 216, 254 n., 276

see also House of Commons, Reform of parliament

Parliamentary History and Debates, VIII, 61. See Hansard

Parnell, Sir Henry, M.P. for Queen's County, VII, 346 n.

arranges for Ricardo's seat in parliament, V, xiv–xvii, VII, 232, 300, 327, 346–8, 359, 363, VIII, 10, 17

on timber duties, V, 102, 104

sinking fund plan, V, 270–2, IX, 175

see also V, 86, 98, 335

Parr, Dr Samuel, VIII, 84, 106

Parsimony:

transfers, does not diminish, demand, II, 309, 326–7, X, 408

country enriched by, I, 278; Malthus denies this, IX, 19–20, see also II, 317, IX, 26

motives for, and effects of, distinguished, II, 9

see also Saving

Patten, Simon N., 'The Interpretation of Ricardo', I, xxi, IV, 8 n.

Patteson, Elizabeth, see Wilkinson, Elizabeth

Patteson, Sarah, see Wilkinson, Sarah

Pattle, Eliza, VII, 216 n.

Pauntley Court, Ricardo's estate, VII, 299 n., VIII, 48, X, 97–8, 105

Paupers: education bill, VIII, 25; literacy among, VII, 303–4, 306; Owen's workhouse for, VIII, 46; 'a million of' (1819), VIII, 139; Horton's plan for emigration of, XI, xv–xvi

Payerne, X, 263

Payne, Mr, V, 463 n.

Peacock & Co., III, 430

Peacock, Thomas Love, IX, 279 & n.

Pearse, John, Governor of Bank of England, M.P. for Devizes:

submits paper to bullion committee, III, 113–19, 140; evidence, III, 356–61, 364–9, 419

defends the Bank against Ricardo, V, 18, 143, and against Grenfell, V, 62

see also V, 461–2

Pearson, Karl, and Morant, G. M., 'The Wilkinson head of Oliver Cromwell', X, 167

Peel, Sir Robert, M.P. for Tamworth, V, 365, VIII, 29 n.

Peel, Robert, M.P. for Oxford University:

Chairman of committee on resumption of cash payments, V, 2, 7, 134–5, 350–4, 364–8

replies to Attwood's attack, V, 186

see also V, 18, 23, 200, 321, 371, 401, VIII, 20, 350–1, IX, 124, 146, X, 370

Peel's bill for resumption of cash payments (1819), V, 2–3, 7–8, 202, 368, VIII, 31 & n.

and ingot plan, IV, 47–8, V, 135, 200, 351, 518, VIII, 20

and increased value of currency, IV, 228–31, V, 310

effects on price of corn, IV, 222, 228

not fully acted on, V, 134, 206–7, 254

Cobbett on, IX, 123 n., 140–1 & n.

Peel's bill (cont.)

Ricardo blamed for ill-effects, VIII, 360 & n., IX, 122; defends himself, V, 515–21

Western's motion for amendment, V, 198, 210, 218, 522–3, IX, 202

and loan of 1819, X, 84–5

see also V, 18, 186, IX, 165 n., 266–7 and under Resumption

Pemberton, Thomas, Increase of the Number of Poor, 1811, X, 402

Penny Cyclopædia, article on Ricardo, X, 37 n.

Pensions, plan for spreading burden, V, 160–1, 191–5, 281–2, see also V, 156, 248–9, 265, 267, IX, 198 n. 3

People, the: their good sense, VIII, 59; on the side of good government, V, 498, VII, 261; an effectual check to government, V, 496–7, VII, 273, 322, VIII, 133; must in the end prevail (Mill), IX, 42; see also V, 500–1, VIII, 303, 336

Pepe, E., X, 355

Peploe, Samuel and Mrs, X, 314 n., 315, 317, 320

Perceval, Spencer, Prime Minister and Chancellor of the Exchequer, VI, 43 n.

his bargain with the Bank in 1808, IV, 51, 53–4, 77, 81–3, 88–90, VI, 261, 283, 333, 337, 347

Ricardo's ingot plan first submitted to, VI, 43–6, 70, VIII, 54, X, 10, 93

see also III, 413 n., IV, 157–8, 193

Perkins family, X, 267, 276

Permanent versus temporary effects, VII, 120, 121–2; see also Short period

Perry, James, editor of Morning Chronicle: publishes Ricardo's first paper, III, 3–4 & notes, X, 7; Cobbett on, V, 41 n.; see also V, xxvii, VIII, 294 & n.

Pestalozzi, Swiss officer, X, 248

Peter the Great's house at Saardam, X, 208

Peterloo, VIII, 54 n. See Manchester massacre

Petty, Lord Henry, Chancellor of the Exchequer, 1806–7, VII, 284 n.

sinking fund plan, IV, 154–7, 175–7, 180, 193

see also IV, 416, VIII, 319, and under Lansdowne, Marquis of

Phelps, John Delafield, VII, 189, 191, VIII, 334 n.

Philalethes, *The Policy of a Restriction on the Importation of Corn*, 1815, VI, 201 n.

Philanthropist, The, VI, 313

Philips, George, M.P. for Wootton Bassett: on benefits of machinery, V, 302, 303; on Ricardo, V, 185; see also V, 352, VI, xxxvi, VIII, 70

Philips, Mr, VII, 316 n.

Phillips, George R., M.P. for Horsham, XI, xi–xii & n.

Phillips, Mr, his lectures on chemistry, VII, 313 & n.

Phillips, Thomas, R. A., portrait of Ricardo, IX, facing p. 1, X, 51–3

Phillips, William, geologist, VI, 180, 215

Physiocrats, VIII, 162. See also Économistes

Picciotto, J., *Sketches of Anglo-Jewish History*, X, 24 n.

Piedmont, revolution in 1821, VIII, 363 & n.

Piggott, Sir Arthur, X, 42–3 & n.

Pilot, The, newspaper, III, 27

Pinkerton, John, *Modern Geography*, 1802, VII, 189–90

Pinsent, Joseph, X, 389

Pisa, IX, 225, 227, X, 322–3

Pissevache, X, 283

Pitt, Joseph, X, 97

Pitt, William:

his sinking fund, IV, 41, 151–4, 158–9, 161–7, 174, 190–4, V, 118–20, 262, 265, VIII, 120

and Bank in 1795, III, 77 n.; renewal of Bank charter, IV, 91–3

views on poor law, I, 107 n.

friend of reform, V, 288; his apostasy, VIII, 63, 77

Pitt (*cont.*)

see also III, 188–9, V, 248, VI, 258, VII, 249, VIII, 61, 319, X, 75 n.

Speeches of, 1806, IV, 159

Place, Francis, VI, xxxv–xxxvi

and chrestomathic school, VI, xxix–xxxi, 112 n., VII, 198, VIII, 198, 212

and Say's visit, VI, 156–7 notes, 160, 161 n.

translates Say, VI, xxvi–xxvii, 160 n.

annotates *Principles*, VII, 183 & n., 189, 235

sends books on sinking fund, VIII, 66 n., 69, 77; comments on 'Funding System', VIII, 83 & n., 105–6, 118–25

and Thomas Evans, VII, 307–8

Westminster election, VII, 357 & n.

list of letters, IX, 399; other letters quoted: to Mill, VI, 161 n., to Bentham, VIII, 113–14 n.

see also VI, xxv, xxxviii, 158 n., VII, 182, 316 n., VIII, 115, 294 n., IX, 173, 288 n.

Illustrations and Proofs of the Principles of Population, 1822, IX, 49 n.; Ricardo reads MS, IX, 47–8, his comments, IX, 49–57, 59, 61–2, recommends publication, IX, 58, 64, 115–16; see also IX, 94, 101, 103, 120

Playfair, John, VIII, 58, 82

Playne, A. T., *History of Minchinhampton*, VIII, 283 n., X, 96 n.

Playne, William, VIII, 283 & n., 293

Pliniana, Villa, X, 296

Plough, I, 82; ploughing in the Netherlands, X, 188, with oxen in Germany, X, 231

Plowden, Francis, *Historical Review of the State of Ireland*, 1801, VIII, 49, 52

Plummer, A., article 'Sir Edward West', VII, 298 n.

Plunket, William Conyngham, M.P. for Dublin University, V, xxii–xxiii, VIII, 148, 350–1 & n., 362 n., IX, 274

Podmore, Charles, stockbroker, VI, 113 n.

Podmore, F., *Robert Owen*, VII, 177 n.

Podmore, Robert, stockbroker, VI, 112 n., X, 123–4

Podmore, Robert, jun., stockbroker, VI, 113 n.

Poland, corn production in, I, 15, 134, 144–5, IV, 265, VIII, 369, 374; see also I, 100 n., 378

Pole, Charles, Deputy-Governor of the Bank, V, 353

Pole, William Wellesley, M.P. for Queen's County, V, 350

Poles, two young, met on the Simplon, IX, 223, X, 289–90 & n., 301. See also Kunatt, Stanislaw

Police bill, Edinburgh, IX, 161–3, 179, see also 137

Police of the Metropolis, report on, 1816, VII, 150 & n.

Political economists, their 'abominable theories' (Lethbridge), V, 169; see also IV, 409, VI, 178, and under Economists, Theories

Political economy:
object of, I, 5, VII, 122, VIII, 270, 278, 286

whether a science, V, 162, 296, VIII, 152–3 n., 331, see also VIII, 100

a guide to taxation, VIII, 79, 132–3, see also V, 44, VIII, 71

true principles of, V, 296, 298, VIII, 207, daily gaining ground, VIII, 163–4

makes progress in parliament, VIII, 150, IX, 166; Brougham 'lectures' the House on, IX, 164, 167, 207; Ricardo is read a lesson in, V, 178

little knowledge of, on Stock Exchange, VI, 150

fashionable with ladies, VIII, 56 n., X, 172

French government prejudiced against, VIII, 225, 228

attacks on, V, 248, 295, 306–7, VIII, 382, 387, IX, 155 & n.

Political Economy Club, X, 50–1; foundation, VIII, 367 & n., 381

subjects discussed: glut, IX, 9–10; machinery, 9 n., 158 n., 159; Say's letters, IX, 36 & n., 158, 172–3 & n.; tax on all goods, and prices, IV, 320, IX, 158–9; riches and value, IX, 312 & n.; national bank, IV, 273; see also IX, 112–13, 116, 120, 264–5

meetings attended by Ricardo, IX, 9–10 & n., 36 n., 172–3 & n., see also IV, 320

Political Economy Club, Centenary Volume, I, lx, VII, 50, 187, VIII, 157, X, 35, 52, 67, 73, 370

Minutes of Proceedings, 1821–1882, IV, 273 n., 320 n., VIII, 367 n., IX, 9 n., 116 n., 159 n., 173 n., 191 n., 265 n., 312 n., X, 51 n.

Poor, the:
sufferings of, in 1816, VII, 61–2, 66–7, 87, 95, 209

public provision for, objections to, VII, 248; sinks price of labour, II, 49, VII, 142

parish relief and savings banks depositors, VII, 12, 63–4 & n., 96, 117, 125–6, 128–9

education of children of the poor supported, VII, 45 & n., but not school feeding, VII, 359–60, 363; see also Education

Poor laws:
report on, 1817, I, 107 n., VII, 150 n., 209, 219, 248–9; committee on, 1819, Ricardo a member, V, xxiv; Sturges Bourne's bill, V, 1, 6–7, VIII, 25, 74–5 n.; settlement bill, VIII, 30, 32; amendment bill, 1821, speech on, V, 113–14; see also IX, 198 n.

pernicious tendency of, I, 105–9, 162, VII, 133–5, 360; ought to be abolished, I, 107, VII, 124–5, see also IX, 54–5, XI, xv–xvi

proper object of, VII, 248

effect of, on quantity of food, VII, 3, 202

see also Parish relief, Public Works

Poor rates, I, 257–62, IV, 217–18, V, 45
Pope, Alexander, *Essay on Man*, VI, 327
Population, I, 78, 98–100, 159, II, 115
  increases faster than capital, VII, 72, VIII, 368; alternately take the lead, IV, 22–3, see also II, 277, 321, VIII, 150–1 & n.
  and fund for maintenance of labour, I, 78, 108–9, 164, 219, 289, 292–3; and wages, I, 125, 406–7, VIII, 273
  and cheap food, I, 373, 409, IV, 19 n., VI, 140, VIII, 255, IX, 239, see also I, 292, VII, 360, X, 408–9
  effect on rent, I, 70–2, 77, 102, 334, see also II, 133–4, VIII, 182
  checks to: prudential, II, 220–1, 262, V, 303, VII, 218–19, VIII, 25, 183–4, IX, 55; artificial, VII, 63, VIII, 71 & n., 80–1, IX, 62 & n.; other restraints on, I, 100, II, 115, VII, 125
  population in Ireland, I, 100 n., VII, 48
  Malthus's principle of, I, 406–7, II, 111, 234, 262, 303, 341, VI, 140, 192, 195–6, 199, 318, see also II, 243, VI, 224, 301, VIII, 195, IX, 323
  comments on Place's book on, IX, 49–57
  see also Demanders, Happiness
Portarlington, Ricardo's constituency, V, xiv n., VII, 355, VIII, 17 n., 162; a 'quiet sort of borough', VII, 311; he 'never set foot in', V, 289
Portarlington, Earl of, V, xv n., xviii; negotiations with, for seat in parliament, VII, 216–17, 232, 293, 306, 308, 327, 346–8, 359, 382, VIII, 327, X, 99
Porter, George Richardson (D.R.'s brother-in-law), X, 60; bequest to, X, 105
  article on Ricardo in *Penny Cyclopædia*, X, 22 n., 37 & n.
Porter, Sarah (D.R.'s sister), see Ricardo, Sarah
Porteus, Dr Beilby, V, 325

Portions:
  division of the whole produce of land and labour into three portions, I, 347, 411
  portion of produce paid to landlords for rent, VII, 81; was previously a portion of the profits obtained from the land, IV, 18 & n., 20
  portions distinguished from proportions (Malthus), II, 195 n.; rent not governed by proportions, II, 196 n.
  see also Proportions
Portugal, I, 137–41, 377–8, III, 190, VI, 86, VII, 276 n.
Positive value, VIII, 394, IX, 1–2, 29, 339, 351
Potato:
  Malthean objections to, IX, 232, 239, see also II, 215
  potato question in Ireland, V, 225, 234, VII, 175–6, IX, 230–2, 237–9, 252–5, 257–61
  see also I, 97, 332–3, V, 528, IX, 56
Potato flour: speculation proposed by Say, VII, 166, 224–6, 230; Lasteyrie's process for, IX, 231, 253, 259, 273
Power-loom, V, 68
Practical men, III, 163, 188, 190, 227, 239, 256, 362, IV, 240; Ricardo too theoretical, Malthus too practical, VI, 295; *Principles* not intended to be a practical book, VIII, 184
Pratt, J. T., *History of Savings Banks*, 1830, VII, 23, 187 n.
Precious metals, see Gold and silver
Press, the:
  free press as check on government, V, 486, 497, VII, 298, 323, 368, IX, 102, XI, xxii, see also VIII, 53, IX, 55
  in Scotland, VIII, 167 & n., IX, 136 & n., 142
  parliamentary reporting, V, xxvii–xxxi
  Hazlitt on periodical press, VII, 28 n., VIII, 185–6; Mill on liberty of the press, IX, 154 n.

Preston, Mr, VIII, 46

Prévost, Pierre, professor of physics at Geneva, IX, 219–20, X, 270 & n., 281, see also I, liv, II, vii, xii

Price:

puzzled to find law of, VI, 348, VII, 71–2, 83–4

early view that price of corn regulates all prices, III, 270, VI, 108, 114; found erroneous, I, 302, 307–8, 315, IV, 21 n., 35–6, 216, VI, 221, 269, VII, 105; Adam Smith's original error, VII, 100

rise in raw produce leaves all other prices unchanged, IV, 20, 236–7, VII, 24; this qualified for raw material contained, I, 117–18, IV, 20 n., VI, 179, 348–9

prices of all commodities cannot be raised by rise of wages, I, 104–5, 126, 303, 307–8, 315, IV, 213–16, 236; none rise, but some fall (ed. 1), I, 61–3, 66; some rise, some fall (ed. 3), I, 34–5, II, 60–4, according to proportion of fixed capital used, I, 46, 239, II, 274, VII, 82–3, VIII, 179–80, 193, and to durability of capital, I, 39–43

regulated by quantity of labour necessary for production, I, 110, 118, II, 34–5; by facility or difficulty of production, IX, 239, see also I, 191, VII, 3, 250; finally settled by competition of sellers, II, 38, VIII, 277

and value distinguished, IV, 60, 236, VII, 288, 297, see also II, 242, III, 360, IV, 373, VI, 54–5, and cp. I, 110 n.

natural and market, I, 88–92, 191, 196, II, 83, 299, VIII, 256–7, 271–2, see also I, 119, 217, 312–13, 317 n., 340–3

natural price regulated by cost of production, I, 301–2, 344, 382–5, 397, II, 34–5, 38–9, 46–9, 52–3, V, 300, VI, 177, 189, VII, 250–1, VIII, 201, 207, see also II, 40–1, 390, IV, 211

Price (*cont.*)

market price regulated by demand and supply, I, 382–5, II, 45, 47, VI, 148 & n., VIII, 272, 286, 302, see also I, 119–20

monopoly price, I, 249–51, 384–5, II, 48–9

absolute price, I, 63; permanent price, VII, 250–1; real price, I, 12, 410, 413 n., 414–16, II, 292, VII, 145, and nominal price, I, 274–5 n., II, 250; relative price, I, 12

relation of price to quantity supplied, I, 104–5, 384–5, V, 171, VI, 90–2, 163; small excess of corn, large effect on price, IV, 28–9, 219–21, 259, 266, V, 318–19

four causes of high price of raw produce, I, 161, VI, 146, 154

distinction between alterations in value of money and in value of commodities, I, 47–51, 63–4, VI, 348, VII, 203

rise or fall in price, due to change in value of money or to difficulty of production, I, 417, II, 412, VI, 233

magic effect of rise in, on industry, IV, 36

price of labour, I, 46, 95–6, 315, II, 60, 248, 368, V, 38, 244, VI, 145, 234, VII, 8, 10, 199

price of wages, I, li–lii, 94 n., 95 n., 96 notes, 111 n., 118, 145, 303 n., II, 63, 231 n., 411, IV, 22, VI, 223, 241, and cp. IX, 325

price of production, VI, 146, 148, 155

prices: determined by mass of commodities on one side and amount of money multiplied by rapidity of circulation on the other, III, 311

of home commodities, how affected by rise in price of imported corn, VI, 206, 212–13

prices of the mass of commodities, I, 423; mass of prices (Bentham), III, 299, 301, 311; general price of goods, I, 169 & n., 228 n.

Bosanquet's opinion on rise of prices considered, III, 236–44

Price (*cont.*)
fall of prices in 1815, VI, 303–4, 328, 343–5; in 1816, V, 419–20, VII, 38; in 1821–2, V, 72–3, 108, 232, 241, IX, 152
resistance to reducing, VII, 67
see also Corn, price of, Remunerating price, Value
Price, R., M.P. for Herefordshire, V, 472, IX, 119, 121
Price, Dr Richard, IV, 151, 184
An Appeal to the Public, 1772, VIII, 64, 66, 320, 332
Price, Uvedale, *Essay on the Picturesque*, 1794, IX, 121
Principal and factor, Law of, V, 292–3
Prinsep, C. R., translates Say into English, VIII, 315 & n., 374 n.
Prisons:
Ricardo's visits to: as sheriff, VII, 276; in Amsterdam, X, 206; in Bologna, X, 312; dungeons in Venice, X, 308
county gaols, VII, 173, bill relating to, 1822, IX, 198
see also IX, 89, 280
Produce, gross and net, I, 178, 421 n.
net, increased by machinery, gross diminished, I, 388–92; McCulloch disagrees, VIII, 383–4, 387–8, 391–2, 399–400, IX, 13; see also VIII, 377
savings and net produce, IX, 131
see also Income, Revenue
Production:
regulates demand, I, 290–2, IV, 178, V, 434–5, VI, 163–4, VIII, 159, 181, 216, 236–7, 258, 273
quantity of productions, not value of, increased by trade, I, 128, 319
decreasing rate of, I, 98–9
whether discouraged by falling prices, VI, 303–5
bounties on, I, 321–6
Malthus on motives for, IX, 10, 13, 15–16, 19–21, 24–6, and cp. VI, 121
see also Cost of production

Productive powers: of labour, I, 98, VI, 191, of the land, I, 126, II, 321, 336
Productive services, Say's doctrine of, VIII, 228, 277, 379–80, IX, 34–5, 170–2 & n.; Ricardo objects to lumping them together, IX, 172 & n., 188 n.
Productiveness:
of labour, on last land cultivated, II, 276, 336; on the land and in manufactures, IV, 38; increased, and profits, II, 373
of capital, VI, 195; of the last capital employed on the land, IV, 347
of industry, and productiveness of capital, VI, 290–1, 294, 297, 320, 323
Professors, their reward regulated by demand and supply, IV, 189
Professorship of moral philosophy in Edinburgh, VIII, 204–5 & n., 215, IX, 205–6
Profits, I, 110–27, 289–93, IV, 3–41
beginnings of theory, IV, 3–4 & n., VI, xxi; corn-ratio theory, I, xxxi–xxxii, xlviii–xlix, VI, 108, 117
fall with growth of capital and population, I, 120, VI, 148–9, 152; Adam Smith's error, I, 289–90, VIII, 380
fall checked by cheap food, I, 132, II, 221–2, IV, 22, 25–6, 37, VI, 94–5, 104, VIII, 208–9; by improvements in agriculture, II, 157, 276, IV, 11 n., 19 n., 346
regulated by difficulty or facility of procuring food, I, 296, IV, 13 n., VI, 144–5, VIII, 194–5, on no-rent land, I, 126, II, 132, 276–7, 285, 363, IV, 347, VII, 78, X, 409; discussed in relation to Otaheite, VI, 289–90, 292–4, 296, 301–2
depend on low price of corn, I, 112–14, II, 125, VI, 168, 194, 205, 291; different effect if low price due to bounty, I, 323–4; difficulty in case of America, IX, 99–100

Profits (*cont.*)

profits of farmer regulate profits of all other trades, IV, 23–4, VI, 104, 133, 170, 194; Malthus disagrees, VI, 117–18, 139–40, 152, 167, 182, 207

lowered by tax on corn, I, 159–60, 166–7, 205, 233, 239, by restrictions on imports of corn, IV, 237–8, V, 33, 38, VI, 108, 110, 113–14, 116, 203; raised by free imports, IV, 35–6, VIII, 357–8

vary inversely with wages, I, 110, 118, 143, 292–3, II, 165, 264–8, 327, 393, 446–7, VI, 226, VII, 57, 155–6, IX, 99, 179; temporary exception, VII, 199; profits and wages always constitute the same value, I, 115, 403–4 & n., 411, IV, 349; rise of wages the only cause for fall of profits, I, 296, VI, 162

depend on proportions, not quantity, II, 345; on proportion of labour needed to support the labourers, I, 48–9, 125–6, II, 217 & n. 7, 258–9, 266–7, 290, VI, 108, 121, VII, 80–1, VIII, 73, 130, who work on no-rent land, II, 278–9, 284, 336, VIII, 194–5; on proportions of net to gross produce, VI, 204

high when capital scanty, VI, 131, 133

table of rent and profit, IV, 17; discussed, I, xxxii & n., VI, 187, 191, 194, 217, 220, 222,

all rent a transfer from profits, II, 123, 157, 186–8, IV, 18, VI, 173, VII, 282–3; profits always rise when rents fall, IV, 14, 21, 35, 38–9

four causes of rise in price of raw produce, different effects on profits, VI, 146, 148–9, 154, and cp. I, 161

taxes on profits, I, 205–14; tax on wages wholly a tax on profits, I, 215, 226–7

also a cause of value, VIII, 194, but an insignificant one, VIII, 279. See also Value

difference with Malthus explained to Trower, VI, 103–5, and cp. 102;

Profits (*cont.*)

further discussions with Malthus, VI, 108–23, 128–34, 139–42, 144–9, 152–5, 162–3, 167–8, 170–2, 174–5

depend upon the arena for the employment of capital (Malthus), VI, 103 & n., 104, and cp. II, 140, 293

the mighty hinge (Trower), VIII, 267, 273

as 'wages of a particular kind of labour' (J. S. Mill), IX, 385–7

see also Distribution

Profits, rate of:

and rate of interest, I, 297, IV, 233, VII, 199

not altered by variations in value of money, I, 50–1, 65, VII, 156, 159

not affected by foreign trade, I, 133, IV, 25–6, nor by colonial trade, I, 345, VII, 202

tendency to equality of, I, 72, 88–9, 119, 129, 307, 416, VIII, 259, 270, 275, IX, 354 n., 358–9; different in different countries, I, 134, II, 86, VII, 176, 186

depends on ratio of production to necessary consumption, VI, 108, 204

diminishes with cultivation of poorer land, IV, 7 & n., 13–17, VI, 209–10, 213–14

see also Rate of interest

Progress: natural tendency towards, I, 265; uniform progress denied by Malthus, VII, 122; see also VII, 24

Progress of society: value of manufactures falls, of raw produce rises, I, 97, VI, 294; rise in value of corn, IV, 212, 235; rise in price of necessaries and rent, I, 70, 225, 334, VIII, 209, and of labour, I, 93–4, 120; see also Society, state of

Promissory notes, III, 415

Property:

sacredness of, I, 204, V, 69, 501–2; the people not hostile to, V, 500–1, VII, 273, 370, VIII, 59

unequal distribution of, IX, 243–4

Property (*cont.*)

effects of subdivision among children, II, 387, VIII, 225, 377

and alterations in value of money, III, 93, V, 107

pillage and destruction of, in 1816, VII, 45, 49

taxes on transfers of, I, 153–5, V, 291, 315

see also Tax on property

Proportions:

value measured by, II, 101, 138, 253, 267, VIII, 278–9, IX, 355–7

proportion of production to necessary consumption determines rate of profits, VI, 108, VIII, 130, see also I, 48–9, 125–6, II, 344–5

of immediate and accumulated labour in different commodities, IV, 379

of the whole produce distinguished from portions by Malthus, II, 195 n., 196–8 & n.

division of the whole produce by, see Distribution

Protecting duties:

justified in case of commodity subject to peculiar tax, IV, 217–19, V, 256–7, VIII, 158, 172–3, see also VI, 181

on corn, IV, 240–53; protection should be gradually withdrawn, IV, 263, V, 138, 173, VIII, 187, 357, IX, 8, 188, 195, see also V, 34, VIII, 103; fixed duty preferable to graduated, V, 83, 86, 88, 91, VIII, 158, 350, 359

Malthus throws off impartiality, VI, 177–8; his arguments for, answered, IV, 9, 27, 33

Irish protecting duties, V, 57–8, 104, 218–19

see also Corn laws, Countervailing duties, Import duties, Restrictions

Protection, arguments for, answered, V, 51

Corn law of 1815 the worst form of protection, IV, 242, 249, V, 173, 183–4

Protection to Agriculture, IV, 201–66

Providence, bounty of, IV, 31, 221. See also Nature, gifts of

Provident Institution at Bath, VII, 130 & n. See Savings banks

Provisions:

four causes of high price of, I, 161, 217–18, VI, 146–7, see also I, 400–1

advantages of cheap, II, 412–13, see also VI, 269

see also Necessaries

Prudential habits, among the labouring class, I, 106–7, II, 221, 262, V, 303, IX, 261

Public Characters of all Nations, 1823, X, 37 n., 38

Public deposits in Bank of England, IV, 51 & n., 99, VI, 334, 348

Public expenditure, second report from committee on, 1807, IV, 53, 78–81, 83–4, 88 n., 89, 91–4, 96–7, 98 n., 136, 139, VI, 282

Public opinion, as check on government, VI, 263, 311, VII, 238–9, 298–9, 322, 368, VIII, 211

Public works for relief of unemployment, V, 32, VII, 116 & n., 121 & n., XI, x–xi

Puget & Co., bankers, V, xvii n., VII, 347, 359, 363

Puller, Richard, XI, xxviii; see under Ravenstone, Piercy (his pseudonym)

Purves, George (pseudonym of Simon Gray), *All Classes Productive*, 1817, VIII, 38 n., 40; *Gray versus Malthus*, 1818, VIII, 38 n.

Quakers, VI, 180 n., VII, 26, 155 n., IX, 182 n.; Wilkinson family and, X, 36, 41–3, 45; birth of Ricardo's children registered with, X, 41–2 & n.

Quantity regulates value, V, 209, see also V, 170–1, VIII, 278, IX, 249, and under Price, relation to quantity

Quantity theory of money, III, 311. See Money

Quarterly Review:
1816: The Poor (Southey), *Records of the Creation* (Weyland), VII, 247
1817: *Essay on Population* (Sumner), VII, 247
1821: Agricultural Report (Senior), IX, 109 & n., 122
Godwin's *Answer to Malthus*, IX, 147, 154
1822: State of the Currency (Coplestone), IX, 249
see also III, 428–9 n., VII, 173, 289 n., 297, VIII, 17 n., 44
Quatrelles L'Epine, *Le Maréchal de Saint-Arnaud*, X, 325 n.
Queen's trial, see Caroline, Queen
Quillacs hotel at Calais, X, 182–3

R.P. (Ricardo Papers), VI, xliii; contents of, X, 386–91; found in 1930, I, viii–ix
Radcliffe, John, VI, 240 & n.
Radicalism, VIII, 107, 129, 284, 314, 328, IX, 122, 148, 160, 292; radical reform, V, 29, VIII, 146; radical review projected, VIII, 16–17 & n.; see also V, xxii n., VII, 62–3 notes, 375
Rae, John, *Life of Adam Smith*, VI, xxxvii, 326
Rae, William, Lord Advocate, and *The Beacon* affair, IX, 136, 142, 187, 204–5, 207
Raguet, Condy, American free-trader, X, 389
Ramsay, George, *Essay on the Distribution of Wealth*, 1836, IV, 306
Ramsgate, Ricardo family at, 1812 and 1813, VI, 84, 85, 96, X, 136 & n.
Randall, Miss Fanny, X, 278–9
Raoul-Duval, Edgar, I, xi, VI, xxvi, xxvii, VII, 230
Raphael, X, 312, 316
Rapidity of circulation of money, and prices, III, 90, 276–7, 311; ratio of circulation (Trower), IV, 322
Rapperschwyl, X, 238, 243

Rate of interest:
not affected by quantity of money, III, 88–9, 92, 143, 150, 194 n., 341, 374–5, except temporarily, I, 298, V, 445
ultimately regulated by rate of profits, I, 110, 296–7, 300, 363, V, 12 n., 130, 346, VI, 108–9, VII, 199, see also II, 331, IV, 346, V, 269 n.
cannot be controlled by any bank, IV, 233
no criterion of over-issue of notes, III, 26, 88, V, 12
market and legal, I, 296–9, V, 338–47; Bank lends below market rate, I, 364
low rate foreshadows stationary state, IV, 234
fall of, in 1820, VIII, 260
Irish and English rates, V, xvii, VII, 216, 347, 355 & n., 363, 382
Ravenshaw, J. G., East India Director, VIII, 263 & n.
Ravenstone, Piercy (pseudonym of Richard Puller), *A Few Doubts as to...Some Opinions on...Political Economy*, 1821, IX, 45, 59–60, 62–4, XI, xxviii
Raw produce:
causes of rise in price of, I, 400–1, VI, 146, 154, VII, 120, 123, see also I, 93–4, 161, VI, 294; effects of rise, I, 115–18
price of, and manufacturing skill, I, 142, 145–6
taxes on, I, 156–75, 183, 252, VII, 115
farmer's capital consisting of, I, 117
see also Corn, Necessaries
Real, see under Exchange, foreign, Price, absolute, Rent, Value, Wages
Redesdale, Lord, V, 351
Redundancy of currency: use of term, III, 61, VI, 22, 25–6, 34–7 & n.; or cheapness of currency, VI, 36, 41–2
as cause of depreciation, III, 63, 74 n.; and of unfavourable exchange, III, 59–60, 107, 109–10, VI, 62–5, 74, 82, 87, see also VI, 27–8

Redundancy of population, I, 390, 394; and redundancy of capital, II, 277, 339, 426–7; redundancy of both together impossible, VIII, 181, 185, 278

Rees, Abraham, *The Cyclopaedia*, 1819, VIII, 61, 67

Reform of parliament:
speech on Lambton's motion for, V, 112–13, VIII, 367 n., on Lord John Russell's motion, V, 283–9, IX, 288, 292; other speeches on, V, 470, 473–5, 484–6, VIII, 330

discourses written as an exercise, V, 489–512, VII, 302, 317, 329, 332, 349–50, 358, 364, 376–7

correspondence with Trower on, VII, 260–1, 266–7, 272–4, 289–90, 298–9, 309–11, 319–24, 340–5, 365–70, 373–5, 381, VIII, 12–16, IX, 267–8, 292

discussions on, at Easton Grey, VIII, 56–9, 61–3, 68, 75, 129–30

reform and revolution, VIII, 49–50, 146

see also V, 26, 29, 493 n., VII, 270, 360, VIII, 152 n., and under Ballot, Borough system, Elections, Representation, Suffrage

Regent, Prince, V, xvii, 28, VII, 208, 372, 382. See also Wales, Prince of, and George IV

Reichenbach waterfall, X, 254, 257

Reid, Hugh G., *Biographical Notice of McCulloch*, VI, xxii, xxiii

Reid, Irving & Co., X, 85, 88, 89

Reid, Thomas, on perception of external objects, VII, 229, 235

Religious opinion, see Free discussion

Rembrandt, X, 206

Remunerating price, for corn, IV, 210–13, 218, V, 49–50, 84–5, 89, 152, 164–5, 182, 244; for provisions, X, 184

Rent, I, 67–84, IV, 9–10, 13–18
the payment for the original and indestructible powers of the soil, I, 67, IV, 18 n.; includes return from

Rent (*cont.*)
capital inseparable from land, I, 261–2 n., see also II, 202

and diminishing returns, I, 70–2, 74–5, 83–4, IV, 211–12

the difference between the produce of two equal capitals, I, 71, 413 n. 2, II, 134, see also I, 83

last portion of land cultivated pays no rent, I, 71, 74, VI, 173; not necessary for theory of rent, I, 412–13 n., VII, 372, 379, VIII, 4, 57, 149–50; last capital pays no rent, I, 72, 328–9, II, 73, 166–7, 172, IV, 240, VI, 177, 198

not a component part of price, I, 77–8, 329, II, 72–3, see also I, 22–3 n.; not part of cost of production, II, 42–5

a transfer, not a creation, of wealth, I, 197, 399–400, II, 116–17, IV, 18, VII, 120, 282–3, VIII, 182; transferred from profits, II, 123, 157, 186–8, VI, 173; Malthus's error in supposing it clear gain, I, 398, II, 166, 223

rise of, a symptom, never a cause of wealth, I, 77–8; rises with growth of wealth and population, I, 102–3, VI, 294; high rent a symptom of approach to stationary state, VII, 16–17

whether high because of difficulty (Ricardo) or of facility (Malthus) of production, VI, 290, 292–4, 296–7, 301–3, 318–19, see also I, 411

whether rent and fertility rise and fall together, I, 75–7, 402–4, II, 121–3, 211

effects of improvements in agriculture, I, 79–83, 412, II, 118, 134–5, 185, IV, 11 n., 19 n., 41, VI, 190, VIII, 182, 184, 208

rent the effect, not the cause of high price of corn, I, 74, II, 71, IV, 212, IX, 197, see also I, 427

tax on, falls wholly on the landlord, I, 173, 175

Rent (*cont.*)
fall in rent due to cheap imported corn
not an evil, II, 161–2, 173, IV, 41
and quantity of capital employed, I,
78; no greater capital required by
farmer who pays a higher rent, II,
75
as share of produce, I, 49 & n., 83–4
& notes, 334, 402–3 & notes, 411,
II, 195–8, IV, 18 & n., IX, 40; not
governed by proportions, II, 196 n.
as surplus produce, I, 75, II, 122–3,
128, 134, 210–12, IV, 11 n., VI,
204, VIII, 182, 209
origin of theory of, IV, 6–7; relation
between profits and, IV, 14, 21, 38;
table of rent and profit, IV, 17,
VI, 187, 191, 194, 217–18, 220;
theory explained in terms of Malthus's measure of value, II, 124–7
'getting rid of', simplifies theory of
distribution, VIII, 194, and cp. IV,
7–8
corn rent and money rent, I, 82–4,
102–3, 157–8, 177, 210–12, 322,
II, 128, VII, 92
real rent, I, 175, VIII, 209
building rent and ground rent, I, 201–
4, see also I, 174
Adam Smith on, I, 327–37; Malthus's opinions on, I, 398–429
rent of mines, like rent of land, effect,
not cause, of high value of product, I, 85; Adam Smith's contrary view criticised, I, 329–32
mine that pays no rent, I, 87 & n.
see also Distribution
Reply to Mr Say's Letters to Malthus
(anon.), X, 405–10; see also
Cazenove, John
Reporting, parliamentary, V, xxvii–
xxxi; imperfections of, V, 49 n.,
111 n., VIII, 196, 371, IX, 284;
Ricardo misrepresented, V, 81 n.
92 n., 129 n., VIII, 356–9, IX, 164,
175; his own transcripts, V, xxx–
xxxi, 231, 309, 332, XI, xxv; committee on, 1878, V, xxix n.; other
reporting, V, 463 n., VI, 336

Reports of committees: see Agricultural committee, 1821, and
1822; Bank of England charter,
1832; Bank restriction act, 1797;
Bullion Report, 1810; Children
in manufactories, 1816; Corn laws,
1814; Education of the lower
orders, 1816, 1818; Finance, 1819;
Grain, 1814; Police of the Metropolis, 1816; Poor laws, 1817; Public
expenditure, 1807; Resumption of
cash payments, 1819; Roman
Catholics, laws on, 1816
Representation of the people:
a necessary reform, V, 286–9, 470,
475, 484, 498–9, VII, 368; household suffrage sufficient, V, 473,
485, VII, 273 & n.; universal
suffrage going too far, V, 29, 502,
VII, 261, 270, 360, 369–70, VIII,
129
Whigs and, VIII, 62, 68, 335–6
see also VII, 321, VIII, 50, 52–3, 148,
227, and under Reform
Republican, The, Richard Carlile's
paper, XI, xxi–xxiv
Restrictions:
on importation of corn: effect on profits, IV, 16 n., 237–8, VI, 108–10,
113–14, 116, 119, 146; effect on
value of money, II, 154–6; con-
flicting interests of landlords and
manufacturers, I, 312–13, II, 199–
200; sudden removal ruinous to
farmers, VIII, 103; see also Corn
laws
on trade: justified to restore natural
relation, VIII, 173; petition against,
V, 42–6; see also VIII, 82, and
Protecting duties
Resumption of cash payments:
Horner's motion for Committee,
1816, IV, 51
Peel's resolutions, 1819, V, 7–8, 18,
490; Ricardo's speech on, V, 9–17,
VIII, 31–2 & n.
committees on, 1819, V, 350–70, see
also IV, 226, V, 44, 522, VIII,
19–21, 23

Resumption of cash payments (*cont.*)
Ricardo's evidence to Commons' committee, V, 371–415, to Lords' committee, V, 416–57
Lords' reports, IV, 227, V, 13–14, 354, 356, 361–4, 367, 370, 403, VIII, 27, 36; Commons' reports, V, 9–10, 12, 14–15, 355–60, 366, 370, VIII, 21, 36–7, see also V, 151; Ricardo's speech on, V, 2–3; Bank directors on, IV, 267–70; merchants' petition against, VIII, 29 n.
cash payments bill (Peel's bill), V, 91; R.'s speeches on, V, 91–100, 105–8, 110; see also VIII, 368
Baring's loans to France and, V, 352 n., VII, 292 n.
attacks on: Cobbett's, VIII, 74 & n., IX, 106 & n., 123 & n., 140–1 & n., 153, 166–7, 176, 250, 267 n.; City opposed to, VIII, 29 & n., 31–2 & n.; Rothschild pressing for deferment, X, 89–90 & n.
Bank opposed to, VII, 292 & n., VIII, 20–1, 134–5 & n.; advised to reduce issues gradually and sell bullion, V, 13, 40, 61–2, 105, 206–7, 518; advice ignored, V, 76, 106, 110, 135–6, 165, 255, 312, 519; their mismanagement, IX, 15, 22, 140–1, 202; cash payments resumed too soon, V, 135, 140–1, 311–12
effect on prices: Ricardo estimates 3% if ingot plan adopted, V, 10–11, 16, 105, 527; 6 or 7% if coin used, 206, 255; later allows 5%, 94, 127, 134, 311, 385, and then 10%, IV, 228, 259 n., V, 142, 150, 165, 204, 255, VIII, 350, IX, 152; Baring says 25%, V, 45–6, 72, 77; Attwood, 30%, 105, 312; Palmer, 50%, 520, 527; others, up to 100%, 252; see also V, 94, 127, 134–6, 209, 312–13, 353, 385, VIII, 186

Resumption (*cont.*)
effect on price of corn, IV, 222–35, 262, on taxation, V, 386, 525
Western's motions: June, 1822, V, 198, 202, 210, 212–18, IX, 202, 207; July, 1822, V, 223–31, Ricardo's speech on, 231–45; in 1823, V, 309, R.'s speech on, 309–21, see also V, xxx & n.
'the Ricardo System', V, 92, VIII, 5, 20, 361
see also III, 427, VIII, 38, 150, and under Ingot plan, Peel's bill
Revenue:
gross and net, I, 347–51, 393–4
labour supported from gross, I, 388, 390, II, 236, but sometimes receives part of net, I, 348 n., 425, II, 381, VII, 378–9, VIII, 311; see also Wages
taxes paid from net, I, 421–4
proportion of, consumed and reproduced, III, 329
pecuniary and real, III, 280–3
capital and revenue, III, 281–2, VII, 121, VIII, 319–20, XI, xi
see also Income, Net revenue, Produce
Revolution:
Malthus's fears of, VIII, 107–8, 129
and Reform, V, 495, 497, VIII, 49–50, 146
revolution in Naples, V, xxii, VIII, 363
see French revolution
Revulsions of trade, I, 265–6; see also VIII, 275
Rhine, X, 215–22, 233–7; swim in, VII, 163
Riazanov, D., X, 382–3
Ricardo, Abigail (D.R.'s mother), *née* Delvalle, X, 24–8; drives David from home, 37–8; her children, 54–61
Ricardo, Abigail (D.R.'s sister), X, 58; visit to Gatcomb, VII, 55, 66; bequest to, X, 105; see also X, 133, 135

Ricardo, Abraham (D.R.'s father), X, 19–26; settles in England, X, 3, 20–1; on Stock Exchange, 3, 21, 23; naturalized, 22; obtains 'Jew brokership', 22; marriage and children, 24, 54–61; his homes, 24–5; sends David to Holland, 3, 31; estrangement from him, 37–8; reconciliation, 38; his will, 25–6; see also VI, 49 n., 56, X, 4–5, 53, 67, 75 n., 104

Ricardo, Abraham (D.R.'s brother), X, 55

Ricardo, Benjamin (D.R.'s brother), X, 59, 105

Ricardo, Birtha (D.R.'s daughter), X, 64; Maria Edgeworth on, X, 168, 170–1; goes on Continental tour, X, 177, 209, 222–3, 235, 237, 256–7, 284, 305, 327, 330–1, 352; see also VIII, 232, 284, IX, 45, 240, 296, X, 105

Ricardo, Daniel (D.R.'s brother), see Ricardo, Francis

Ricardo, David:

birth and childhood, X, 3–4, 29–30; at school in Holland, X, 30–3; employed on Stock Exchange at fourteen, X, 4; studies science with a friend, X, 6, 34–5; speaks Dutch, X, 194, 209, 214, and a little French, VII, 161, 165, IX, 213, X, 117, 181, 220, 255, 271, 333; his education 'neglected', VII, 190, 196, 305; difficulty of writing, VI, 314–15, 326, VII, 53, 65–6, 83, 305, 327, VIII, 55, 141; worst of memories, VIII, 7, 295, see also IX, 45

Jewish background, X, 16–32, 37–9; Unitarian connections, X, 39–41; doubts on taking sacrament as Sheriff, X, 42–3

marries at twenty-one, X, 5, 36–8; estranged from parents, X, 37–9; his children, X, 61–4; visits Osman at Cambridge, X, 136–40; opposes Fanny's marriage, VIII, 325, 334–5, X, 161–4; his fiftieth

Ricardo, David (cont.)

birthday, X, 164 5; his grandchildren, VII, 89, 177, 223, VIII, 329

homes in London: in childhood, X, 29–30, at Mile End, VI, xix, 47, 53 & n., X, 47, 118, Upper Brook Street, VI, facing p. 1, 52–3 & n., 59, 82, VII, 1, 13, 17–18, X, 48, 105, 336 n.; his counting-house, VI, 19, X, 74; country house, see Gatcomb Park

Clubs, X, 49–51; Geological Society, VI, xxx, 205–6, X, 6, 144; King of Clubs, VI, 87 & n., 220, VIII, 18, IX, 151; Brooks's, VIII, 28 & n., 163; Political Economy Club, VIII, 381, IX, 9–10, 36 n., 113, 158–9 & n., 172–3 & n., 264–5, 312

early visits to Holland, X, 33, 205, 207, see also IX, 210; relatives there, X, 201–2 & n.; proposed visit to Paris in 1803, X, 117; visit to Continent in 1817, VII, 160–5, 167–9; tour with family in 1822, IX, 209–29, 234–51, X, 175–352; a bad traveller, VII, 170, X, 247, 345

on the Stock Exchange, X, 6, 67–74, 123–4; loan contractor, X, 75–91; presentation from subscribers, X, 125–8. See also Loans

landed property, X, 95–9, see also V, 167, VII, 187 n., 230, VIII, 238, IX, 263; other investments, X, 99–102, see also VIII, 35, IX, 203–4; total estate, X, 102–4; coat-of-arms, VI, xli, 20 n., X, 54

Sheriff of Gloucestershire (1818), VII, 221, 223–4, 251–2, 255–6, 258–9, 276–8, 283 & n., 296, 372, VIII, 134, X, 42–3, XI, xii

speaks at Bank Court, V, 461–7, VI, 335–6, 341, 343, 346, VII, 19 & n.; enjoys attacks on the Bank, VI, 268–9

speaks at East India Company meetings, V, 475–8; refuses directorship, VIII, 250–4, 262–3, 281–2, 292

Ricardo, David (*cont.*)

enters parliament, V, xiii–xix, X, 11. See Parliament, seat in

finds speaking in public difficult, VI, 335, 343, 346, VII, 11, 381–2, VIII, 21, 38–9, 47 n., 142, 357, IX, 198, X, 51; but not in conversation, VII, 65, IX, 230, X, 168–9, 170; defect of hearing, VIII, 253, X, 299

his modesty, I, xix, VI, 241, 331, VII, 190, VIII, 60 n., X, 13; shyness, IX, 235, X, 140; no romance in his composition, X, 282; 'imposed upon by everyone', X, 244, 343, see also X, 117

alleged interested motives, V, 81–2, 87, 471, VIII, 147–8, see also VII, 5; Western's insinuations answered, V, 317–18, 526–7

his candour and liberality, VIII, 346, IX, 230; perfect sincerity and love of truth, II, 12, and cp. X, 169; no affectation or pretension, V, xxxii

his principles of toleration, IX, 278; supports Catholic emancipation, VIII, 350–1, 369, and free religious discussion, V, 280, 324–31, XI, xxii; opposed to Six Acts, VIII, 146–7; deplores persecution of the Queen, VIII, 299, 303–4; votes for liberal causes, V, xxii; arouses hostile feelings in County, VIII, 156–7 n. See also Reform of parliament

supports Chrestomathic School, VI, xxix–xxxi, 112–13, VII, 184, 190, 198, VIII, 191, 197–9, and Brougham's Infant school, but not school feeding, VII, 359–60, 363, 371; establishes school for the poor in Minchinhampton, VII, 45 & n., IX, 328–9

and Savings banks: Tetbury, VII, 26, 187 n., 220, City of London, VII, 34 & n., 46, 49–50 & n., Westminster, VII, 47, 49–50

views on public and private charity, I, 73 & n., VII, 248–9, see also I, 107, IX, 223

Ricardo, David (*cont.*)

on shooting as a sport, VII, 318–19, see also VI, 300, VII, 309; 'the barbarities of fishing and hunting', V, 122

his cautious driving, X, 168, and cp. VII, 361, VIII, 231–2; his horses too well fed and too little worked, VII, 365

not a particle of a farmer, VII, 207, see also VI, 150; as a gentleman does not reduce wages, VIII, 307

first reads *Wealth of Nations*, VII, 246, X, 7, 35–6; re-reads, VII, 88–9, 100, 111, 115; see also VII, 2

walks with Mill, VI, xxxiv, VII, 263, 266, 277, VIII, 7, 8, 10, IX, 210, X, 264; with Trower, VII, 147, 268, 273, 275; with Bentham, VII, 277, VIII, 191

his Benthamite principles, V, xix, VI, xxviii, IX, 52, 239, 259

'the Ricardo school', Sismondi on, VIII, 376–7 & notes

his 'peculiar opinions', VI, 178–9, 188, VII, 203, 214; 'paradoxical', II, 60, VII, 215, 222; 'new and unusual language', I, 19, II, 191–2, 194, see also II, 64, 117, 119, 126, 166, 331, VIII, 331, IX, 283

'abundantly theoretical', V, xxxiii, IV, 352, V, xxv, 93, 128 n., 270, see also V, 46, 109, 266, XI, xv; too theoretical, Malthus too practical, VI, 295; 'a visionary', VIII, 197; imagines strong cases, VIII, 184, 235, and cp. I, 121, IV, 312; 'dropped from another planet', V, 56, 85; 'the Oracle', V, 40, IX, 123 n., 141 n.

his library, X, 399–402; reads Bayle's *Dictionary*, VII, 190, 196, VIII, 49, Berkeley, VII, 277–8, Clarendon, IX, 45, History of Ireland, VIII, 49, Locke and Hume, VII, 197, 205–6, 229, books of travel, VII, 189, 259, IX, 218, Turgot and Montesquieu, VII, 382–3, Warburton and Beattie, VII, 277–8

Ricardo, David (*cont.*)
portraits and appearance, X, 51–3,
frontispieces to vols. V, VIII, IX
illness and death, IX, 388–92, X, 12;
his will, X, 104–6; his tomb, X, 12
Brougham's sketch, V, xxxii–xxxiv;
Cobbett on, V, 40–1 n., VIII,
74–5 n.; Mrs Grote on, IX, 288 n.;
J. Hume and Huskisson on, V,
332; Mallet's sketch, VIII, 152 n.,
X, 51–2; Malthus on, II, 12; Sis-
mondi on, IX, 244 n.
obituaries and biographies: *Annual
Biography and Obituary* (Moses
Ricardo), X, 1–15; *Encyclopaedia
Britannica* (McCulloch), X, 370;
General Biographical Dictionary
(John Gorton), X, 38, 39 n.;
Gentleman's Magazine, X, 103;
Globe and Traveller, IV, 7; *A
Centenary Estimate* (Hollander),
X, 17 n., 18 & n., 20, 37 n., 81 n.;
Memoir (McCulloch), in succes-
sive versions, X, 369–70, 375;
Penny Encyclopædia (G. R. Porter),
X, 37 n.; *Public Characters*, X,
37 n.; *Scotsman* (McCulloch), X,
369; *Sunday Times*, X, 37 n., 40,
51; *Tablettes Universelles* (Say),
X, 57 n., 103 n.; *The Times*, X, 20;
Windsor Express (James Hitch-
ings), VI, xxxv n.

WORKS

Absolute Value and Exchangeable
Value, 1823, IV, 357–412; see also
IV, 308, X, 392 n.
Defence of the Plan of Voting by
Ballot, 1824, V, 487–94, 504–12;
see also VII, 302 n., 327 n., X,
368
Economical and Secure Currency, 1816,
IV, 43–141. See below, *Proposals
for an Economical and Secure
Currency*
*Essay on the Influence of a low Price of
Corn on the Profits of Stock* ('Essay
on Profits'), 1815, IV, 1–41, VI,
178–9 & n.

Works, *Essay* (*cont.*)
relation to *Principles*, I, xiii, xxx–
xxxiv, lvi n., 69 n., 81 n., 271 n.,
IV, 8, see also I, lvii, 268 n., VI,
242 n., 249
draft shown to Trower, VI, 102,
103–4, 183–4; Malthus sees MS,
VI, 176, 182–3, 187, 216
Mackintosh on, VI, 182; Mill and
Say think it obscure, VI, 249, 270,
338–9; McCulloch on, VII, 105 n.
West's pamphlet and, IV, 4–6, VI,
179–80
editions and translations, IV, 8, X,
360–1, 371, 375–6, 378, 380, 381–5;
table of corresponding pages, IV,
419
see also IV, 14 n., 26 n., X, 400
Fragments on Torrens, 1818, IV,
303–18; see also VII, 316 n., 372,
376–7, X, 392 n., 397
Funding System, article in *Supplement to Encyclopaedia Britannica*,
1820, IV, 143–200
invitation to contribute, VIII, 54,
72, 78; instructions from Mill, VIII,
57–61, 66–7, 83, 105–6; writing
of, VIII, 75–9, 141, 144, 188; correspondence with Place on, VIII,
83 & n., 118–25; McCulloch on,
VIII, 137–8; Trower on, VIII,
319–20, 332; question of payment, VIII, 240, 242–3 & n.
editions and translations, X, 368,
375–6, 378, 381; table of corresponding pages, IV, 421
see also VI, xxxv, xxxvi, VIII, 69,
81, 127, 131, 238, 262, 307, X, 355
High Price of Bullion, The, 1810, III,
47–127, note on, III, 5–12
reviewed by Malthus, III, 11, 99 n.,
VI, 24 n.; Bosanquet on, III, 207,
215, 229 n., 248; sent to Perceval,
VI, 43 n.
ed. 3 with Additions, III, 8; ed. 4
with Appendix, III, 11, V, 351;
editions and translations, X, 356–9,
368, 371, 374–6, 378, 380–5; table
of corresponding pages, III, 435–6

Works, *High Price* (*cont.*)
see also III, 176 n., 248 n., VI, xxxiv–xxxv, 4, 6, 7, 11, 22, 41, 165, 203, VII, 31 n., X, 390, 400

Journal of a Tour on the Continent, X, 175–352; see also VI, xviii, IX, 208, 209 & n., X, 371

Letters to McCulloch, ed. Hollander, X, 372–3; see also I, xxxvii, VI, xx n., xxiii, VII, 37 n., 93 n., VIII, 173 n., IX, 320 n., 345 n., X, 387

Letters to Malthus, ed. Bonar, X, 370, 383; letters misdated, IV, 3 n., VI, xxi & n., 226 n., VII, 135, 148; see also VI, xx, VII, 201 n.

Letters to Trower, ed. Bonar and Hollander, X, 371; see also I, vii, III, 36 n., 406, V, 142 n., VI, xxiv–xxv, IX, 71 n., 166 n., 174 n., 278 n.

Letters written during a Tour on the Continent, 1891, X, 180, 371. See *Journal of a Tour*

Minor Papers on the Currency Question, ed. Hollander, X, 373–4; see also III, 9 n., 345, 380 n., 413, IV, 274 n., 308, 326, VI, xvii n., 1, IX, 31 n., 168 n., 331 n., 358, X, 387, 389, 401, XI, xvii n.

Note on Prices and Taxation, 1821, IV, 319–22; see also I, 214 n.

Notes on Bentham's *Sur les Prix*, 1810–11, III, 259–341; see also III, 427, IV, 7 n., VI, xxviii n., 14–20

Notes on Blake's *Observations on the Expenditure of Government*, 1823, IV, 323–52, see also X, 400; review of Blake's *Observations*, IV, 325–6, 353–6, see also X, 392 n.

Notes on the Bullion Report, 1810, III, 343–78, see also III, 10 n., 427, X, 387

Notes on McCulloch's article 'Exchange', VIII, 85–93

Notes on Malthus's 'Principles of Political Economy', II, 1–463
first reading of Malthus, VIII, 179–85, annotated, VIII, 207–9, 212, 215–17, 228–30, 283, 296, 301; two notes sent to Trower, VIII, 304–7,

Works, *Notes on Malthus* (*cont.*)
323; MS sent to McCulloch, VIII, 298–9, 318, 325, 333–4, 338–40; seen by Malthus, VIII, 308, 314–15, 334, 336, 349, 373, by Trower, VIII, 393, again by McCulloch, IX, 135, 138, 148

publication advised by Mill, VIII, 292–3, 296, 333, by Trower, VIII, 320–1, 345–6, 395; his own doubts, VIII, 297–8, 305, 342, and McCulloch's, VIII, 340, XI, xiii

discovery of MS, II, xv–xvi, X, 387; first publication, II, xv–xviii, 118 n., 231 n., X, 373

see also I, liii, lv, lvii, lix, 49 n., 83 n., 87 n., 349 n., VIII, 312, 352, 363, 382, IX, 1

Notes on Trotter's *Principles of Currency and Exchange*, 1810, III, 379–403; see also X, 387

Observations on…an Article in the 'Edinburgh Review', 1811, III, 99 n., 99–127; see also X, 358–9

Observations on Parliamentary Reform, V, 487–503; see also VII, 302 n., 332 & n., 336, 376, X, 368, 375, 391

Observations on Trower's Notes on Trotter, 1811, III, 405–9

Observations on Vansittart's Propositions respecting Money, 1811, III, 411–23; see also X, 387

Plan for a National Bank, 1824, IV, 271–300
first outlined in 1815, IV, 45–6, 114; written in 1823, IX, 325–6, 329, 331, 334; published posthumously in 1824, IV, 272, XI, xxvi; MS of, IV, 274, X, 391; editions and translations, X, 367; pirated edition, XI, xxix; table of corresponding pages, IV, 422; see also I, 361–3, IV, 359–60, 415, VI, 165–6, X, 15, 402

The Price of Gold (*Morning Chronicle*, 1809), III, 13–46; note on, III, 3–6; editions, X, 373, 385; see also III, 82 n., 88 n., X, 7–8, 355, 390

Works (*cont.*)

Principles of Political Economy, 1817: writing of, I, xiii–xix; first stages, VI, 262–3, 309, 315–16, 321; instructions from Mill, 330, 339–40, VII, 60; expects to be stopped by theory of price, VI, 348–9; problem of value, VII, 20, 71–2, 82–4; work suspended, VII, 36, 53, resumed, 65–6; MS of first part of *Principles* sent to Mill, 73, 82, 85–6; writing the section on taxation, VII, 84, 87–8, 91–2, 115 & n., Mill's comments, 106–8; re-reads Adam Smith, Say and Malthus, VII, 88–9, 100–1, 115, 120; last section sent to Mill, 111–12, and one chapter to Malthus, 137, 139–40, 145, 176, 179

arrangement and division into chapters, I, xxii–xxx, see also X, 403–4; printing, VII, 140, 147; cancels, X, 403–4, XI, xxx; publication, I, xix, VII, 148

Malthus's first comments, VII, 176, 312

reviews: McCulloch in *Edinburgh Review*, VII, 278–82, 285–6, 288, 289 n., 291, 295, 296–7, gets off first edition, VII, 312, 337, 351, VIII, 152 n., see also VI, xxi, VII, 319; *Scotsman*, VII, 219–20 n.; *British Review*, I, 60–1 n., VII, 219–20 & n., 222, 231, 235, 256, 259, 289 n.; *Blackwood's Magazine*, VII, 316 & n., 326, 332, 362

Torrens' 'Strictures' on, in *Edinburgh Magazine*, VII, 179 & n., 315–16 & notes, 338, answered by McCulloch, VII, 315–16 & n.; Ricardo's lost reply, VII, 316 n., 364, 376, see also IV, 305–8, 315–18

notes on, by Place, VII, 179 n., 183 & n., 189; Say's notes on, see below, French translation

see also II, 171 n., VI, xviii n., xxi, VII, 144 n., 155 n., 227, VIII, 173 n.

Works, *Principles* (*cont.*)

ed. 2, I, xlix–liii, VII, 162, 327–9, 370, 383 & n., VIII, 11; changes: in chapter on value, I, xxxvii–xliii, VII, 331, 333, on corn importation, I, 267, 318, 428–9, VII, 271, 354, on currency, I, 353–4, 356–61, VII, 353, on durabilities of capitals, I, 31, 53, 58, 60–1, VII, 338, 377, on the Irish labourer, I, 100 n., VII, 334, on no-rent land, I, 413 n., VII, 371–2, 379, on rent, I, 412–13, VII, 282–3, on taxation, I, 152, 242, VII, 280–1, 286, 334, 337–8, 353, on Torrens, I, 96–7 n., 271, VII, 179–80; see also VII, 358 n., VIII, 10, 37, 150, 221, 237, X, 377

ed. 3, I, liii–lx, VIII, 315, see also, 333, 346; McCulloch's suggestions, VIII, 341; rewriting of chapter on value, I, xxxvii–xlix, VIII, 194, 229, 261, 279–80, 283–4, 344; alterations in: due to Malthus, I, 35 n., 43 n., 47 n., 49 n., 81 n., 83 n., 335, 404, II, 64, 118, 121–3, 197 n., IX, 178, due to Say, I, 249 n., 264 n., 279–85, 287–8 n., 348 n., 349 n., II, 382, VII, 378–9, VIII, 301 & n., 315, see also 344–5; new chapter on machinery, I, lvii–lx, 386–97, VIII, 373 & n., 377, 381–92

printing, VIII, 333, 342; publication delayed, I, liv, VIII, 341 & n., 379; Say on, IX, 31

'becoming a text-book', VII, 309, VIII, 82; read by few (Mallet), VIII, 152 n.; not many converts, VIII, 227, 376, 377 n.; not understood in France, VIII, 224 & n.

list of editions and translations, X, 362–5, 368, 371–2, 374–8, 379–85, see also 355–6; table of corresponding pages, I, 443–7

see also I, 426 n., II, vii, IV, 146, 203 n., 272, 320, V, 362, VII, 8 n., 228 n., VIII, 71, 94, 320, IX, 46, 223

Works, *Principles* (*cont.*)

French translation by F. S. Constancio, with Notes by J. B. Say, VII, 361 & n., 362, 364, 370–1, 375, 378–9, VIII, 4, 136; sales of, VIII, 225, 227; see also I, l, 348–9, 413, II, x, 382, VIII, 5, X, 374–6, XI, xxix

Proposals for an Economical and Secure Currency, 1816, IV, 43–141

Grenfell suggests writing, VI, 241–2, sends books and papers, 257–61, 265–7, 275–8, 281–5, 288; reads MS, 285–7, urges publication, 305, 313

doubts whether to publish, VI, 294–5, 312–13; Malthus comments on MS, VI, 298–303, 315; Mill's advice, VI, 324, 329–34, 337–8, VII, 4–5, 7

MS revised, VI, 335, 343, 347–8; publication, VII, 10, 13–15, 16, 19; ed. 2, VII, 24–5; payment for, VI, xxxv, VII, 14; reviewed by McCulloch, VII, 353–4, VIII, 1–3, 5, 10, 20, 23–4

passages quoted, in *Principles*, I, 356–61, VII, 353, VIII, 4–5, 20, in speech, V, 205–6

list of editions and translations, X, 361–2, 367–8, 371, 375–6, 378, 380–1, 383–5; table of corresponding pages, IV, 420

see also III, 11, IV, 272, 415, V, 351, 355, 364, 390, 463 n., 465 n., VI, xxxiii, 342, VII, 39, 42, VIII, 36

Protection to Agriculture, 1822, IV, 201–70

a sort of minority report, IV, 203, welcomed by the government, IV, 204–5, V, 155; attacked by Attwood, V, 162–4; reviewed in *Scotsman*, IX, 183

editions and translations, IV, 205, X, 365–6, 378, 381, 383, 385; table of corresponding pages, IV, 421–2

see also IV, 326 n., 361, V, xxv, IX, 166 n., 181 n., 203 n., X, 118

Works (*cont.*)

Reply to Mr. Bosanquet, 1811, III, 155–256, note on, III, 10–12

reviewed by Malthus, III, 11, 99 n.; Mushet on, III, 169 n.

editions and translations, X, 359–60, 368, 371, 375–6, 380, 381, 385; table of corresponding pages, III, 436–7

see also III, 169 n., 427, IV, 320, V, 371–2, VI, 14, VII, 384, VIII, 91 n., 126, 140, 340, X, 358, 400

Speech on Mr. Western's Motion, 1822, V, 198 n., X, 366–7

Three Letters on the Bullion Report (*Morning Chronicle* 1810), III, 129–53, note on, III, 8–9; editions, X, 373; see also X, 355

Two Papers on Parliamentary Reform, V, 487–512

letter to a newspaper on Peel's bill (1821–2), V, 515–21, X, 392 n.

commonplace books, X, 393–8; see also IV, 307 & n., 308, 315

lost notes and papers: on Grey's speech on reform, VIII, 6 & n., 8–9; importation of corn, VIII, 199; price of gold, III, 33–4 & n; profits, VI, 102–4, see also I, xxxi, IV, 3–4; reply to Torrens on value, VII, 316 n., 360, 364, 372, 376–8, VIII, 8, see also IV, 307–8; on Say's *Letters to Malthus*, VIII, 284, 292, 298, 301 & n., 315, 341 & n., 344–5, see also VIII, 305, X, 405

mistaken attributions to, VIII, 165 n., 173 n.

Ricardo's books and pamphlets, numbers printed, X, 356–75

Ricardo Memorial lectures, 1824, VI, xxii, IX, 301 n., 391 & n., X, 370

Ricardo Papers (*R.P.*), VI, xliii; contents of, X, 386–91; discovery of, I, viii–ix

Ricardo Tracts, in Goldsmiths' Library, X, 400, 402

Ricardo, David (D.R.'s son), X, 62–3;
at Cambridge, VIII, 284, 293,
297, IX, 44, X, 136; inherits Gatcomb Park, X, 105; see also VI,
128, 239–40, 243, 255, VII, 52,
VIII, 241–2, X, 50, 118, 242, 259,
265

Ricardo, David Israel (D.R.'s uncle),
X, 19 & n., 30

Ricardo, Esther (D.R.'s sister), first
wife of W. A. Wilkinson, X, 59–
60; visits Gatcomb, VII, 61, 66;
her marriage, VII, 325, 330; death,
IX, 279, 296–7; letter from, X,
133–5; see also VI, 264, 349, VII,
6–7, 55, X, 44, 105

Ricardo, Fanny (D.R.'s daughter),
wife of Edward Austin, X, 62; her
marriage, VII, 324–5, X, 161–4,
Ricardo opposed to, VII, 330, 334–
5, 350; her death, VIII, 183 & n.;
bequest to, X, 105 n.; see also
VII, 55, 107, 136, X, 54

Ricardo, Fanny, wife of Moses,
D.R.'s brother, née Wilkinson, X,
44, 56; leaves her father's home, X,
121–2; bequest to, X, 106; see also
VI, 323, 332, VII, 7, X, 111, 209,
225, 336

Ricardo, Francis or Daniel (D.R.'s
brother), X, 58–9; as Ricardo's
clerk, X, 74; executor of his will,
106; bequest to, 105; see also VI,
112 n., VII, 14, IX, 45, X, 115–17,
336, 347

Ricardo, Frank, (D.R.'s grandson),
X, ix, 61, 64

Ricardo, Frank, jun. (D.R.'s great-
grandson), discovers Ricardo
papers, I, viii, xi, II, xv, VI, xx,
xxiii, X, 64, 386–7; see also X,
17 n., 52 n., 54 n., 127

Ricardo, Hannah (D.R.'s grand-
mother), née Abaz, X, 19, XI, xxix

Ricardo, Hannah (D.R.'s sister), wife
of David Samuda, X, 56; visits
Gatcomb, VII, 66, IX, 306; death
of her two children, VII, 239–40;
bequest to, X, 105

Ricardo, Hannah (D.R.'s cousin), X,
106

Ricardo, Harriett (D.R.'s daughter-in-
law), wife of Osman, née Mallory,
VII, 144 n., 186 & n., X, 61;
Ricardo's 'own dear child', X,
348–9, 352; death of infant, VII,
268–9, 279, 284; loses her mother,
IX, 263, X, 264–5, 268, 335, 355;
Maria Edgeworth on, IX, 230,
X, 168, 171; Mill's affection for,
VII, 182, 318, 330, 335, VIII, 11,
50–2, 263, IX, 114–15 & n., 118,
120; see also VII, 306, 328, VIII,
48–9, 183, 284, IX, 125, 209, X,
179

Ricardo, Henrietta (D.R.'s daughter),
wife of Thomas Clutterbuck, X,
62, VI, 100; her children, VII, 89,
101, 109, 113, 116, 307, 315, VIII,
329, IX, 234, X, 259, 280; moves
from Bath to Hardenhuish, IX,
296, 328, X, 315; bequest to, X,
105; see also VI, 49, 51, 125, 219,
312, 324, VII, 15, 92, 136, 262,
VIII, 56, 183, 213, 332, 400 n.,
IX, 14, 44, 144, 250, 262, 264, X,
136, 209–10, 219, 253

Ricardo, Henry David (D.R.'s grandson), X, 63

Ricardo, Lt.-Col. Henry George
(D.R.'s great-grandson), of Gatcomb, X, 63; see also X, ix, 50,
53 n., 54 n., 399, 400 n.

Ricardo, Isaac (D.R.'s brother), X,
56

Ricardo, Jacob (D.R.'s brother), X,
57–8; and French Rentes, X, 101;
letters, 129–32; bequest to, 105;
see also VI, 112 n., X, 23, 25 n.,
242, 390

Ricardo, John Lewis (D.R.'s nephew),
X, 58; Anatomy of the Navigation
Laws, X, 58; see also IV, 147

Ricardo, Joseph (D.R.'s brother), X,
54–5; bequest to, X, 105; see also
VII, 15, X, 25 n.

Ricardo, Joseph (son of David Israel),
X, 32

Ricardo, Joseph (D.R.'s cousin), X, 106

Ricardo, Joseph Israel (D.R.'s grandfather), X, 19, XI, xxix

Ricardo, Mary (D.R.'s daughter), X, 63; studies political economy, IX, 114, 118, 125, 331; Maria Edgeworth on, X, 168, 170–1; on the Continental tour, X, 177, 182, 189, 194, 196, 198, 200–1, 205, 209, 211–12, 217–18, 231, 234, 237, 240, 249, 251, 255–6, 262, 264, 269, 284, 286, 293, 295–7, 305, 318, 327, 331, 352; bequest to, X, 105; see also VIII, 232, 284, IX, 45, 219, 240, 296

Ricardo, Mortimer (D.R.'s son), X, 63–4; at Eton, X, 267, 389; at Cambridge, X, 136; estates left to, X, 105; see also VI, 240, IX, 44–5, 296, X, 164, 229, 242, 266, 336

Ricardo, Moses (D.R.'s brother), X, 56

at school in Holland, X, 33

as doctor, VII, 294, 330, 350, 357, 360, 376, 382, IX, 279, X, 44, 47, 118

visits Gatcomb, IX, 375–6

his ill-health, VII, 294, 296, 305, 309, X, 225, 229, 315, 336, 342

bequest to, X, 105–6

author of *Memoir of David Ricardo*, III, 3, X, 14–15; intended to write a fuller biography, X, 16; publishes *National Bank*, IV, 273, 275 n.

see also VI, 84, VII, 14, 80, 302, 315, VIII, 10, 84, IX, 391, X, 35 n., 51

Ricardo, Moses Israel (D.R.'s uncle), X, 19, 30, 32

Ricardo, Osman (D.R.'s son), X, 61; at Cambridge, X, 136–40; his marriage, VII, 144 n.; at Hyde, VII, 182 & n., 186 & n., 190–1; moves to Bromesberrow Place, VIII, 48–9; letters to, IX, 209, X, 179, 198; in D.R.'s will, X, 104–5, 106, 127; and Ricardo Tracts, X, 400–1; see also VI, 10 n., 13, 219,

Ricardo, O. (*cont.*)
VII, 55, 262, 293, 299 n., 303, 361, VIII, 263, 332, 400 n., IX, 13–14, 44, 103, 122 n., 296, X, 97, 109, 112, 118, 168, 259–60, 344, 386

Ricardo, Percy (D.R.'s grandson), X, 24 n., 54, 59

Ricardo, Peter W., X, ix, 53, 400 n.

Ricardo, Priscilla Ann (D.R.'s wife), *née* Wilkinson, X, 36 & n.

marriage displeases relations, X, 38

her father's legacy, 45, 118

attends Quaker meetings, 41–2, 45–6

her child noticed by Princess, 112

insists on move to West End, VI, 52, 93, X, 48

school at Minchinhampton, X, 169

'her warmth and energy on trifling occasions', X, 115–17

her kindness, VII, 7–8, X, 168

thinks Ricardo always imposed on, X, 343

reckons Mill immoderate, VII, 303

her letters from the Continent, X, 209–10, 241–2

carried over a mountain, X, 249, 251, 283–6, 326

portrait by Heaphy, X, facing p. 1, 53

Ricardo's bequest to, X, 105, and cp. 46

see also VI, 47, 90, 115–16, 118, 323, VII, 17, 72, 84, 89, 186, 190, 201, 324–5, 332, VIII, 58, 183, 308, 310, 400, IX, 116, 213, 230, 233, 296, 326–8, 379, 391, X, 61, 64, 147–8, 188, 198, 214, 234, 237, 258–9, 295–6, 299, 324, 328–9, 340–1, 344, 346

Ricardo, Priscilla (Sylla), D.R.'s daughter, wife of Anthony Austin, X, 62; her marriage, VII, 12–13 & n., 19–30, X, 163; her children, VII, 136–7, 139, VIII, 329, 400 n.; her cheerful spirits, IX, 264, 296, 376; bequest to, X, 105; see also VI, 113, 115–16, VII, 7, 54, 56, 61, 70, 72, 113, 187 n., 262, 325 n., IX, 124 n., 250, 262, 389, X, 266, 348

Ricardo, Rachel (D.R.'s sister), second
wife of W. A. Wilkinson, X, 59;
visits Gatcomb, VII, 328, 336,
VIII, 284; bequest to, X, 105; see
also X, 133
Ricardo, Raphael or Ralph (D.R.'s
brother), X, 59
and Mill, VI, 251, VII, 61, 315, IX,
219
visits Gatcomb, VII, 55, 66, 326
on the continent with D.R. in 1817,
VII, 160, 165, X, 220
introduced to Say, VI, 250, 273,
312
marriage, VIII, 22 & n., 25, 240
bequest to, X, 105
see also VI, 112 n., 151, VII, 14, 167,
295, 339, VIII, 10, 143, 214, 223,
X, 74
Ricardo, Rebecca (D.R.'s sister), wife
of Isaac Keyser, X, 56–7; see also
VII, 240, X, 105
Ricardo, Rebecca (D.R.'s cousin),
Mrs Da Costa, X, 206 n.; visit to,
in Amsterdam, X, 206–7, 211–12;
see also X, 19, 30
Ricardo, Rebecca Israel, X, 18 n.
Ricardo, Miss S., X, 18 n.
Ricardo, Sabethaz, X, 202 n.
Ricardo, Samson (D.R.'s brother), X,
60–1
and foreign loans, X, 57–8, 101, 351,
390
visits Gatcomb, VII, 66
republishes *Plan for a National Bank*,
IV, 273, X, 367
bequest to, X, 105
letter quoted, VIII, 298 n.
see also X, 51, 347
*Observations on the pamphlet of J. H.
Palmer*, X, 60; *A National Bank*,
IV, 273, X, 60
Ricardo, Samuel Israel (D.R.'s uncle),
X, 19, 30
Ricardo, Sarah (Sally), D.R.'s sister,
educational writer, wife of G. R.
Porter, X, 60, 105; declines a
present, 133–5; see also VI, 264,
309, 311, 322, 349, VII, 6

Ricardo, Solomon (D.R.'s brother),
X, 61
'Ricardoes' (gold ingots), V, 368–9.
See Ingot plan
Rich and poor countries, I, 266, 373–8,
VI, 141
Rich class, see Classes
Richardson, Overend, and Co., dis-
count brokers, IV, 280 & n.
Richardson, Thomas, evidence to the
bullion committee, III, 377–8, to
law merchant committee, IV,
280–1 & n.
Riches:
case in which real riches are augmented
by increase of money, III, 318–19,
VI, 16–17
imaginary, pleasure derived from,
VIII, 187
see also II, 235, and under Wealth
Riches and value, I, 273–88
Say's definition criticised, I, 279–81,
287–8 n., VI, 271–4, VIII, 299,
379, IX, 169–71, 188–91
see also I, 429, II, 192–3, 203, 207
Rio de Janeiro, VIII, 92
Rive, Charles-Gaspar de la, professor of chemistry at Geneva, X,
270–1 & n., 272, 281, see also IX,
218–20
Roads:
as relief works, V, 32, VII, 116 & n.,
121, VIII, 155, 283
road construction in Holland, IX,
209–10, X, 213–14; under the
Prussians, X, 222; in Italy, IX,
225–6, X, 326–31, 335
excellence of Simplon road, IX, 221,
226, X, 288–9
want of streets in Venice, IX, 222
see also II, 368–9
Robarts, M.P. for Worcester, VII, 101
Robarts, Curtis & Co., bankers, X,
68 n., 80
Robarts, Lubbock & Co., bankers, X,
68 n.
Robertson, Alexander, M.P. for Gram-
pound, on East and West India
sugars, V, 297, 476–7, 479–83

Robertson, W., *History of Scotland*, X, 398

Robins, John, X, 81 n.

Robinson, Frederick John (President of the Board of Trade till 1823; thereafter see under Chancellor of the Exchequer):
his liberal principles, V, 42, 44–5, 146, 248, IX, 269
on scope of agricultural committee, V, 48, 81
on corn laws, V, 51, 78
see also V, xx, 68, 86, 188, 218, 250 n., 335, 350, 492 n., IX, 270 n., 273, 274

Robinson, Sir George, M.P. for Northampton, V, 185

Rocca, son of Madame de Staël, X, 279

Rockingham, Lady, VII, 264 n.

'Rodborough Simplon', X, 168

Rogers Ruding library, IX, 150 n.

Rogers, Samuel, VIII, 152 n.

Roget, Peter Mark, VII, 191 & n., 193

Roman Catholics:
Plunkett's motion for claims of, V, xxii–xxiii; franchise bill, 1823, V, 329 n., 330 n.; report on laws relating to, 1816, VII, 146 & n.
Catholic emancipation, V, xv, xxii & n., xxiii & n., VIII, 50, 350–1, 362–3, 369, see also VIII, 289, 304

Rome, IX, 227, X, 319–20

Romilly, Lady, VII, 198, 206, 328 & n.

Romilly, Sir Samuel, M.P.:
elected for Westminster, VII, 269, 270 n.
his system of reform, VII, 273
his suicide, VII, 328 & n., 345–6, 357 n., 370, and moving will, VII, 376, 383
see also V, 335, VII, 198, 285, 305, X, 42, 50, 281
Memoirs of, VII, 189 n., 250 n.

Romilly, William, IX, 220, X, 281–2

Rose, George, M.P., his bill for Savings banks, VII, 33, 45, 63, 128, 133, 141, 152–3, 173, 209; see also III, 63 n., 429

Rosenhagen, A., VI, 46 & n.

Ross-on-Wye, VIII, 231, IX, 27, 113

Rosser, Henry Blanch, young friend of Bentham, VIII, 113–17; *The Question of Population*, 1821, VIII, 114 n.

Rossi, Pellegrino, X, 270, 270–1 n.; see also IX, 219, 245, X, 375–6

Rothschild, Nathan Meyer: opposed to ingot plan, V, 357; loan of 1819, X, 85–90, see also V, 21 n., 58 n., VIII, 30 n.; French loan of 1823, X, 57; see also III, 427–8

Rotten boroughs, VII, 110. See Borough system

Rotterdam, merchants' houses fit for princes, X, 195–6; see also IX, 211, 241

Rousseau, Jean Jacques: *Confessions*, VII, 60; *Émile ou de l'éducation*, VIII, 11; *Nouvelle Héloïse*, VII, 303, 306, 318, 328, 330, 336, IX, 220, X, 61, 282, 394 n., 395–6

Royal Military College, Bagshot, J. S. Mill attends lectures at, VII, 313–14, 326; Torrens's son at, VII, 315

Rubens, VII, 160, 163

Rulikowski, IX, 223, X, 290–1 n.

Rumbold, Charles Edmund, M.P. for Great Yarmouth, V, 185

Run on Bank for gold, witnessed by Ricardo in 1797, III, 365, see also 98; danger of, under Ingot plan, V, 455–6. See also Panics

Rush, Richard, VII, 285

Russell, Lord John:
contempt for political economy, IX, 155 & n.
motion on reform of parliament, V, xix, 283–9, 488–90
on taxation as cause of distress, IV, 257–8 & n.
on the Queen's trial, VIII, 220–1

Russell family, X, 173

Russia: imports of corn from, VIII, 369, IX, 155 n., of tallow, V, 291, 294; see also III, 290, IV, 28, V, 77, 103, 110–11, 404–5, VI, xxxvii, 79 & n., 80

Rutherford, A. W., *Hints from Holland*, 1811, annotated, X, 401 & n.
Ruxton, Mrs, IX, 256, 257, X, 32 n., 172

Saardam, X, 208
Sachseln, X, 252–3
St Andrews University, adopts *Principles* as text-book, VIII, 82
Saint-Arnaud, Comte de, later Marshal of France, X, 325 n.; young officer met on the Continent, X, 324–5, 327, 330, 332–3, 340–2, 345; story of his ancestry and wealth, X, 337–8; 'not what he represented himself to be', 351; see also X, 178, 334, 339
St Germains, Earl of, V, 351
St James's Park, walks in, VI, xxxiv
St Martin, X, 273, 276
St Maurice, IX, 220, X, 283
St Michel, X, 340
St Quintin, Catherine, wife of Ricardo's son David, X, 63
St Quintin, William Thomas, X, 63
Salisbury, VI, 124
Salmon, W. W., X, 96 n.
Salvador, Mr, X, 201
Samuda, David (D.R.'s brother-in-law), X, 56; visits Gatcomb, VII, 66, IX, 327–8, 335; executor of Ricardo's will, X, 25 n., 105; see also VII, 14
Samuda, Hannah (D.R.'s sister), see Ricardo, Hannah
San Carlos, Duke of, X, 273
Sargans, X, 240
Sarnen, good-humoured host at, X, 250
Sarzana, X, 324–5
Saunders, Dr, VII, 110
Savile, Mrs, VII, 109–10, 113
Saving:
and accumulation of capital, I, 131, 151 n., 166–7, II, 8–9, 383, 390–3, 402, III, 281–2, V, 438, VI, 16
power of saving increased by machinery, I, 390, 396
motive for, I, 133, IX, 25, 131

Saving (*cont.*)
can only be from unproductive expenditure, II, 417; only from net revenue, I, 347–8
saving is spending, II, 449, VIII, 181, X, 409
cannot be a cause of stagnation, disagreement with Malthus, II, 325, IX, 24, 26–7; see also VII, 121
see also Parsimony
Savings Banks:
Rose's bill, VII, 33–4, 45, 63 & n., 116–17, 125–6, 128–9, 133, 141, 152–5, 173, 209, VIII, 202, 210
parish relief to depositors, VII, 12, 63–4, 96, 117–18, 125–6, 129–30, 133–5, 141–2, 149, 248
plan for life-annuities through, V, 121 & n., 128–9
investment of deposits, VII, 152–4
correspondence with Mallet on, XI, xvii–xxi
Bath, VII, 23, 153; Chichester, VII, 155 n.; City of London, VII, 49–50 & n., 153–4, 180; Godalming, VII, 12, 23 & n., 34, 46, 96, 209, VIII, 202; Hertfordshire, VII, 174; Southampton Row, XI, xviii; Southwark, VII, 26; Tetbury, VII, 26, 187 n., 220–1; Westminster, VII, 34 & n., 47 n., 49
Say, Jean-Baptiste, VI, xxv–xxvii
meetings with, VI, 156–7, 160–1, 275, in Paris, VII, 168, 231, IX, 244
Professor of industrial economy, VIII, 291; his lectures, VIII, 225, 291, IX, 191–2, 223; see also X, 290
difficulty in conversation, VI, 161, 219, IX, 244–5 & n., 248; reasons by exclamations, VIII, 260–1; his profound thinking and egregious blunders, VIII, 302; does not understand the new doctrines, VIII, 374, IX, 244, 249
his golden maxim, I, 242, VII, 334, 338
misunderstands distinction between quantity of, and value of, labour, VIII, 149, 161

Say, Jean-Baptiste (*cont.*)
confuses utility, value and riches, I,
279–88, VI, 247–8, 271, VIII,
280–1, 298–9, 379, IX, 168–71;
defends his views, IX, 32–6, 63,
188–91; see also VIII, 276, 312,
IX, 64
misunderstands no-rent land, I, 413 n.,
VIII, 4, 57, 149–50, see also VII, 372
on gross and net revenue, I, 347 n.,
VII, 378–9
on stagnation and counter-commodities, VIII, 227–9, 260–1
demand limited only by production,
I, 290, IV, 178, VI, 163–4, 168,
VIII, 258–9, IX, 13, see also II,
311, VII, 121
doctrine of productive services, VIII,
228, 260, 277, 379–80, IX, 34–5
on price of corn regulating all prices,
VII, 105
his currency plan, VI, 165–6 & n.,
see also IV, 272
and Ricardo's *Principles*: on ed. 1,
VII, 178, ed. 3, IX, 31–6, 46,
63–4, 154, 158, 168; his 'Notes' in
French edition, I, 348–9 notes,
413 n., II, 382, VII, 178, 361, 364,
370–1, 375, 378–9, VIII, 4–5, 7,
10, 136–7, 149–50, IX, 244, X,
374–6, 379–80, see also X, 374–6,
379–80; alterations due to, in
ed. 2, I, 413 n., VII, 372, 379, VIII,
4–5, 7, in ed. 3, I, 249 n., 264 n.,
279–85, 287–8 n., 348 n., 349 n.,
II, 382, VII, 378–9, VIII, 301 & n.,
315, see also VIII, 341 n., 344–5,
IX, 46
letter read to Political Economy
club, IX, 36 & n., 158 n., 172–3;
elected to, IX, 173 n., 191 & n.
speculation in potato-flour, VI, xxv,
VII, 166, 168, 224–6, 230, see
also X, 95 n.
list of letters, IX, 399
see also I, 5, IV, 343, VI, 250, 273,
312, 336, VII, 186, 201 n., VIII,
22, 212, 270, 275, 331, IX, 187,
195, X, 57–8, XI, xi

WORKS
Catéchisme d'Économie politique, 1815,
VI, 245 & n., Ricardo on, I,
287–8 n., VI, 247–9, 264–5, 269,
Say's reply, VI, 271–4; ed. 2,
1821, IX, 169, 173 & n., 188–190;
see also VI, 255
Cours complet, 1828–9, IX, 32 & n.
Lettres à M. Malthus, 1820, VIII,
227 & n., 280–1; Ricardo on, VIII,
227–8, 276–8, 284, 379–80, IX,
170–2, his 'Notes' on, I, lvii, VIII,
292, 298, 301–2 & n., 305, 315,
341 n., 344–5; Malthus on, VIII,
259–61; McCulloch on, VIII,
313; Say complains of misunder-
standings, IX, 36; translation in
New Monthly, VIII, 249; Cazenove's *Reply*, X, 401 n., XI, xxx,
Ricardo's 'Notes' on the *Reply*,
X, 405–10; see also II, 338, VIII,
225, 229, 249, 285
Mélanges et correspondance, 1833, VI,
xxvii, 273, IX, 31 n., 188 n.
Œuvres diverses, 1848, VI, xxvi, xxvii,
165 n., 273, VIII, 291 n., IX, 31 n.,
244 n.
Traité d'Économie politique:
ed. 1, 1803, IV, 178, VI, xxv, VIII,
7
ed. 2, 1814, I, 6–7, 69 n., 73–4 n.,
155, 186–90, 227 n., 235–8, 242–4,
254–6, 264 n., 275 n., 279–80 n.,
285–8, 290, 299–300 n., 307 n.,
316–20, 344, 347, 349–50 n., 352 n.,
355 n., 372 n., 379, 383, IV, 71,
VI, xxv, 156, 160–1, 163–4, 168,
VII, 89, 101, 105, 108, 112, 115,
121
ed. 3, 1817, VI, 270, 321, VII,
166 & n., 168, 178 & n., 219, 222,
231, 235, X, 399
ed. 4, 1819, I, lvii, 279–84, 421 n.,
II, 14, 311, VII, 227, VIII, 136,
149, 225, 228, 298–9, 312–13, 315,
341 n., IX, 32, 46, 171, 190, X,
399
ed. 5, 1826, I, 249 n.

Say, Jean-Baptiste, *Traité* (*cont.*)
  Ricardo reads, VI, 163–4, re-reads
    while writing *Principles*, VII, 89,
    101, 112, 115, comments on, VIII,
    228, 298–9, IX, 46, 171; altera-
    tions to meet Ricardo's objec-
    tions, VI, 321, VII, 166, 178,
    227, VIII, 136, 315; McCulloch
    on, VIII, 312–13; reviewed with
    R.'s *Principles* in *British Review*,
    VII, 219, 222, 231, 235, see also
    VI, 255
  intended translation by Place, VI,
    160 & n.; Prinsep's translation,
    1821, VIII, 315 & n., reviewed in
    Scotsman, VIII, 374
  obituary of Ricardo in *Tablettes
    Universelles*, 1823, X, 57 n.; 'Notice
    sur Ricardo', X, 103 n.
  articles, 'De l'Angleterre', 1815, VII,
    94; 'De la crise commerciale de
    l'Angleterre', 1826, X, 58 n.
  unpublished letters to Francis Place,
    VI, xxvi n.
  Un professeur d'Économie politique,
    by A. Liesse, IX, 192 n.
Say, Louis, VII, 226 & n.; *Considéra-
    tions sur l'industrie et la législation*,
    1822, IX, 245, 248–9
Scale of discounts, 1782–97, IV, 415–
    18, see also III, 358 n., IV, 279
Scarce books, I, 12
Scarcity, as source of value, I, 12,
    194, 250, 276–7, II, 204; see also
    III, 309–10
Scarlett, James, M.P. for Peter-
    borough: Poor-law bill, V, 113;
    superabundance no cause of agri-
    cultural distress, V, 141; see also
    V, 185, IX, 198
Schaffhausen, X, 235–8
Scheveling, X, 203
Schmidt, C. A., X, 376
Schneider's hotel, Florence, X, 314,
    319–20
Schools: Brougham's Infant School,
    VII, 356–7, 359–60, 363, 371;
    Charterhouse, VI, 129, X, 61–3;
    Dissenting Academy, Daventry,

Schools (*cont.*)
    VII, 171 n.; Eton, VII, 138, X, 63,
    267, 389; Ets Haïm, Amsterdam,
    X, 31–2; Fellenberg's, Hofwyl,
    X, 262; Haileybury, see East-
    India College; Harrow, VII, 138,
    X, 267; Lancasterian system, VI,
    112 n., VII, 45 n., 155 n., X,
    402; Minchinhampton, Ricardo's
    schools at, VII, 45 & n., IX, 328–9,
    X, 169; Owen's Infant School, VII,
    150; Talmud Tora, Amsterdam,
    X, 31–2; Westminster, VII, 138;
    see also VI, 126, and Chrestomathic
    School
Schwediaur, Francis Xavier, VII, 167
    & n.
Schwetzingen, X, 228–9
Schwyz, X, 245
Scotland:
  banks, III, 228, 235, 399
  burgh system, VIII, 326
  cash accounts, I, 365–6
  juries, VIII, 167, IX, 136, 142
  long farm leases, VI, 174–5, 177, 297
  press, VIII, 167, IX, 136, 142
  Say's visit to, IX, 187
  Scotch linen laws petition, V, 290
  see also I, 256, 351, III, 286–7, VIII,
    400
Scotsman, The, McCulloch's news-
    paper, VI, xxii, VII, 291, VIII,
    167 & n., IX, 204–5
  Ricardo subscribes to, VIII, 28, 142–
    3, 157
  his papers on reform published post-
    humously in, V, 489, 494
  Principles reviewed in, VII, 219–20 &
    n., 222
  Malthus's *Principles* reviewed in,
    VIII, 178 & n., 185
  articles: on agricultural distress, 1821,
    VIII, 337, 341; corn laws, VIII, 197
    & n.; Edinburgh police, IX, 137
  see also V, 515, VII, 259, VIII, 25 n.,
    82, 139, 205 n., 223, 239–40, 319,
    359 n., 390–1, IX, 140 n., 142,
    155, 277, 301 and under McCulloch,
    J. R., articles in *Scotsman*

Scott, Mr, surgeon, VI, 349
Scott, Sir Walter, Maria Edgeworth's visit to, IX, 259 & n.; see also VIII, 58, 204, IX, 136 n., 232
Ivanhoe, VIII, 152 n., 155–6; *New Tales of my Landlord*, VIII, 37 & n., 40, 44; *Quentin Durward*, IX, 294; *The Heart of Midlothian*, X, 169
Scrope, George Poulett, X, 63
Sebright, Sir John, M.P., IX, 148
Secheron, X, 264, 269, 270, 282
Sedgwick, actor, X, 112
Seditious Meetings Prevention bill, speech on, V, 28–9
Seignorage on coinage: principles of, III, 222–6; no objection to a moderate one, I, 371–2, V, 362; necessary if gold coinage retained under ingot plan, V, 401–7, 431; in France, III, 179; see also IV, 114, VII, 265, IX, 331
Selection of Speeches at County Meetings, 1822, V, 469 n.
Seligman, E. R. A., 'On some neglected British Economists', IX, 27 n.
Senior, Nassau William, meets Ricardo at Political Economy Club, IX, 312 n.; article on agriculture in *Quarterly Review*, 1821, IX, 109 & n., 122; *Conversations with... Distinguished Persons*, 1878, III, 261 n.
Sens, X, 346
Sentinel, The, newspaper, IX, 187 & n.
Seoane, J. A., X, 355
Sequeira, Rebecca Henriques de (D.R.'s grandmother), wife of Abraham Delvalle, X, 27
Serbelloni, Villa, X, 294, 296
Servants in Ricardo's household:
Mrs Cleaver, on Continental tour, X, 177, 182, 197, 235, 237, 297, 313, 328, 343–4
Darby, gamekeeper, X, 159–60, 265 & n., and cp. VII, 319
Thomas Darby, X, 159–61
John Drysdale, footman, X, 104 n., see also IX, 208

Servants (*cont.*)
Catherine Harrison, maid, her adventure, X, 144–59
Pamela, maid, X, 111
William Pike, butler, X, 104 n.
William Primmer, coachman, X, 26
Mary Rundle, X, 26
Thomas, X, 110, and cp. 350
Servants, menial: whether preferred to commodities, VII, 70, VIII, 102; see also I, 392–3, 395, 424, VI, 155, 164, VIII, 184
Services productifs, see Productive services
Servoz, X, 274
Seymour, Lady, *The Pope of Holland House* (John Whishaw), IV, 204 n., V, 128 n., VI, 66, 87, 135 n., 139 n., VII, 54 n., 144 n., 185 n., 251 n., 270 n., 291 n., IX, 109 n., X, 50 n.
Sewers, Ricardo member of committee on, V, xxvi, IX, 284 & n.
Sharp, Richard (Conversation Sharp), VI, xxxvi–xxxvii
Ricardo succeeds him as member for Portarlington, V, xv, xvi, xviii, VII, 311, VIII, 17–18
his travel hints, X, 179, 246, 296, 298 n., 301 n.
letters, VII, 291, VIII, 17
see also V, 352, VI, xix, 28–9, 31, 48, 59, 66–7, 71–2, 77, 82, 87, 90, 244, VII, 252, 263, VIII, 70, 152 n., 163, 204, 214, X, 49, 50, XI, xxvii
Shchepkin, M., X, 381
Sheet-anchor, Ricardo's, the invariability of precious metals, VI, 348
Sheffield Telegraph, XI, xxviii
Shepherd, Henry John, M.P., VIII, 56
Shepherd, Lady Mary, visits Gatcomb, VIII, 56 & n.; Maria Edgeworth on, X, 172
Shepherd, William, stockbroker, X, 126–8
Sheppard, Edward, X, 96
Sheppard, Phillip, Ricardo buys Gatcomb from, X, 95–6; dispute with, about a servant, X, 159–61
Sherborne, Lord, V, 469–70, VIII, 330

Sheriff, office of, VII, 255–6, 258–9, VIII, 113, 134, 148, 164; in Scotland, IX, 136; see also under Ricardo, Trower

Shitabroy, Rajah, VII, 237

Short period, VI, 170, see also VI, 153

Short time work prevents mobility of labour, VIII, 316

Shuman, courier on Continental tour, IX, 213–14, X, 177, 182–3, 185, 187, 191, 200, 204, 215–16, 221, 234, 244, 248, 263, 274, 297–8, 310–11, 342

Sicily, vote on, in 1821, V, xxii

Sidmouth, Lord (Henry Addington), IV, 153–4, 165, VI, 261

Sieber, N., X, 381

Sieveking, Heinrich, *Karl Sieveking*, III, 434 & n.

Sieveking, Karl, 'Geschichte des Pfund Sterlings' (MS), III, 434 & n.

Silberling, Norman J., 'Ricardo and the Bullion Report', III, 6–7, X, 91–4

Silberner, E., III, 266

Silk manufacture Acts, see Spitalfields

Silk trade with Bengal, IV, 251, V, 197, 478

Silver:
    whether gold or, the standard, III, 28–33, 36–46, 84–5 & n., VI, 4–6; silver the main currency under William III, I, 370–1; still the standard (Lauderdale), VIII, 45 & n.; preferable to gold as standard, IV, 63, 67 n., V, 428, 432, VI, 301, change of opinion, V, 390–1, 427; preferred by Malthus, VI, 299, and by Locke, III, 65–6; the currency of Hamburg, III, 180
    silver picked up on the sea-shore in a day, II, 81, IV, 406, VIII, 179; see Value, measure of, Malthus's
    price of, III, 29–32, 44, 85, VIII, 45; under the mint price in 1816, VII, 28–9; low price from forced abundance, I, 229
    exports to East Indies, III, 171–2, 249

Silver (*cont.*)
    law against coining, III, 36–7, 68–9; legal tender of coins limited, III, 42, 46, 66, 85; checks against excessive circulation of, I, 371 n.; debasement of, III, 30, 37–9, 70; recoinage (1816), V, 386–7, see also X, 201
    see also America, Spanish; Gold and Silver

Simond, Louis, met in Geneva, X, 270–3 & n., 281–2, IX, 218–20; his book on Switzerland, X, 239 & n., 246, 255 n.; articles on Fellenberg's school, X, 262 n.

Simonde, J. C. L. (later Sismondi, *q.v.*), *De la richesse commerciale*, 1803, I, 380–1 & n., 399, II, 105, X, 399

Simplon road, IX, 221–2, 226, 234, X, 288–9, see also X, 168

Sims, Miss, VIII, 308, 310

Sinclair, Sir John, VI, xxxvii
    his currency plan, VIII, 186, 386
    plan to reduce national debt, VIII, 187
    list of letters, IX, 400
    Correspondence of, 1831, VI, xxxvii, 143 n., 150 n., 151 n., VIII, 186, 386; *Memoirs of*, by his son, VI, xxxvii
    Address to the Owners...of Land, 1822, IX, 156
    History of the Public Revenue, ed. 3, 1803–4, VIII, 66
    Observations on the Report of the Bullion Committee, 1810, III, 139–45, 359, 428 n.
    On...the National Calamity, 1817, VII, 151 & n.
    Code of Health, 1807, *of Agriculture*, 1817, *of Finance* (never written), VI, 143

Sinking fund, IV, 149–67
    when real and when a delusion, IV, 172–84, VIII, 118–23; real in origin, V, 267, VIII, 67; has become a delusion, IV, 194, V, 20, 26, 62, 79–80, 194, 243, 265, VII, 94 & n.; ought to be abolished, IV, 99, VIII, 78, IX, 180

Sinking fund (*cont.*)
conditions for efficiency, I, 248–9, V, 262–5, VIII, 122
the savings bank of the nation, VII, 17; injustice of inroads on, IV, 40–1, VII, 105–6
not a cause of glut, IV, 178–80
whether it turns revenue into capital, IV, 183–4, VIII, 319–20
cannot be used both to annoy an enemy and to pay a debt, IV, 198, V, 25, 251, 268–9
application of, to reduction of borrowing, IV, 171–3; recommended by Ricardo, V, 4–5, X, 81–2, 85, see also V, 21–2 & n.
and land-tax, V, 259–61; and pensions plan, V, 160–1, 194–5, 248–9, 267
Stanhope's, IV, 149; Pitt's, IV, 151–3, 191–2, 194, V, 118–20, 262; Addington's, IV, 153–4; Petty's, 154–7; Perceval's, 157–8; Vansittart's, 158–67, V, 118–20, 262–3, VI, 91 & n.; Parnell's plan, V, 270–3, IX, 175 & n.
commissioners of, I, 362–3, IV, 182–3, 191, 194–5, V, 120 n., 194
speeches on, V, 4–6, 20–2, 24–5, 64–7, 115–20, 248–51, 259–65, 266–73, see also 129–30
article on, for *Encyclopaedia*, VIII, 54, 72, 75–8; see Ricardo, David, *Funding System*
see also III, 272–3, V, 101, 147, VI, 178, VII, 38, 260, VIII, 33, 110, 135, 147, IX, 269
Siordet, I. M., *Letter to Sir John Sinclair*, 1811, X, 401
Sirven affair, IX, 374
Sismondi, J. C. L. Simonde de, VIII, 22
discussions with, IX, 218, 220, 235–6, 243–4 & n., 248, X, 270, 278, 281
views on rent, I, 399–400
on unequal distribution of property, IX, 243–4 & n.
Ricardo's twenty-five readers, VIII, 376–7 n.

Sismondi (*cont.*)
too sentimental for McCulloch, VIII, 24–5
Malthus's letter to, VIII, 375–7
see also I, lv, 5, VIII, 224 n., 366, 382, IX, 219, X, 279, 322, 375–6, 409
Nouveaux principes d'économie politique, 1819, VIII, 22 & n., Ricardo on, VIII, 57, 80, McCulloch on, VIII, 24–5, 38, 40, 383, Torrens on VIII, 376–7 & n.; ed. 2, 1827, IX, 244 n.; see also VIII, 109, X, 399
Études sur l'économie politique, 1837, IX, 244 n.
articles: on power of consuming and power of producing, VIII, 376, see also 224 n.; 'Sur la balance des consommations avec les productions', IX, 244 n.; on J. Barton, IX, 245 & n.
see also Simonde
Six Acts, Ricardo votes against, V, xxii, 28–9, VIII, 146; see also VIII, 110, 133
Skarbek, Count Frederick, X, 290 n.
Slater, James Henry, VIII, 323, IX, 144, 383
Slavery, in the West Indies, V, 483, in the East Indies, V, 297, 300
Smaler, Richard, VI, 113 n.
Smart, William, *Economic Annals 1801–1820*, VII, 116 n.; *1821–1830*, V, xxiv n.
Smiles, S., *A Publisher and his Friends, Memoir of John Murray*, IX, 107 n.
Smith, Adam, *Wealth of Nations*:
first reading of, X, 7, 35–6, VII, 246; re-read, VII, 88–9, 100, 107–8, 111–12, 115, 246, see also III, 7, VII, 2, X, 390–1, 399; *Principles* patterned on, I, xxiii–xxv
on greater productivity of labour in agriculture, II, 20, IV, 37, VI, 178, see also IX, 193; confines labour of nature to agriculture, I, 76–7 n.
compares banks with highways, III, 55
on bullion and foreign exchanges, III, 112

Smith, Adam (*cont.*)
  colonial trade, I, 340, VII, 100
  consumption as sole end of production, V, 219
  his authority quoted by country gentlemen for high duties on importation of corn, I, 317
  demand for necessaries limited, for luxuries unlimited, I, 293, 295–6, IX, 19; effects of demand on prices, VI, 148 & n.
  depreciation of coinage through excess of paper, I, 354–5, III, 148–51; depreciation of colony currency, I, 356; observations on debased coinage apply to depreciated paper, III, 96–7, see also 76–7
  effectual demand, power and will to purchase, VI, 58, 142, and cp. 56
  and export of surplus goods, I, 291 n.
  his free trade principles, I, 338, V, 43
  on gold and silver, I, 366, III, 52–3
  on value of gold, corn, and labour, I, 373–8, see also 18–19
  overrates advantages of gross revenue, I, 347–9, II, 382, VII, 379
  on labour as standard of value, I, 416, IV, 409, IX, 363, 380; alternates between standards, I, 13–14
  legacy duty, I, 153–4
  theory of money, III, 220, 327–8; paper money and taxation, III, 236–7
  natural price, II, 38, 46, 52, VIII, 202, IX, 65, see also I, 375–6; real and nominal price, I, 274–5 n.
  difficulty of estimating rate of profits, I, 296–7; profits in different employments, IV, 12 n.
  rate of interest not regulated by quantity of money, III, 25–6, 88–9, 143–4, 150, 194 n., V, 12 & n.
  on rent of land, I, 327–37; strict and popular senses of rent, I, 67–8; building rent and ground rent, I, 201–4; rent of mines, I, 329–32
  effects of restrictions on export of precious metals, I, 228–9, 310

Smith, Adam (*cont.*)
  on seignorage, III, 179–81, 222
  low value of silver in Spain, I, 228–9
  his maxims of taxation, and the land-tax, I, 181–6, see also I, 204, 235; taxes on raw produce fall on rent, I, 183–4, 252, IV, 33–4 n., 239, see also I, 199; but malt tax falls on consumer of beer, I, 252–3; taxes on wages, I, 215–16, fall on landholders and consumers, I, 222–8, 232–6
  on value, I, 11–23, 309, see also III, 284, IX, 2, 190; his original error, I, xxxv–xxxvi, 22–3 n., VII, 100, 377, regards rent as component of price, I, 77–8, 329, II, 42–5, see also IV, 315–17
  value and riches, I, 273, 276–8, 286 n., 429; criticised by Say, I, 285–7
  real value of wages, I, 19–20
  on evaluating different kinds of work, I, 21 n.
  worshipped in Edinburgh, VII, 295
  his errors: on bounties on exportation, I, 304–5 & n., 310–17, VII, 100, 107–8; on capital employed in foreign trade, I, 350–1, see also 129; on carrying trade being not of choice, but of necessity, I, 294; on colonial trade raising profits, I, 344–5, VII, 100, 202; on the peculiar nature of corn, I, 313, 413–14 & n.; on corn being always of the same value, I, 374, V, 210–12; identifies low value of money with high value of corn, I, 336–7; supposes price of corn regulates all other prices, I, 302, 307–8, IV, 21 n., VII, 105; food production always yields rent, I, 327–9, 332–3; thinks profits depend on accumulation without reference to population, I, 289–91, VIII, 380; rise of wages raises price of all commodities, I, 46
  Cobbett on, IX, 267 n.

Smith, Adam (*cont.*)

David Hume's supposed notes on, I, vii, XI, xxvii

Louis Say's notes on, IX, 245, 248

Buchanan's ed. with Notes, 1814, VI, 159 & n.; see also I, 77 n., 216–20, 251–2, 254, 314–15, 334, 355–6, 370, VII, 101, IX, 206, X, 399

Cannan's ed., 1904, I, lxii

McCulloch's ed., IV, 6–7 & n.

proposed edition with notes by Malthus, VI, 159–60 n., 169; Malthus's questions to his pupils on, VI, 159 n.

see also I, 151 n., 365, II, 26–7, III, 58, 81, 145, 163, 188, 253, IV, 7, VI, xxxvii, 34, 95, 120, 272, 316, VII, 40, 98, 106, 180, 219, VIII, 24–5, 189, 225, 286, IX, 22, 164, 187, 210, X, 21, 53

Theory of Moral Sentiments, X, 399

Smith, Sir Charles, X, 277

Smith, George, M.P., V, 185

Smith, John, M.P. for Midhurst, banker: on inroad of machinery upon labour, V, 30 & n.; supports ingot plan, V, 359; see also V, xxvi, 37, 292, VII, 356, VIII, 45

Smith, J. B., Barclay & Co., III, 430

Smith, Joseph, *Catalogue of Friends' Books*, X, 43 n.

Smith, Kenneth, *The Malthusian Controversy*, XI, xxviii n.

Smith, M. F. L., *Tijd-affaires in effecten aan de Amsterdamsche Beurs*, X, 19 n.

Smith, Robert (father of Sydney Smith), IX, 60, 89 n., 108 & n.

Smith, Robert, M.P. for Lincoln, V, 277

Smith, Sydney, IX, 89 n.

visits Gatcomb, IX, 46, 63, 89–90

tolerates all religions but not atheists, IX, 60

on Ricardo's driving, X, 168

cousin of Trower, VI, xxiii, IX, 108

letter quoted, VII, 251 n.

articles by, IX, 89, 108

see also V, 352, X, 50

Smith, Thomas, accountant: his evidence on ingot plan, V, 360; *Essay on the Theory of Money*, 1807, III, 9 n.; *Reply to Mr. Ricardo's Proposals*, 1816, V, 360 & n.

Smith, Thomas, of Easton Grey, Ricardo's country neighbour, VI, 135 & n., VII, 187 & n.; Unitarian, VII, 171 n., X, 40, 169, 350 n.; first meeting at Malthus's, VI, 164; visits from, VII, 54, 56, VIII, 276, 282, X, 169–71; visits to, VII, 171, VIII, 56, 61–3, 75, 334 n., IX, 263–4; his collection of pamphlets, VIII, 62–3, 77, 84, 106; his death, IX, 232 n., 328; letters quoted, VII, 54 n., 186 n., X, 50, 298, 389; see also V, 128, VI, xxxii, 66 n., 244, 295, VII, 15, 35, 61, 90, 114, 144 n., 185, 191–2, 206, 223, 275, VIII, 107, XI, xii n.

Smith, Mrs Thomas (Elizabeth Chandler), VI, 135 & n.; her autograph collection, VI, 139 n., 164–5, 169; is widowed, IX, 232–3, 240, 251, 262–4, X, 337, 349; see also VII, 35, 189, X, 32, 389

Smith, William, geologist, VII, 119 n.

Smith, William, M.P. for Norwich, V, 296, X, 77 n., 285

Smithies, Rev., on the 'calculating economy of Mr Ricardo', IX, 267 n.

Smollett, Tobias, his tomb at Leghorn, X, 322

Smuggling, I, 378, II, 452, III, 183, V, 268, VII, 303, IX, 147, X, 169–70, 189, see also IV, 190

Smyth, Professor William, VI, 72, 196, 215, 219, 220, 240, 243, VII, 223, 252, 311, VIII, 114

Soap, as one of necessaries of labourer, I, 20, 224, 234, 275, IV, 257

Society for Mutual Improvement, VIII, 115, 117

Society for the Suppression of Vice, V, 277–8

Society, state of, stationary, retrograde, and progressive, I, 176–7, III, 274,

Society (*cont.*)
IV, 22–3; see also I, 108–9, IV, 234, VII, 16–17, and under Progress of society
Soetbeer, A., *Die Hamburger Bank*, III, 176 n.
Solly, Edward, merchant, V, xxiv, 174, 181–2, 185, VIII, 374
Somerset, Lord R. E. H., M.P. for Gloucestershire, VII, 272 n., VIII, 156 n.
South Sea Company, IV, 83, 149, VI, 276, IX, 198 & n.
Southey, Robert, his reveries on political economy, VII, 247 & n.
Spade husbandry, II, 238–9, V, 31, 35, IX, 56
Spain:
  rate of exchange with her colonies, III, 171, VIII, 126, 141, see also I, 195–8
  drain of gold to, VI, 122, 298
  value of silver in, I, 228
  war in, IX, 268–9, 274, 294, 315, 372, 378–9; sympathy with the Spanish people, V, 274 & n., IX, 213, X, 57
  see also VIII, 294 & n.
Spanish America, see America, Spanish
Spanish and Portuguese ancestry of Ricardo, X, 17–19
Spanish funds, IX, 256, 262, 372, 379
Specie payments: Horner's motion on, 1816, IV, 51 & n., 65, VII, 28, 30 & n.; under Peel's bill, VIII, 32, 35–6, 39. See Resumption of cash payments
Speculation, V, 131, 141, 341–2, 449, VII, 16, 352, VIII, 39, see also III, 122; excess of, leading to stagnation, V, 385; see also Over-trading, Potato flour
Speculators, and real capitalists, III, 134–5; speculators in corn, IV, 253–4, V, 85, 90
Spence, William, II, 360 & n., IV, 178, VI, 132
Spenceans (followers of Thomas Spence), VII, 307 n.

Spezia, X, 326
Spicer, John, stockbroker, VI, 112, X, 126–8
Spicer, John William, VIII, 347
Spinoza, X, 31–2
Spitalfields silk manufacture Acts, V, 220, 292, 295–7, 306–9, IX, 318
Spring-Rice, Thomas, M.P. for Limerick, V, xxvi
Staël, Baron de, IX, 236, 242, 248, X, 351
Staël, Madame de, IX, 218, 242, X, 269, 278 n., 279; *Considérations sur la révolution française*, 1818, VII, 274, X, 397
Stafford, VII, 264
Stagnation:
  and glut, IX, 10, 25
  caused by produce not being adapted to wants, II, 415–16
  cannot arise from saving, IX, 26–7
  increase of consumption no remedy for, IX, 16, and cp. II, 307
  and counter-commodities, VIII, 227–8, 260
  commerce more liable to, than agriculture, IV, 254–5, see also VIII, 159
  in 1815–16, VI, 328, 345, VII, 49, see also II, 441, VII, 192
  in 1819, V, 384–5, 398–9
  in 1821, IX, 16, 21–2, 26–7
  abroad in 1817, VII, 161, 164
  correspondence with Malthus on, IX, 9–11, 15–17, 19–27
  see also Glut
Stamp duties: on bank notes, IV, 73, 94–5, 120–34, 295, VI, 258–61, 265–8; on transference of property, I, 204; see also V, 315
Standard of currency:
  necessity of a fixed standard, V, 254; perfect currency defined in terms of, IV, 55
  standard inevitably variable, III, 391, IV, 62–3, V, 205–6, 209, 442; gold the least variable, I, 45–6, III, 65 n., V, 388, 427, VII, 42–3

Standard of currency (*cont.*)
'commodities generally' as, IV, 61, V, 374, mass of commodities, IV, 59
corn as (Western), V, 210–11, 238–9, 313
currency without a standard, IV, 59, 62, 64, see also III, 255, V, 519
bank notes the standard in 1809, III, 79; ancient standard restored in 1819, V, 232
value of, altered by Bank's gold purchases in 1819, V, 312
when currency was depreciated 30%, R. would have lowered the standard, IX, 73–4; but not in 1819, when only 5%, V, 43, 73, 208
see also Double standard, Gold standard, Money, standard of, Silver

Stanhope, first Earl of, plan for a sinking fund, IV, 149
Stanhope, third Earl of: his Banknotes Act, VI, 45, 88, V, 316; on gold, as standard of currency, VI, 54, as circulating medium, 54 n.
Star, The, newspaper, V, 57, 58, 464
Stationery, Ricardo member of committee on, V, xxvi
Staubbach waterfall, X, 257
Steam-engines, I, 31, 32, 53, 69, II, 74, 87, 361, IV, 33, 87 n., 393, V, 179, 500, VII, 157–9, VIII, 171, 192, 384, 389–90, IX, 193
Steam-packet, IX, 241, X, 181–2, 196
Steers, James, Ricardo's partner as loan-contractor, VI, 112 n., X, 79–82, 123–4, 125 n.
Stephens, Mr, X, 169
Steuart, Sir James, *Inquiry into the Principles of Political Œconomy*, 1767, III, 33 n.; on pound and guinea, III, 32–3; on measurement, III, 72–3; currency without a standard, IV, 59 & n.; see also I, 5, III, 7, 81, VI, 34, 40, VII, 202, X, 390
Stewart, Dugald, VI, 156, VII, 211, 229, 235, 312, VIII, 58, IX, 5
Stirling, A. M. W., *Coke of Norfolk*, IX, 265

Stock Exchange:
Ricardo as jobber, X, 67–74; loans and, 79–94, 125–8; see also V, 338, VI, xxiii, 84, 112 n., 116, 143, 149–50, 340, 345, VII, 14, X, 3–6, 129
fraud on, in 1803, X, 123–4; hoax in 1814, VI, 105–7, see also X, 124
Waterloo and, VI, 231 n., 233, X, 83–4
'List of members', VI, xxiv n.
Stockholders, see Fundholders
Stock Jobbing, The Art of (1819), X, 69 n.
Stock notes, Vansittart's project, VII, 260 & n.
Stocks, price of, relation to rate of interest, V, 266, 269 n., 344–5. See also Annuities, Bank post bills, Bank of England, stock of, East India stock, Exchequer bills, French funds, India bonds, Navy bills, Omnium, Ordnance bills, South Sea Company, Spanish funds, Treasury bills
Stoke Newington, X, 25
Stokes, Charles, stockbroker, VI, 270 n., VII, 14
Stokes, John, X, 97
Stones, duties on, IX, 284, 291 & n.
Storer, H. S., *Delineations of the County of Gloucester*, picture of Gatcomb Park, VII, ix, 1
Stourton, Lord, *Letters on... Agriculture*, 1821, IX, 68, 87
Strachey, Mr and Miss, X, 169
Street, John, stockbroker, X, 126–8
Strickland, Mr and Mrs, IX, 232
Strike of keelmen at Newcastle, VIII, 99
Stroud, coach for Gatcomb, VII, 277, 331, VIII, 310; see also VIII, 295, X, 63
Stuart, Lady Jane, VII, 213 n.
Stuart, Mr, petition against duties on stones, IX, 291 & n.
Stuart, Sir John, friend of James Mill, VIII, 105 & n.; see also VII, 213 n.
Stuart-Wortley, James Archibald, M.P. for Yorkshire, singular argument for low bank-rate, IV, 234 & n.; see also V, 57 n., 86, 129, 148, 351

Stuckey, Vincent, country banker, supports ingot plan, V, 359; see also III, 234–5, 385

Sturge, Charlotte, *Family Records*, character of Mrs Ricardo, X, 45–6

Suasso, Abraham Lopes, X, 201–2 & n.

Suasso, B. L., X, 201–2 & n.

Subsidy, foreign, effect on exchanges, VI, 39, 41, 64–5, 73–8, 83, 89, VII, 43, on wages, VIII, 174, 177, 195; see also VI, 236, 241, 255–6

Sudbury silk weavers, V, 295

Suffrage, household, V, 473, 485, VII, 273 & n.; universal, V, 29, 485, 502, VII, 270, 360, 369–70; see also Ballot, Reform

Sugar:
East and West India, V, 188–90, 297–301, 477, 479–81, IX, 273, 277
as necessary of labourer, I, 20, 104, 306, 406
sugar from beetroot, 'absurd scheme of Buonaparte', V, 51, 90–1, VIII, 356; see also IV, 248, V, 153

Sumner, Mrs Charles Richard, *née* Maunoir, X, 272–3 & n.

Sumner, George Holme, M.P. for Surrey, V, 48, 86; his *Life of C. R. Sumner*, X, 273 n.

Sumner, John Bird, later Archbishop of Canterbury: gives up political economy for theology, VII, 247–8; reviews Malthus on Population, VII, 247 & n. 2; *Treatise on the Records of the Creation*, 1816, VII, 247 & n. 4

Sun, The, newspaper, VII, 28 & n., 30

Sunday Times, Obituary of Ricardo, X, 40 n., 51

Sunninghill, VI, 240 n.

Supply, regulates value, VIII, 279; follows close on heels of demand, VIII, 302. See Demand and supply

Surplus produce:
both rent and profits come out of, II, 128, 134
yielded by land in form of rent not an advantage, I, 75, VIII, 182, 209

Surplus produce (*cont.*)
and rent, distinguished by Ricardo, II, 122–3, 213, VIII, 182, 209, identified by Malthus, II, 122–3, 128, 223, IV, 11 n.; 'by the laws o-nature terminates in rent' (Malthus), II, 123, 210
limited by fertility, II, 130
transmission of, to descendants, II, 319–20
increased by rise in price of corn, Malthus's notion, VI, 185, 187, 190–2, 194–6, 199, qualified, 201, 207–8; controverted, 189, 192–4, 196–8, 203–5, 209–10
wages as, II, 218
see also Net surplus, Rent as surplus produce

Surrey County meetings: for the Queen (1821), VIII, 348 & n.; Trower shouted down (1822), IX, 165 & n.; see also IX, 268

Susa (Suze), IX, 228, X, 337–40

Suspension of cash payments, 1797, III, 169, 376, IV, 99, 283, V, 208–9, 216, 236–7, 350. See also Bank Restriction Act, Resumption

Sutherland, L. Stuart, III, 427 n.

Sutton, Mr, X, 83

Swatman, Edward, X, 136, 138

Sweden, III, 183–4

Sweden, Crown Prince of, X, 319–20

Swift, Jonathan, XI, xxx, see also VII, 122, VIII, 114

Sykes, Daniel, M.P. for Kingston-upon-Hull, V, 102, 147, 277

Takabatake, Motoyuki, X, 384

Talbot, Mr, VI, 93–4

Ta-li Kuo, X, 385

Tallow and candles, duties on, V, 146–7, 291, 294, see also V, 219, VIII, 372

Tarn, A. W., and Byles, C. E., *Guardian Assurance Company*, IX, 105 n.

Taste, influence on value, I, 194, see also I, 89–90, VI, 119, and under Wants and tastes

Tattlock, Thomas, III, 430

Taunton, Mrs, IX, 18

Tavistock, Marquis of, M.P. for Bedfordshire, V, 23, 26

Taxation, I, 150–5; a difficult subject, IV, 15 n., VIII, 132–3; neglected by economists, VIII, 71, 79–80, 130–1, IX, 69, 87

tends to diminish accumulation, I, 152 & n., 222, VII, 171, VIII, 168, 170, and production, I, 185, VIII, 154–5; an incentive to send capital abroad, V, 33, 38; a choice of evils, I, 167, 185; injurious to all classes, V, 137, 154, 168

and prices, I, 168–72, 228, III, 240–2, 328, V, 54, 74; whether tax on all commodities can raise prices with same quantity of money, IV, 320–2: it can (early view), III, 238, 242–3, it cannot, I, 168–9, 213, early view revived, I, 169 n., 213–14 n., IX, 158–9

ability to pay taxes, and cheap corn, I, 8, IV, 39–40, V, 83, 88–9, VII, 104

tax on bread: raises price of all commodities (early view), III, 270, see also III, 243; raises price of bread only, I, 254; does not diminish consumption of bread, I, 237 n.

tax on corn: raises price of corn twice (early view), VI, 206; falls on consumers of corn, I, 159, V, 258; lowers rate of profit, I, 166, 205, 239

tax on gold, I, 191–200

on ground rents, I, 203–4

on houses, I, 201–4, III, 138

on income, see Income tax

land-tax, I, 181–90; different effects if levied in proportion to rent or to produce, I, 181–3; does not fall on landlord, VIII, 79; Adam Smith on, I, 183–4; Say's view of, I, 186–90; sinking fund and, V, 259–61

tax on law proceedings, V, 147

on leather, V, 124–5, 127

Taxation (cont.)

on luxuries, I, 241–4, VIII, 177, 189–90, 195–6, see also I, 204, 233

on malt, I, 252–4, V, 26, 52, 101 & n., 294–5, 301–2, IX, 147

taxes on necessaries: shifted from the poor to the rich, I, 235–6; paid by consumer, not landlord, IV, 33–4 n., VI, 173; effects on comforts of labourers, V, 26–7, VIII, 168–71, 174, 176–7, 189–90, 195–6

tax on profits: effects on prices of different commodities, I, 205–10, VIII, 153–4; leaves corn rent unaltered, I, 211–12, VII, 91–2

tax on property, IV, 122 n., 155, V, 20–1, 23, 187, VII, 27, VIII, 190; on transfer of property from the dead, I, 153, landed interest exempt, V, 291; on sale of land, I, 154–5; see also IV, 86 n.

taxes on raw produce, I, 156–72; paid by consumer, I, 157, 159, 160, 196, 257, IV, 240, 255–6, VI, 173, VII, 38, 115; Adam Smith's incorrect view, I, 183–4, 252; affect corn rent but leave money rent unaltered, I, 157–8, 212, 322, VII, 92

taxes on rent cannot be shifted, I, 173, 175

taxes on revenue do not diminish demand, I, 237

tax on salt, I, 237, IV, 257, V, 84, 89, 147, 192, 194–5

special commodities proper for taxation, I, 240

tax on wages: compared with tax on necessaries, I, 215; diminishes rate of profits, I, 214, 226–7; Adam Smith's error on effects of, I, 222–5, 232–3; Buchanan's view criticised, I, 216, 218–22, VII, 108

war taxes, I, 244–8, IV, 155–7, 185–90, VIII, 170, 174–7

McCulloch accuses Ricardo of encouraging ministers to taxation, VII, 281, 286, 349; passages altered in *Principles*, ed. 2, I, 152 n., 242 n., VII, 334, 337–8, 353

Taxation (*cont.*)

Adam Smith's maxims, I, 181–2, 204, 235

taxation and agricultural distress, IV, 255–9, V, 84, 89, 91, 124, 131–2

Tax on capital to pay off national debt, Ricardo's proposal, V, 38, 187, 271, 472. See National debt, Ricardo's plan to pay off

Taylor, C. W., M.P., IX, 147

Tea:

tax on, I, 240, V, 23, 189; as labourer's necessary, I, 20, 104, 306, VIII, 275

tea-trade, V, 481

a Dutch tea, X, 211

Teixeira, Mr, X, 211–12

Temple, Earl, M.P. for Buckingham-shire, V, 47

Teniers, VII, 163

Tennant, Smithson, VI, 90 & n., 135; Whishaw's *Account* of, VI, 244 & n.

Terry, Christopher, VI, 277, VII, 15

Tetbury, savings bank, VII, 187 n.; see also VIII, 295

Thanet, Earl of, V, 369

The Times:

reporter does not understand Ricardo, V, 129 n., IX, 164

breach with Owen, VII, 177 & n.

Hardcastle's letters to, VIII, 3 & n.

parliamentary reports, V, 67, 92, 95, 98, 100–3, 111, 114, 117–18, 121, 157, 223, 352, 368

see also VII, 131, VIII, 6, 36, 59, XI, xxviii

Theories: age of, V, 109; abominable theories of political economists (Lethbridge), V, 169; wild dreams of theorists, III, 195, and cp. V, 371; fanciful and impracticable theories (Lord Liverpool), IX, 269 n.; see also V, 143

Theorist, Ricardo accused of being a, IV, 352, V, xxv, 93 & n., 128 n., VIII, 347; 'abundantly theoretical', V, xxxiii; 'disregards experience', VIII, 152 n.; *Principles* not intended to be practical, VII, 378

Theory of Money (anon.), 1811, X, 400

Thiele, Ottomar, X, 378

Thistlewood, Arthur, VIII, 163 n.

Thompson, Thomas, country banker, III, 228

Thompson, William, M.P. for Calling-ton, V, 185

Thomson's *Annals of Philosophy*, VI, 244 & n.

Thornton & Power, merchants, III, 431

Thornton, Edward, Minister at Ham-burg, III, 430–1

Thornton, Henry, VI, 87–8

joint author of Bullion Report, III, 413–14 & n.

on unfavourable balance of trade, III, 59–61; unfavourable exchange, 75–7; export of gold coin, 58–9, 81

Enquiry into Paper Credit, 1802, III, 4, 58–62, 64 n., 75–7, 79–81, 83, 95, 100, 208, 365, X, 390

Substance of Two Speeches...on the Report of the Bullion Committee, 1811, III, 84 n.

see also III, 364 n., VI, 42, VII, 109, X, 49

Thornton, John, IX, 104 & n. 3

Thornton, Samuel, Governor of the Bank of England:

evidence on public expenditure, IV, 77–8, 91–4, V, 12 n.

on profits of the Bank, IV, 97 & n., 102–3, VI, 276, 283

on stamp duties, VI, 258

supports Ingot plan, V, 14, 363

see also VI, 288

Thornton, Stephen, Brothers & Co., Russia merchants, VI, xxxvii, IX, 104 n.

Thorpe, Mr, V, 353

Thoun (Thun), X, 258–61

Thrashing machine, burned to the ground, VII, 45; see also I, 82, 251, V, 90, 211, 525, VI, 187

Tierney, George, M.P., Whig leader, VI, 67 n.

on resumption of cash payments, V, 2, 8, 10, 14–15; member of the committee, 350, 354, 365

letter to, on bullion payments plan, VI, 67–71, see also V, 351

on the surplus profits of the Bank, IV, 102

see also IV, 166, VI, 306, VII, 252, 260, 305, VIII, 146, X, 93, 396

Tillotson, John, D.D., *Works*, 1712, V, 327 & n., see also 325

Timber duties, V, 102–4, 110–11, 306, VIII, 371

Time, as cause of variation in relative value, IV, 370, 381–3, 403, VIII, 193

owing to different proportions of fixed and circulating capital, I, 31, II, 58

or to different durabilities of fixed capital, I, 38–9, 43, 58–9, and of circulating capital, I, 31, 53 n., 61 n.

or to different times taken to bring to market, I, 34, 37, VIII, 142, 344

profits as compensation for time, IV, 375; denied by McCulloch, IX, 366–8

Time bargains, and continuation, whether illegal, V, 338–45; see also X, 19 n.

Tintoretto, IX, 222

Tithes, I, 176–80

fall wholly on the consumer, I, 176, IV, 255

justify countervailing duties, IV, 217–18, 243, V, 45

like other taxes hinder production, VIII, 155

McCulloch on, VIII, 203–4, 222, 229; extension of tithes to exempted lands, VIII, 237–8

valuation of, IX, 31, 39–40, 70, 88–9

see also I, 188, V, 304, VIII, 214, IX, 146, 199

Titian, IX, 222, X, 304, 307, 309

Tobacco, I, 406, VIII, 275; tax on, V, 23

Token currency:

silver as, V, 16; coined by the Bank, IV, 102; see also V, 14, VI, 86

gold tokens, Baring's proposal, V, 92, 96, see also V, 403 n.

Tooke, Horne, VIII, 152 n.

Tooke, Thomas, VI, xxxvii–xxxviii, IX, 250

evidence on agriculture, IV, 221, 228, 231, 259, V, xxiv, 214, 520, VIII, 366–7 & n., 370–1 & n., 373–4, IX, 67, 86, 106, 108

on resumption of cash payments, V, 361–2

draws up merchants' petition, V, 42 n.

Mallet on, VIII, 152 n.; Cobbett on, IX, 106 & n.

and Political Economy Club, IX, 158–9 n.

visit to Gatcomb, IX, 5, 14, 18, 27, 41, 105

letters from, VIII, 366, 371, IX, 104, XI, xxvi

see also V, 369 n., VI, xxvii n., IX, 46, 219, 224, 229, 266, 301, 345, 362

On High and Low Prices, 1823, IX, 250 & n., 314, 370

Letter to Lord Grenville, 1829, IV, 418

Some Account of the Free Trade Movement (anon.), 1853, V, 42 n.

Tooke and Newmarch, *History of Prices*, III, 8 n., V, 42 n., 369 n., IX, 106 n., 202 n.

Tooke, William Eyton, IX, 107 & n.

Tories, V, xx, VI, xxii, VII, 260, VIII, 25, 163 n., 205

Torrens, Robert:

first meeting with, VI, 215, 219

alterations due to, in *Principles*, ed. 2, on unequal durability of capitals, I, 31, 53, 58, 61, VII, 338; other additions to placate him, I, 96–7 n., 271, VII, 179–80, 333, 349; his intended review of *Principles*, IV, 305, VII, 179 & n., 180, 288, 309, 316 n.

Torrens, Robert (*cont.*)
controversy with, on value and capital, IV, 305–18, VII, 253, 315–16 & n., 338, 354, 364, 372, 376–7; his measure of value (quantity of capital employed), IV, 375, 393–5, IX, 355–7, 359; his lost paper on value, VIII, 128, 138 & n., 142

early view that price of corn regulates all prices, VI, 212–14, 269; later adopts Ricardo's views, VII, 24, 35–6, see also VIII, 163–4, IX, 120

his error on glut and counter-commodities, VIII, 227, 260

'labour of capital', IX, 369

opposed to ingot plan, VIII, 83

disagrees with Malthus on depreciation, VI, 205 & n., 215, 218–19; criticises his *Political Economy*, VIII, 185–6 & n., 226, 261–2

meets McCulloch in Edinburgh, VII, 315–16 & n., 354

and election of 1818, XI, xi–xii, of 1820, VIII, 156–7 & n.

interest in *The Traveller*, IV, 7, VIII, 185–6 & n., 226, 261–2, 316, and *The Champion*, IX, 114 & n., 120, 122

letter to, XI, xi; lost correspondence with, VII, 180

his letters to Place quoted, VII, 179 n., 316 n.

see also IV, 320, VII, 31–2, 34 n., 177, VIII, 29 n., 143, 190, 229, 313, 367 & n., 373, 378, 381, IX, 159, 207, 312, 334

Comparative Estimate . . . with Strictures on Mr. Ricardo's Proposal, 1819, VIII, 83 & n.

Essay on the External Corn Trade, 1815, IV, 5, VI, 185 n.; few sold, VII, 141; Ricardo on, I, 96–7 n., VI, 188, 205–6, 212–13, VII, 179–80; Malthus on, VI, 185–6, 201–2, 211–12, 223–4; ed. 2, VIII, 164; see also I, li, 93 n., 271 n., VI, 269, VII, 31 n., VIII, 82, X, 399

Torrens (*cont.*)
Essay on Money, 1812, VI, 215, 219 & n., VII, 31 n., X, 399

Essay on the Production of Wealth, 1821, IV, 393–5, VII, 35, 141, 251, 316 n., VIII, 22, 47, IX, 46, 66, 68, 77, 113, 293; Malthus on, IX, 79–80, 87, 112; see also IV, 308

Letter to the Earl of Liverpool, 1816, VII, 24

Letters to the Earl of Lauderdale in *The Sun*, 1816, VII, 28, 30

'Strictures' on Ricardo's theory of value in *Edinburgh Magazine*, 1818, IV, 306–8, VII, 179 n., 315–16 & n., 324, 326, 332, 338, 360, 362, 364, 376; McCulloch's reply, VII, 354; Ricardo's lost answer, VII, 360, 364, 372, 376–7, VIII, 8 & n.; see also X, 397

articles: on Owen in *Edinburgh Review*, 1819, VIII, 82 n., 159 n., 163–4, 227, 376 & n.; in *The Champion*, 1821, IX, 114, 120, 122

Tournay, X, 187

Towers, J. L., *Resumption of Cash-Payments*, 1811, X, 401

Townsend, John, letter from, XI, xxi

Trade:
increases enjoyments, not value, I, 319, II, 395, IV, 25–6

home and foreign, I, 133, 318–19

sudden changes in the channels of, I, 263–72

periods of prosperity and adversity (Malthus), VII, 122

see also Foreign trade

Tradesman, The, III, 9 n.

Tradesmen, V, 285

Trade Unions, see Combination of workmen

Traveller, The, Torrens's newspaper, V, xix, VIII, 185 & n., 316

articles on Malthus's *Political Economy*, VIII, 186 n., 226, 262

Treasury bills, IV, 282, 283 n.

Trevelyan, G. M., *British History in the Nineteenth Century*, X, 39 n.

Trinity College, Cambridge, Ricardo's sons at, X, 61–3; visit to, 136–40; see also VIII, 114

Tritton, John Henton, banker, III, 372–3

Trotter, Coutts, *Principles of Currency and Exchanges*, 1810, III, 115; 'Notes' on, III, 8 n., 379–403; 'Observations on Trower's Notes on', 405–8; see also X, 401

Trower, Hutches, VI, xxiii–xxv
'Friend to Bank Notes' controversy in 1809, III, 4–5, 21–46, 81 n., 88 n., X, 7–8

early chats on political economy, VII, 246; walks in Kensington Gardens, VII, 268, 273, 275; simple explanation to, on profits of capital, VI, 103–5, on value, IX, 1–3, 38, 87

advice from, on composition, VI, 326

correspondence with, on parliamentary reform, V, 490–3, VII, 266–8, 272–4, 289–90, 298–9, 309–10, 319–24, 326–7, 340–5, 360, 364, 366–71, 373–4, 381, VIII, 12–16

and Notes on Malthus, VIII, 201, 218–20, 320–2, 346, 395

and Savings Banks, VII, 12, 23 & n., 26, 33–4 & n., 96, 117–18, 128–9, 141–2, 149

on Loans, VI, 237–8, VIII, 30–1

on the management of the poor, VIII, 42–3

Sheriff of Surrey, VII, 255, VIII, 148, 164, 347, 348 n.; magistrate, VII, 96, 173, VIII, 70, 109, 131–2, IX, 312; East India proprietor, VI, 96 n., 343 n.

visit to, VIII, 162; never visited Gatcomb, IX, 377, 382–3, 338–9

list of letters IX, 400–1

see also VII, 15, 34 n., VIII, 130, X, 50, 78 n., 79, 103 n., 162, 177, 179

Christianity in India [1813], VI, 96; 'Note on prices and taxation', IV, 319–22; 'Notes on Trotter', III, 405–9

Trower, Mrs Hutches, VIII, 71, 80–1, 113

Trower, John, stockbroker, VI, xxiv, VII, 45, VIII, 35, 368, IX, 28, 40, 383, X, 82 & n., 85

Trower, Walter John, IX, 28 & n.

Tso-liang Chen, X, 385

Tucker, Mr, V, 483

Tudela, Abraham, VIII, 349 n.

Tunbridge Wells, VI, 92, 232

Turgot, A. R. J., I, 5, 238, 280 n.; his *Œuvres*, and *Life* by Condorcet, VII, 365 & n., 382, X, 399

Turin, VII, 216 n., IX, 227–8, X, 335, 338–9

Turkey, V, 495, IX, 39, X, 247

Turner, Dawson, X, xxx n.

Turner, Samuel, VII, 27 & n., VIII, 368; *Considerations upon Agriculture...and the pamphlet by David Ricardo*, 1820, V, 254, IX, 197 & n.; *Letter...to Robert Peel*, VIII, 42, 45

Turnip husbandry, I, 80–1

Turton, Sir Thomas, V, 466

Tuscany, Grand Duke of, X, 311–17, 320

Umbrellas in Milan, X, 298

Unemployed fixed capital, I, 265

Unemployed labourers, VII, 194. See under Employment of labour

Unitarians, Ricardo and, X, 39–41; see also VI, 135 n., VII, 171 n., VIII, 84 n.

Universal suffrage, would be going too far, V, 29, 485, 502, VII, 270, 360, 369–70; see also VIII, 99, 107

Upper Brook Street, Ricardo's house in, VI, facing p. 1, 52–3 & n., 82, VII, 1, 13, 17–18, X, 48, 105, 336 n.

Usury laws: Onslow's bill for repeal, V, 109–10, 323, 335–6; Ricardo's evidence, 1818, V, 337–47, VII, 305; report on, V, 336; see also I, 296–7, V, 97, 222, 511, VIII, 17 & n., 341 n.

Utility:

the foundation, not the measure of
value, I, 11, 280 n., III, 284, VI,
247; dispute with Say on, I,
279–80 n., VI, 271, VIII, 276–7,
280, 299, 379, IX, 32–5, 168–71,
188–90, see also VIII, 260, IX,
64; Bentham on, III, 284

no standard for, in nature, VII, 242,
see also VII, 302

iron and gold, utility and value contrasted, I, 283, IX, 33, 168

and riches, I, 281, VIII, 379, IX, 169

Utrecht, X, 212–13

Vagrant bill, IX, 181

Value:

chapter on, I, 11–51, first version, I,
52–66; absolute and exchangeable
value, IV, 357–412; see also I,
xxx–xlix

in early state of society, I, 12, 22–4,
26–7, 38 n., 42, 53–4, 58 n., 62 n.,
112, IV, 315–18, IX, 2

regulated by quantity, not value, of
labour, I, 11–20, 24–5, 46–7, 118,
II, 34–5, 79, 100–2, IV, 397, VIII,
142, 149, 179

this not disturbed by rent, I, 67–78;
but modified by accumulation of
capital, I, 22–3 & notes, VII,
377–8, by the use of machinery,
I, 30–8, 53, 56, II, 58, by different
proportions of fixed and circulating capital, I, 66, IV, 318, by unequal durabilities of fixed capital,
I, 38–9, 43 & n., 58–9, VIII, 339–
40, or of circulating capital, I, 31,
53 n., 61 n., by the time taken to
bring to market, I, 34, 37, IV,
404, VIII, 180, 192–4, 344, by the
rise or fall of wages, I, 30, 33–6,
56–8, 60–3, IV, 317–18, 368,
384–5; all exceptions come under
time, VIII, 193, IX, 356

profits also a part of value, IV, 373,
389, 392, VIII, 194, IX, 350–2,
356, 387, but an unimportant part,
I, 36, II, 59, VIII, 279–80

Value (cont.)

discussion with Torrens on value,
1818–19, IV, 305–18, VII, 253,
315–16 & notes, 338–9, 354, VIII,
138, 142

value and price, early distinction,
VI, 54–5; later, II, 242 & n., VII,
297, 378; latest, IV, 236, 373

puzzled by law of relative value, VII,
20, 71, 83–4

sheet-anchor the invariability of
precious metals, VI, 348–9, of
money, I, 47, 63, see also I, 87 n.,
II, 82–3

absolute value, IV, 361–412; letters
on, IX, 297–300, 306–11, 341, 346,
352, 356, 364, 377–8, 383

distinguished from exchangeable
value, IV, 398

measure of, a desideratum, IV, 395–
6, mass of commodities as, IV, 400

see also I, xlvi–xlvii, 21, 43 n., 63,
V, 209, VIII, 279, 339, 344

exchangeable value, defined, I, 92, IV,
398; papers on absolute and, IV,
361–412; value in exchange, I, 11

natural, IV, 375, or necessary, I, 415

positive, IX, 339, 351, and exchangeable, VIII, 394, IX, 1–2, 29

proportional, IV, 380

real, and exchangeable, II, 399, IX,
38, 68, 87, and nominal, II, 26–7,
and relative, I, 42–3, IV, 394, and
money price, IX, 83; real exchangeable value, II, 206 & n.

relative, II, 304, or exchangeable,
VII, 20, and absolute, I, 21, VIII,
279, 339

value and cost, I, 47 n., II, 31, 34–5,
100–2

and riches, I, 273–9, II, 192–3, 203, 207

and utility, I, 279–80 n., 281–3,
287 n., see also I, 11, III, 284, and
under Say, J.-B.

and wealth, II, 33–4, 375, VII, 312

value in use, I, 11. See Utility

definition of value, difference with
Malthus, VIII, 229, 261, 278–9,
see also IX, 352

Value (*cont.*)

simple explanation to Trower: on positive and exchangeable value, IX, 1–3, 38, 87, on differences with McCulloch, IX, 377, and with Malthus, IX, 378

scarcity and, I, 12, see also I, 90, 119, 194, 209, II, 204

relative 'utility' of two definitions of value, VIII, 261, 278

see also Price

Value, measure or standard of:

earliest statement, III, 65 & n.

no invariable standard known, I, 17 n., 43, 275, II, 288, IV, 370, V, 217, IX, 346; no such thing in nature, IV, 404, IX, 387

variety of circumstances the difficulty, I, 44–5, IV, 368–9, 386–7, IX, 303–4, 319

search for an invariable standard, IV, 392, IX, 331, like measures of length and time, IV, 380, 391, 401, IX, 356, see also VII, 43

quantity of labour bestowed the least variable measure, I, 14, 46–7, II, 35, 66, VIII, 279, IX, 325, 344; doubtful whether for a day or a year, VIII, 344

medium between extremes preferred, VIII, 193, requiring both labour and capital, IV, 371–3, IX, 361, for a year, IV, 405; imperfections acknowledged, IX, 346–7, 352, 375

gold as a just mean, I, 45–6, 87 & n., IV, 389–90, 406, IX, 386; see also II, 82–3

McCulloch's measure: quantity of labour, estimated by capital employed, IV, 376–9, 410–12, IX, 303, 330–1, 343–4, 354 n., 361; labour bestowed on agent of production, not on product, IX, 356, 359

cause of value different from measure of, IX, 344, 358, 377, see also IX, 178, 185

Value, measure of (*cont.*)

Malthus's measures discussed, II, 28–35, 66–7, 90–1, 94–102, 175–7, 206–7, 410–11, IV, 361–4, 371–3, 378–9, 390–3, 406–10, IX, 280–3, 297–300, 304–13, 318–25, 336–41, 345–66, 378, 380–2

(1) labour commanded, II, 28–35, 175–6, 410–11, IX, 280 & n., 322, 324, 348

(2) pay of a day's labour, IV, 361–4, 371, 392, 407, IX, 304, 319, 378

(3) mean between corn and labour, II, 95–9, 207, VIII, 233–4, 305–7, IX, 79, 84–5, 91–2, 100, abandoned, IX, 293

(4) silver (or gold) picked up in a day on the sea-shore, II, 81–2, IV, 365, 406, VIII, 179, 343, IX, 298, 305, 347–8, 354, 361, 363–4, 386; how profits are regulated in this case, VIII, 64–5, 73, 108

(5) the constant labour that produces the wages and profits in a commodity, IX, 280–3, 304–5, 307–10, 323–5, 338–40, 350–1, 382, intuitive proof, IX, 308

see also I, 18–19, II, 242, 281, VIII, 180–1, 193–4, IX, 290, 312, 334

Mill's: quantity of labour worked up, IV, 375–6; includes 'labour of machines', IX, 325 n., see also IX, 312

Say's: corn, I, 275 n.; quantity of things commanded, IX, 170

work done by natural agents and machines adds to value, I, 285–7

Adam Smith's: the toil and labour of acquiring, I, 12–13, 17, 309

the quantity of labour commanded, I, 14, 16–17

corn and labour, I, 18–19, 20, 377

Torrens's: quantity of capital employed in producing a commodity, IV, 375, 393–5, VII, 315 n., 354, IX, 355–6, 359, see also IV, 307

Value, measure of (*cont.*)
  other measures discussed:
    shrimps, result of immediate labour only, IV, 365, 367–71, 386, 388–90, 402–3, IX, 298, 347–8, 356, 361, 363–4, 381
    oak-tree, result almost entirely of accumulated labour, IV, 377–8, 388, 410–11, IX, 303, 330–1, 343–4, 354 n., 359, 361; wine mellowed by age, IV, 369–70, 375–6, 387, 402–3, IX, 303, 330, 343, 359
    cloth, mean between the extremes, IV, 369–71, 376, 382, 386–9, 403, IX, 298, 365
  real measure of value, I, 21 n., II, 95, 206–7, IX, 81
Vandamme, General, X, 184–5
Vandyke, VII, 163
Van Lancken's collection of paintings in Antwerp, X, 191
Vansittart, Nicholas (see also Chancellor of the Exchequer):
  Propositions on the Bullion Report, III, 411–23
  his plan of finance, 1813, IV, 158–67, 198–200, V, 262–3, VI, 91–2 & n., 334, VIII, 120–2, see also IV, 175, 182, 193, VIII, 319
  project of stock notes, VII, 260 & n.
  in committee on Resumption, V, 350, 352 n., 354, 365
  see also II, 433 n., III, 262, 429, VII, 252, 292 n., VIII, 350 n., IX, 6, 270, X, 82, 90 n., 189
  Outlines of a Plan of Finance, 1813, IV, 40, 159 n.
Varese, X, 292
Velocity of circulation of money, see Rapidity
Venice, IX, 222, X, 306–10
Verbal Disputes, Observations on, 1821 (anon.), IX, 27 & n., 38
Verona, eve of the Congress, IX, 222, X, 302–6; Juliet's tomb, X, 305
Veronese, Paul, IX, 222, X, 304
Viner, Jacob, IV, 147 n., VI, xx n., IX, 61 n., 72 n.

Vizard, William, the Queen's Solicitor, VII, 264, 346, 355
Void in the currency, III, 24, 60, in the circulation, 61
Voltaire, correspondence with d'Alembert, IX, 335, 374–5; see also VI, 332, VII, 102
Volunteers, Ricardo as captain in the, X, 46–7, 118; see also X, 402, XI, ix
  Bank Volunteers, IV, 97 n.

Wada, Saichiro, X, 384
Wade, R. W., stockbroker, VII, 14
Waentig, Heinrich, X, 378
Wages, I, 93–109
  and proportion of capital to population, I, 98, 165, II, 252, 265, 302–4, 321, III, 389, IV, 22–3, V, 32, see also II, 8, VIII, 170–1, 258
  corn wages fall, money wages rise, with growth of population, I, 101–4, II, 132–3, see also I, 305–6, II, 137, 259, VI, 189, VII, 202, 214 n.
  increase in, implies full employment, II, 412
  fall of, in 1816, VII, 75, 193, 199; in 1820, VIII, 290, 307; in 1822, V, 228; inadequacy of, for married men, V, 1, VII, 118, 124, 133
  fall of, in 1821, without men out of work, IX, 20, 25, and cp. 40
  should be sufficient to provide for periods out of work, VII, 248
  bad system of Gloucestershire clothiers, VIII, 316
  fixing of, opposed, V, 292, 296, 307, IX, 318; should be left to competition, I, 105, VIII, 316
  petition of Spitalfields silk weavers, V, 292, 295, 306–8
  and fund for maintenance of labour, I, 164–5, 196, 219–22, 225–6, 289, 292–3, 306, VIII, 258, IX, 24
  and machinery, I, 16, 387–8, 392, IV, 35, VIII, 171 & n.
  hand weavers' petition, V, 302–3

Wages (*cont.*)

market price of labour regulated by supply and demand, I, 94, 382, II, 268, see also I, 15, 96–8, 101, 104, 163–4, II, 413, V, 114, 303, VII, 57, 72, 78

natural price of labour regulated by price of food and necessaries, I, 93, 95, by difficulty or facility of producing food, I, 218, 296, VII, 57, 80–1; general rule modified, I, 160–6, 217, VI, 146; see also I, 118, 302, II, 78, 291, IV, 179, 236–7, 347, V, 33, 50, 241, VI, 108, VII, 72, 78, VIII, 234

natural price of wages different in different countries, I, 96–7, see also IX, 82, 282–3, 305

not part of net produce, I, 347–8, III, 283; opinion modified, I, 348 n., 425, II, 380–1, IV, 366, VIII, 257–8, 311; see also VII, 378–9 and under Revenue, gross and net

case of wages spent on unproductive consumption, IX, 16–17, 21, 24–6

nominal and real, disagreement with Malthus on, II, 249–50, 258–9, 278, 322–4, VII, 81 & n., 214, see also I, 19

and cheap parish labour, VII, 142, XI, xvi

poor-rates and, II, 49, V, 113–14

the great regulator of population (Malthus), VI, 155, (Ricardo), VIII, 169, see also I, 218–20, 292, 406–7

price of wages, I, li–lii, 94 n., 95 n. 3, 96 notes, 111 n., 118, 145, 303 n., 334 n., II, 63 n. 5, 231 n., 411, IV, 22, VI, 241, IX, 325; value of, II, 126

Adam Smith's view that rise of wages raises all prices refuted, I, 46, 61–3, 302–3, 307, 315, see also I, 104–5, 126, IV, 213–16, 236

curious effect of rise of wages: some prices lowered but none raised (*Principles*, ed. 1), I, 63, 66, VII,

Wages (*cont.*)

82–3, 98; later view (ed. 3), some prices are raised, I, 35 & n., 43 & n., II, 62–4. See also Value, effect of rise of wages on

wages and profits: division by proportions, I, 125–6, 420–1, II, 61–2, 138, 194–5, 258–9, 266–7, 290, VII, 80–1, VIII, 194–5, on no-rent land, II, 196–7, 278, 284, 336

always constitute the same sum, I, 115, 120, 226, 404, 411; if wages rise profits fall, I, 205, 296, II, 266, VI, 162, VII, 57, 155–6, IX, 179; fall of, increases profits, I, 132, IV, 22, but not rent, IV, 11

provision system of, V, 218

real wages, II, 258–9, VII, 214, and nominal, II, 249, 322–4, VII, 81 & n., and money wages, VII, 81; real value of, I, 19, and nominal value of, I, 50, 65; real and nominal price of, I, 274–5 n.

in rich and poor countries, I, 373, 376, VI, 147; in a dearth, VII, 200–1, see also VII, 194

subsistence wages, I, 93, 159, 217, 305, 382, V, 50, IX, 17, 54

taxes on, I, 215–27, VIII, 169–70, are in effect taxes on profits, I, 226

raised by tax on raw produce, I, 159–61, 166, VIII, 195–6, and on other necessaries, I, 243; not affected by tax on luxuries, I, 243–4

raised by combination of workmen, VII, 203

see also Distribution, Labour

Wages fund, see Fund for the maintenance of labour

Wakefield, C. M., *Life of Thomas Attwood*, VIII, 370 n.

Wakefield, Edward, Ricardo's land agent, VI, xxxviii, X, 96–8

evidence on agriculture, IV, 211, 260, IX, 67

negotiations for seat in parliament, V, xiv–xvi, VII, 86, 216–17, 232–3, 254–5, 346–7, 355

Wakefield, Edward (*cont.*)
  letters from, VII, 216, 232, 252, 346,
    see also X, 390; letter to Place
    quoted, VII, 182 n.
  see also VII, 299 n., VIII, 48–9, X,
    104 n., 267
  Account of Ireland, 1812, V, xiv n.,
    VI, xxxviii, VII, 347 n.
  *Address on Management of Landed
    Property*, X, 96–7 n.
Wakefield, Edward Gibbon, VII, 216
  & n., 217, 232–3, X, 53
Waldshut, X, 233–5
Waldstetter, Lake of, X, 245–8
Wales, Prince of, VII, 208, X, 111.
  See also Regent, and George IV
Wales, Princess of, X, 112. See Caro-
  line, Queen
Walesby, Lincs., Malthus's living at,
  VI, 35 n.
Walker, Col. Alexander, VIII, 106
  & n.
Walker, George, merchant, III, 430
Walks in London: Green Park, VIII,
  191; Hyde Park, VI, xxviii n., VII,
  277; Kensington Gardens, V,
  490–1, VI, xxxiv, VII, 263, 266,
  268, 273, 275, IX, 210, 345, X,
  264; St James's Park, VI, xxxiv
Wallace, Professor at Sandhurst, VII,
  292 n., 304 n.
Wallace, Thomas (Vice-President,
  then President, of the Board of
  Trade):
  reduction of timber duties, V, 102,
    110
  navigation laws amendment bill, V,
    190, 197
  warehousing bill, V, 220, 275
  Ricardo's tribute to, V, 246–7
  see also V, xx, 335
Wallas, Graham, *Life of Francis Place*,
  IV, 145 n., VI, xxix, VII, 183 n.,
  357 n., 363 n., VIII, 105 n., 199 n.,
  X, 34 n.
Wallenstadt, Lake of, X, 239–40
Walpole, Sir Robert, IV, 149, V, 118,
  130
Walters, David, VI, 113 n.

Wants and tastes of mankind: effects
  on price, difference with Malthus,
  VI, 132, 134–5, 141, 147–8, 155,
  VII, 70, 122; see also I, 263, II,
  24–5, 415 & n., IV, 343–4
War:
  outbreak of, effects on commerce, I,
    263, IV, 255, on agriculture, I,
    266, 272
  whether to be financed by taxes or by
    loans, I, 244–7, IV, 185–90, VIII,
    147, 170
  dependence on foreign supplies of
    food in time of, V, 54–5, see also
    IV, 264–6
  increase of wealth and profits during
    (1813), VI, 93–4
  termination of: effects on demand for
    labour, I, 265, 393–4, VII, 49, 67,
    on farmers, II, 110, on land-
    holders, VI, 345, on rate of interest,
    VII, 199, on Bank, IV, 52, on price
    of gold and silver, VI, 119, 299, 318,
    344, VII, 28; see also I, 90, II, 439
Warburton, Henry, F.R.S., VII, 275 n.
  on price of seat in parliament, VII, 276
  visits Gatcomb, VII, 56, 187, VIII,
    276, 282–3
  letter from, VII, 275
  see also IV, 204, V, xv n., VI, 244,
    295, VII, 28–9, 52, 54, 61, 139,
    185, 206, 252, 361, IX, 107, 148,
    312, X, 49, 216
Warburton, William, VII, 277
Ward, George, loan contractor, X, 85
Ward, William, Bank director, V,
  354–5, VIII, 21 & n.
Warehousing system, V, 85, 90, 220,
  275, see also IV, 29 n.
Warrender, Sir George, M.P., X, 187,
  190
Washington, George, bust of, IX, 228
Waterloo, battle of:
  effect on price of stock, V, 5, VI,
    231–3, 235, 237–8 & n., X, 83
  family visit to battlefield, X, 186,
    188–91
  Saint-Arnaud's views on, X, 333
  see also V, xv n., VI, 239, 280, 316

Wathen, George, X, 265 n.

Watson, James, radical, VIII, 129

Watson, Richard, Bishop of Landaff:
Address to the People, 1798, antici-
pates plan for paying off national
debt, V, 41
Apology for Christianity, 1776, X,
394
Apology for the Bible, 1796, X, 395
Anecdotes of the Life of, 1817,
VII, 258 & n., 261, VIII, 323,
335

Watt, James, VIII, 82

Wealth:
real wealth, I, 425, III, 144; no
difference to, whether products be
exported or consumed at home,
III, 330; Malthus's definition, II,
14–15
two ways in which it may be increased, I, 278–9; also increased
by use of paper money, I, 361, and
cp. III, 272
progress of: effects on profits, I, 120,
IV, 11, 14, 18, 23, on rent, I, 77–8,
VI, 181, 204, VII, 16–17, on wages,
I, 94, 102, 112, see also I, 265, II,
414; impeded by corn-laws, IV,
32, 39, VII, 270–1. See also Progress of society
and value distinguished, I, 276, II,
33–4, 375, 420–1, see also VII,
312, IX, 248–9
distribution of circulating medium
and, III, 120
see also Riches

Webb Hall, George, secretary of the
Board of Agriculture, IV, 241 &
n.; his reveries, IX, 153 & n.,
165 n.

Weddle, Mrs, VII, 264 & n.

Wellesley, Marquis: his administration in India, VII, 241–4; Lord-
Lieutenant of Ireland, IX, 124 n.,
145, 153; see also VIII, 241

Wellington, Duke of:
battle of Waterloo, VI, 232, 235,
239, X, 190, 333
on Ricardo's speech, V, 17 n.

Wellington, Duke of (*cont.*)
in committee on resumption of cash
payments, V, 351, 354, 365
see also X, 255, 259
Civil Correspondence, V, xiv

Werner, I., X, 381

Wesen, X, 239

West, Edward, *Essay on the Application of Capital to Land*, 1815, VII,
297–8 & notes; anticipates theory
of rent and profits, I, 5, IV, 5–6,
VI, 179–80 & notes; see also VII,
289, IX, 109 n., X, 400

West India Dock system, V, 104

West Indies: depressed state of property, X, 350 & n.; merchants, III,
429 n., V, 476, VI, xxxvi; planters,
V, 153, 219; slavery, V, 483; see
also III, 350 and under Jamaica,
Sugar

Western, Charles Callis, M.P. for
Essex:
motion for agricultural committee,
1816, V, 319 n., VII, 27, IX, 265
Ricardo's notes and speech on his
resolutions on currency (1822), V,
223–45
motion on resumption of cash payments (1822), V, 198, 202, 210–18,
IX, 202, 207; (1823), V, 309, 322,
Ricardo's speech, V, 309–21, see
also V, xxx, XI, xxv
imputes interested motives to Ricardo, V, 317, 320, 526–7, IX,
250, X, 103 & n.
see also V, 86, 101 n., 153, 155,
158 n., IX, 260, 293, X, 177, 185,
392 n.
Second Address to the Landowners,
1822, V, 317, 320, IX, 250 n.,
X, 402, XI, xxv; Ricardo's notes
on, V, 522–8

Westminster election (1818), VII,
269–70 & n., 273 & n., 357–8 & n.,
360, 363–4; *Authentic Narrative of*,
VIII, 125 & n.; see also V, 474,
484, 486, 491, VIII, 57

Westminster Infant School, VII, 356–
7 & n., 359–60, 363

Westminster Reform Dinner, Ricardo's speech at, 1822, V, 474–5; 1823, 484–6, see also IX, 288 n.
Westminster Reformers, VI, xxxv, VII, 357 & n.
Westminster Review, VIII, 17 n.
Westminster School, VII, 138
Weston, Ambrose, *Two Letters*, 1799, VII, 260 n.
Wetenhall, James, *The Course of Exchange*, VI, 79, 174, 176; tables of gold prices, III, 78 n., V, 462 n., VI, 85, 95
Weyland, John: *The Principles of Population and Production*, 1816, I, 99 n., VII, 46 n., 48, 63, 95; his review of J. B. Sumner's *Records of the Creation*, VII, 247
Wheatley, John, letter to, IX, 71–4
Essay on the Theory of Money, 1807–1822, IX, 71–2 n., see also III, 7 n.
Plan to Relieve the Country, 1821, IX, 72 n.
Whewell, William, X, 63–4
Whigs:
Ricardo on, VIII, 6, 56, 62–3, 75, 206–7, 295, 316–17, 335–6, IX, 45; would be neither Whig nor Tory, VII, 260
Mill on, VII, 373–4, VIII, 8–9, 58–9, 68, 106, 327–9, IX, 41–2
and Tories in Scotland, VIII, 325, IX, 136 n., 187 n.
see also VII, 270 n., 274, 357, VIII, 221, 294
Whishaw, John, VI, 66 n.
on Ricardo's speech against Brougham, V, 128 n.
visits Gatcomb, VIII, 107, 129
discussions on reform, VIII, 61–3, 68, 75, 77
letters to Ricardo, VI, 243, VII, 264; letters quoted, to Th. Smith, IV, 204, VII, 144 n., 270 n., IX, 109 n., to Horner, III, 9 n., VI, 159 n.
see also VI, 87, 90, 196, 220, 240, 255, 295, VII, 14, 54–5, 57, 61, 90, 148, 169, 171, 174–5, 185, 188,

Whishaw (*cont.*)
192, 206, 223, 250 & n., 252, 275, 280, 284, 295, 311, 355, 357, VIII, 57, 152, IX, 251, X, 50, 314 n.
Life of Mungo Park, 1815, VI, 244–5 n.
Some Account of Smithson Tennant, 1815, VI, 244 & n.
see Seymour, Lady, *The Pope of Holland House* (John Whishaw)
Whitbread, Lady E., IX, 143
Whitbread, Samuel, M.P., VI, 232 & n.
White, Joseph, X, 98
White, William, X, 98
Whitehead, Rev. W. B., *Prosecution of Infidel Blasphemers, briefly vindicated in a letter to David Ricardo, Esq., M.P.*, XI, xxii n.
Whiteleaf Oak, Ricardo's estate, X, 104–5
Whiting, Mrs, X, 144, 156–7
Whitmore, John, Governor of the Bank of England, evidence to bullion committee, III, 193 n., 227–8, 356–61, 364–9
Whitmore, William Wolryche, M.P. for Bridgnorth:
his system of duties on corn, V, 88; moves for lowering import price, 196, 256
motion for equalisation of sugar duties, V, 297, 301, 479
member of agricultural committee, 1822, V, 138, IX, 176–7
see also V, 91, 185, 277, VIII, 357
Letter on Agriculture, 1822, IX, 176–7 n.; ed. 2, 1823, IV, 326 n., X, 400
Wigram, William, chairman of East India Company, IX, 330, 373 n.
Wilberforce, William, M.P. for Bramber:
on Ricardo as an economist, V, 40–1 n.
attacks Ricardo on free discussion of religion, 280 n., 324–5, 328
petition on slavery, V, 483
see also VIII, 221 n.
Life of, by his sons, V, 280 n.

Wilbraham, Edward Bootle, V, 369 n.

Wilderspin, S., *Educating the Infant Poor*, 1824, VII, 357

Wilkes, Charlotte (Mrs Jeffrey), VIII, 205, X, 272 n.

Wilkinson (family of D.R.'s wife), X, 43–6; crest, VI, 20 n.

Wilkinson, Alfred, X, 44

Wilkinson, Conrad, X, 60

Wilkinson, David, X, 59

Wilkinson, Edward, surgeon (D.R.'s father-in-law), X, 36, 43

his 'detestable disposition', X, 111 & n.

letter to, X, 119

his death, X, 44

his will, X, 45

Wilkinson, Edward, jun., X, 43–4

Wilkinson, Elizabeth (D.R.'s mother-in-law), *née* Patteson, X, 43, 45 n., 120

Wilkinson, Esther (D.R.'s sister), see Ricardo, Esther

Wilkinson, Fanny, see Ricardo, Fanny

Wilkinson, Horace, X, 60

Wilkinson, Canon Horace Ricardo, X, ix, 43 n., 60, 109, 117, 119

Wilkinson, Josiah Henry (D.R.'s brother-in-law), X, 44

resentment against father, X, 44–5 & n., 121

owns Oliver Cromwell's head, 'his real head', X, 173–4

visits Gatcomb, VIII, 49, 51, 244

correspondence with, X, 109–19, see also VIII, 46–7 n., X, 95, 317 n., 319–20

bequest to, X, 105

Wilkinson, Norman, X, 118

Wilkinson, Priscilla Ann (D.R.'s wife), see Ricardo, Priscilla Ann

Wilkinson, Rachel (D.R.'s sister), see Ricardo, Rachel

Wilkinson, Robert, X, 45

Wilkinson, Sarah (D.R.'s sister-in-law), *née* Patteson, X, 44, 105, 109–11

Wilkinson, William Arthur (D.R.'s nephew), X, 44, 59–60

Wilkinson, W. A. (*cont.*)

Ricardo's clerk on the Stock Exchange, X, 74, 115–17

married Ricardo's sisters: Esther, VII, 325, X, 59, Rachel, X, 59

Wilkinson, William Ernest, X, 60

Wilkinson Papers, X, 386

Wilks, Mark, *Historical Sketches of . . . India*, 1810–1817, VII, 183, 195, 204

Will and power to purchase, II, 36–7, 307, 311–14, VI, 58, 131–3, 141, 155, 209. See also Demand

William, John, *Memoirs of T. Belsham*, VII, 171 n., VIII, 75 n.

Williams, Samuel, III, 183 n., 429 n.

Wilson, C. H., *Anglo-Dutch Commerce and Finance*, X, 21 n.

Wilson, John: contest for Edinburgh professorship, VIII, 204–5 & n., 215, IX, 205–6

Works, ed. Ferrier, VIII, 205 n.

Christopher North, A Memoir of John Wilson, by Mrs Gordon, VIII, 205 n.

see also under Mullion, Hugh and Mordecai

Wilson, Sir Robert, dismissal from army, IX, 88, 110, 123–4

Wilson, Thomas, M.P. for London, V, 189, 192, 292, 351

Windham, William, speech against reform, 1809, VI, 307 & n.; see also VIII, 152 n.

Windsor Express, obituary of Ricardo, VI, xxxv n.

Wine:

fall in price, V, 72 & n.

committee on wine trade, VIII, 204 & n., 214 & n.

letter to a wine merchant, X, 141–3

wine from a wreck, X, 169–70

see also II, 358, VI, 129, VII, 164, IX, 97, X, 163

Wisdom of our ancestors, V, 176, 178–9, 283, 475

Wodehouse, Edmond, M.P. for Norfolk, on Ricardo's good character but bad economics, V, 321–2; see also V, 86, 196, IX, 177, 265

Wollaston, William Hyde, F.R.S.,
VII, 185 & n.; see also V, 352,
IX, 148

Wood, Colonel Thomas, M.P. for
Norfolk, V, 269 n.

Wood End, Ricardo's property, X, 97

Woodfall, William, parliamentary reporter, V, xxvii

Woodrow, John, plan for savings
banks, V, 121, XI, xxi; pamphlets
on, V, 128 n.; his petition, 128

Woodward, H. B., *History of the
Geological Society*, VI, 206 n.,
VII, 119 n., X, 29 n., 35 n., 49 n.,
144 n.

Wooler, Thomas Jonathan, VIII, 329

Woollen manufacturers, I, 90–1, IV,
71 n., 251, V, 57

Wootton Bassett, V, xvi n., VII, 264

Worcester: Ricardo declines standing
for, VII, 101–2, 110; music-week
at, IX, 101; see also VII, 66, 71,
74, IX, 104, X, 61, 351

Working classes, see Classes

Wotton-under-Edge, VII, 187 n.,
VIII, 295, 400 n., X, 62

Wright, John, editor of *Hansard*,
correspondence with, V, xxix–xxx,
XI, xxv
volume of MS Speeches, V, xxx n.

Wright (*cont.*)
biography of Huskisson, IX, 270 n.,
but see XI, xxix

Wynn, Charles Watkin Williams, V,
xxiii n.

Wynne, Henry, VII, 175, 265

Wynne, Mrs (Malthus's sister-in-law),
VII, 175 n., 265

Wyvill, Marmaduke, M.P. for York,
V, 277

Yamamoto, Toyokichi, X, 384

Ya-nan Wang, X, 385

Yate, Walter Honeywood, X, 97,
105 n.

Year, assumed as period of production and consumption, I, xlii & n.,
xlv, 59, 61, 150, II, 64–5; as mean
period for measure of value, IV,
405, see also IV, 364, 389, IX, 386

Yonge, C. D., *Life of Lord Liverpool*,
X, 90 n.

York, Duke of, VII, 208 & n.

Yoshida, Hideo, X, 385

Zinke, G. W., I, liv n., II, vii n., IX,
49 n.

Zug, X, 245, 253

Zurich, X, 236–8, 242–4

Zyst, Moravian establishment, X, 213